C-3267   CAREER EXAMINATION SERIES

This is your
PASSBOOK for...

Urban Park Ranger

Test Preparation Study Guide
Questions & Answers

NATIONAL LEARNING CORPORATION®

COPYRIGHT NOTICE

This book is SOLELY intended for, is sold ONLY to, and its use is RESTRICTED to individual, bona fide applicants or candidates who qualify by virtue of having seriously filed applications for appropriate license, certificate, professional and/or promotional advancement, higher school matriculation, scholarship, or other legitimate requirements of education and/or governmental authorities.

This book is NOT intended for use, class instruction, tutoring, training, duplication, copying, reprinting, excerption, or adaptation, etc., by:

1) Other publishers
2) Proprietors and/or Instructors of "Coaching" and/or Preparatory Courses
3) Personnel and/or Training Divisions of commercial, industrial, and governmental organizations
4) Schools, colleges, or universities and/or their departments and staffs, including teachers and other personnel
5) Testing Agencies or Bureaus
6) Study groups which seek by the purchase of a single volume to copy and/or duplicate and/or adapt this material for use by the group as a whole without having purchased individual volumes for each of the members of the group
7) Et al.

Such persons would be in violation of appropriate Federal and State statutes.

PROVISION OF LICENSING AGREEMENTS – Recognized educational, commercial, industrial, and governmental institutions and organizations, and others legitimately engaged in educational pursuits, including training, testing, and measurement activities, may address request for a licensing agreement to the copyright owners, who will determine whether, and under what conditions, including fees and charges, the materials in this book may be used them. In other words, a licensing facility exists for the legitimate use of the material in this book on other than an individual basis. However, it is asseverated and affirmed here that the material in this book CANNOT be used without the receipt of the express permission of such a licensing agreement from the Publishers. Inquiries re licensing should be addressed to the company, attention rights and permissions department.

All rights reserved, including the right of reproduction in whole or in part, in any form or by any means, electronic or mechanical, including photocopying, recording, or by any information storage and retrieval system, without permission in writing from the Publisher.

Copyright © 2024 by
National Learning Corporation

212 Michael Drive, Syosset, NY 11791
(516) 921-8888 • www.passbooks.com
E-mail: info@passbooks.com

PUBLISHED IN THE UNITED STATES OF AMERICA

PASSBOOK® SERIES

THE *PASSBOOK® SERIES* has been created to prepare applicants and candidates for the ultimate academic battlefield – the examination room.

At some time in our lives, each and every one of us may be required to take an examination – for validation, matriculation, admission, qualification, registration, certification, or licensure.

Based on the assumption that every applicant or candidate has met the basic formal educational standards, has taken the required number of courses, and read the necessary texts, the *PASSBOOK® SERIES* furnishes the one special preparation which may assure passing with confidence, instead of failing with insecurity. Examination questions – together with answers – are furnished as the basic vehicle for study so that the mysteries of the examination and its compounding difficulties may be eliminated or diminished by a sure method.

This book is meant to help you pass your examination provided that you qualify and are serious in your objective.

The entire field is reviewed through the huge store of content information which is succinctly presented through a provocative and challenging approach – the question-and-answer method.

A climate of success is established by furnishing the correct answers at the end of each test.

You soon learn to recognize types of questions, forms of questions, and patterns of questioning. You may even begin to anticipate expected outcomes.

You perceive that many questions are repeated or adapted so that you can gain acute insights, which may enable you to score many sure points.

You learn how to confront new questions, or types of questions, and to attack them confidently and work out the correct answers.

You note objectives and emphases, and recognize pitfalls and dangers, so that you may make positive educational adjustments.

Moreover, you are kept fully informed in relation to new concepts, methods, practices, and directions in the field.

You discover that you are actually taking the examination all the time: you are preparing for the examination by "taking" an examination, not by reading extraneous and/or supererogatory textbooks.

In short, this PASSBOOK®, used directedly, should be an important factor in helping you to pass your test.

URBAN PARK RANGER

DUTIES:
Under supervision, patrol city parks, perform crowd control functions, enforce compliance with departmental rules and regulations and health and sanitary codes, issue summonses and make arrests; provide informational, educational, and safety services to the general public through tours, field trips, and workshops; may act as a staff assistant to an Associate Urban Park Ranger; may assist in the operations of a communications center; perform related work.

SCOPE OF THE EXAMINATION:
The written test will be of the multiple-choice type and may include questions on comprehension and interpretation of written material concerning park rules, regulations, laws, environmental education, maps, and other related material; forms completion, preparation of reports and other written communication; planning and organizing activities; and other related areas.
The test may include questions requiring the use of any of the following abilities:

Written Comprehension: understanding written sentences and paragraphs. An Urban Park Ranger might use this ability when reviewing an incident report.

Written Expression: using English words or sentences in writing so that others will understand. An Urban Park Ranger might use this ability when recording the details of an incident.

Deductive Reasoning: applying general rules to specific problems to come up with logical answers. It involves deciding if an answer makes sense. An Urban Park Ranger might use this ability when deciding if an individual is in violation of laws, rules, and regulations and what enforcement action to take.

Inductive Reasoning: combining separate pieces of information or specific answers to problems to form general rules or conclusions; thinking of possible reasons for why things go together. An Urban Park Ranger might use this ability to interpret the intentions of guidelines and protocols, and how they relate to an incident.

Information Ordering: following correctly a rule or set of rules or actions in a certain order. The rule or set of rules used must be given. The things or actions to be put in order can include numbers, letters, words, pictures, procedures, sentences, and mathematical or logical operations. An Urban Park Ranger might use this ability when deciding the next appropriate action to take when confronting a disorderly individual.

Memorization: remembering information, such as words, numbers, pictures and procedures. Pieces of information can be remembered by themselves or with other pieces of information. An Urban Park Ranger might use this ability to recall the details and features of local flora and fauna.

Number Facility: adding, subtracting, multiplying and dividing quickly and correctly. An Urban Park Ranger might use this ability to calculate time on patrol and miles driven in patrol vehicles.

Problem Sensitivity: being able to tell when something is wrong or likely to go wrong. It includes being able to identify the whole problem as well as elements of the problem. An Urban Park Ranger might use this ability to choose the appropriate action when attending to an individual who is in need of medical assistance.

Spatial Orientation: determining where you are in relation to the location of some object or where the object is in relation to you. An Urban Park Ranger might use this ability when using park roads and structures to convey exact locations within the park.

Time Sharing: the ability to shift back and forth between two or more sources of information. An Urban Park Ranger may use this ability when writing a summons and educating the individual on the rules and regulations.

HOW TO TAKE A TEST

I. YOU MUST PASS AN EXAMINATION

A. WHAT EVERY CANDIDATE SHOULD KNOW

Examination applicants often ask us for help in preparing for the written test. What can I study in advance? What kinds of questions will be asked? How will the test be given? How will the papers be graded?

As an applicant for a civil service examination, you may be wondering about some of these things. Our purpose here is to suggest effective methods of advance study and to describe civil service examinations.

Your chances for success on this examination can be increased if you know how to prepare. Those "pre-examination jitters" can be reduced if you know what to expect. You can even experience an adventure in good citizenship if you know why civil service exams are given.

B. WHY ARE CIVIL SERVICE EXAMINATIONS GIVEN?

Civil service examinations are important to you in two ways. As a citizen, you want public jobs filled by employees who know how to do their work. As a job seeker, you want a fair chance to compete for that job on an equal footing with other candidates. The best-known means of accomplishing this two-fold goal is the competitive examination.

Exams are widely publicized throughout the nation. They may be administered for jobs in federal, state, city, municipal, town or village governments or agencies.

Any citizen may apply, with some limitations, such as the age or residence of applicants. Your experience and education may be reviewed to see whether you meet the requirements for the particular examination. When these requirements exist, they are reasonable and applied consistently to all applicants. Thus, a competitive examination may cause you some uneasiness now, but it is your privilege and safeguard.

C. HOW ARE CIVIL SERVICE EXAMS DEVELOPED?

Examinations are carefully written by trained technicians who are specialists in the field known as "psychological measurement," in consultation with recognized authorities in the field of work that the test will cover. These experts recommend the subject matter areas or skills to be tested; only those knowledges or skills important to your success on the job are included. The most reliable books and source materials available are used as references. Together, the experts and technicians judge the difficulty level of the questions.

Test technicians know how to phrase questions so that the problem is clearly stated. Their ethics do not permit "trick" or "catch" questions. Questions may have been tried out on sample groups, or subjected to statistical analysis, to determine their usefulness.

Written tests are often used in combination with performance tests, ratings of training and experience, and oral interviews. All of these measures combine to form the best-known means of finding the right person for the right job.

II. HOW TO PASS THE WRITTEN TEST

A. NATURE OF THE EXAMINATION

To prepare intelligently for civil service examinations, you should know how they differ from school examinations you have taken. In school you were assigned certain definite pages to read or subjects to cover. The examination questions were quite detailed and usually emphasized memory. Civil service exams, on the other hand, try to discover your present ability to perform the duties of a position, plus your potentiality to learn these duties. In other words, a civil service exam attempts to predict how successful you will be. Questions cover such a broad area that they cannot be as minute and detailed as school exam questions.

In the public service similar kinds of work, or positions, are grouped together in one "class." This process is known as *position-classification*. All the positions in a class are paid according to the salary range for that class. One class title covers all of these positions, and they are all tested by the same examination.

B. FOUR BASIC STEPS

1) Study the announcement

How, then, can you know what subjects to study? Our best answer is: "Learn as much as possible about the class of positions for which you've applied." The exam will test the knowledge, skills and abilities needed to do the work.

Your most valuable source of information about the position you want is the official exam announcement. This announcement lists the training and experience qualifications. Check these standards and apply only if you come reasonably close to meeting them.

The brief description of the position in the examination announcement offers some clues to the subjects which will be tested. Think about the job itself. Review the duties in your mind. Can you perform them, or are there some in which you are rusty? Fill in the blank spots in your preparation.

Many jurisdictions preview the written test in the exam announcement by including a section called "Knowledge and Abilities Required," "Scope of the Examination," or some similar heading. Here you will find out specifically what fields will be tested.

2) Review your own background

Once you learn in general what the position is all about, and what you need to know to do the work, ask yourself which subjects you already know fairly well and which need improvement. You may wonder whether to concentrate on improving your strong areas or on building some background in your fields of weakness. When the announcement has specified "some knowledge" or "considerable knowledge," or has used adjectives like "beginning principles of…" or "advanced … methods," you can get a clue as to the number and difficulty of questions to be asked in any given field. More questions, and hence broader coverage, would be included for those subjects which are more important in the work. Now weigh your strengths and weaknesses against the job requirements and prepare accordingly.

3) Determine the level of the position

Another way to tell how intensively you should prepare is to understand the level of the job for which you are applying. Is it the entering level? In other words, is this the position in which beginners in a field of work are hired? Or is it an intermediate or advanced level? Sometimes this is indicated by such words as "Junior" or "Senior" in the class title. Other jurisdictions use Roman numerals to designate the level – Clerk I, Clerk II, for example. The word "Supervisor" sometimes appears in the title. If the level is not indicated by the title, check the description of duties. Will you be working under very close supervision, or will you have responsibility for independent decisions in this work?

4) Choose appropriate study materials

Now that you know the subjects to be examined and the relative amount of each subject to be covered, you can choose suitable study materials. For beginning level jobs, or even advanced ones, if you have a pronounced weakness in some aspect of your training, read a modern, standard textbook in that field. Be sure it is up to date and has general coverage. Such books are normally available at your library, and the librarian will be glad to help you locate one. For entry-level positions, questions of appropriate difficulty are chosen – neither highly advanced questions, nor those too simple. Such questions require careful thought but not advanced training.

If the position for which you are applying is technical or advanced, you will read more advanced, specialized material. If you are already familiar with the basic principles of your field, elementary textbooks would waste your time. Concentrate on advanced textbooks and technical periodicals. Think through the concepts and review difficult problems in your field.

These are all general sources. You can get more ideas on your own initiative, following these leads. For example, training manuals and publications of the government agency which employs workers in your field can be useful, particularly for technical and professional positions. A letter or visit to the government department involved may result in more specific study suggestions, and certainly will provide you with a more definite idea of the exact nature of the position you are seeking.

III. KINDS OF TESTS

Tests are used for purposes other than measuring knowledge and ability to perform specified duties. For some positions, it is equally important to test ability to make adjustments to new situations or to profit from training. In others, basic mental abilities not dependent on information are essential. Questions which test these things may not appear as pertinent to the duties of the position as those which test for knowledge and information. Yet they are often highly important parts of a fair examination. For very general questions, it is almost impossible to help you direct your study efforts. What we can do is to point out some of the more common of these general abilities needed in public service positions and describe some typical questions.

1) General information

Broad, general information has been found useful for predicting job success in some kinds of work. This is tested in a variety of ways, from vocabulary lists to questions about current events. Basic background in some field of work, such as sociology or economics, may be sampled in a group of questions. Often these are principles which have become familiar to most persons through exposure rather than through formal training. It is difficult to advise you how to study for these questions; being alert to the world around you is our best suggestion.

2) Verbal ability

An example of an ability needed in many positions is verbal or language ability. Verbal ability is, in brief, the ability to use and understand words. Vocabulary and grammar tests are typical measures of this ability. Reading comprehension or paragraph interpretation questions are common in many kinds of civil service tests. You are given a paragraph of written material and asked to find its central meaning.

3) Numerical ability

Number skills can be tested by the familiar arithmetic problem, by checking paired lists of numbers to see which are alike and which are different, or by interpreting charts and graphs. In the latter test, a graph may be printed in the test booklet which you are asked to use as the basis for answering questions.

4) Observation

A popular test for law-enforcement positions is the observation test. A picture is shown to you for several minutes, then taken away. Questions about the picture test your ability to observe both details and larger elements.

5) Following directions

In many positions in the public service, the employee must be able to carry out written instructions dependably and accurately. You may be given a chart with several columns, each column listing a variety of information. The questions require you to carry out directions involving the information given in the chart.

6) Skills and aptitudes

Performance tests effectively measure some manual skills and aptitudes. When the skill is one in which you are trained, such as typing or shorthand, you can practice. These tests are often very much like those given in business school or high school courses. For many of the other skills and aptitudes, however, no short-time preparation can be made. Skills and abilities natural to you or that you have developed throughout your lifetime are being tested.

Many of the general questions just described provide all the data needed to answer the questions and ask you to use your reasoning ability to find the answers. Your best preparation for these tests, as well as for tests of facts and ideas, is to be at your physical and mental best. You, no doubt, have your own methods of getting into an exam-taking mood and keeping "in shape." The next section lists some ideas on this subject.

IV. KINDS OF QUESTIONS

Only rarely is the "essay" question, which you answer in narrative form, used in civil service tests. Civil service tests are usually of the short-answer type. Full instructions for answering these questions will be given to you at the examination. But in case this is your first experience with short-answer questions and separate answer sheets, here is what you need to know:

1) Multiple-choice Questions

Most popular of the short-answer questions is the "multiple choice" or "best answer" question. It can be used, for example, to test for factual knowledge, ability to solve problems or judgment in meeting situations found at work.

A multiple-choice question is normally one of three types—
- It can begin with an incomplete statement followed by several possible endings. You are to find the one ending which *best* completes the statement, although some of the others may not be entirely wrong.
- It can also be a complete statement in the form of a question which is answered by choosing one of the statements listed.

- It can be in the form of a problem – again you select the best answer.

Here is an example of a multiple-choice question with a discussion which should give you some clues as to the method for choosing the right answer:

When an employee has a complaint about his assignment, the action which will *best* help him overcome his difficulty is to
   A. discuss his difficulty with his coworkers
   B. take the problem to the head of the organization
   C. take the problem to the person who gave him the assignment
   D. say nothing to anyone about his complaint

In answering this question, you should study each of the choices to find which is best. Consider choice "A" – Certainly an employee may discuss his complaint with fellow employees, but no change or improvement can result, and the complaint remains unresolved. Choice "B" is a poor choice since the head of the organization probably does not know what assignment you have been given, and taking your problem to him is known as "going over the head" of the supervisor. The supervisor, or person who made the assignment, is the person who can clarify it or correct any injustice. Choice "C" is, therefore, correct. To say nothing, as in choice "D," is unwise. Supervisors have and interest in knowing the problems employees are facing, and the employee is seeking a solution to his problem.

2) True/False Questions

The "true/false" or "right/wrong" form of question is sometimes used. Here a complete statement is given. Your job is to decide whether the statement is right or wrong.

SAMPLE: A roaming cell-phone call to a nearby city costs less than a non-roaming call to a distant city.

This statement is wrong, or false, since roaming calls are more expensive.

This is not a complete list of all possible question forms, although most of the others are variations of these common types. You will always get complete directions for answering questions. Be sure you understand *how* to mark your answers – ask questions until you do.

V. RECORDING YOUR ANSWERS

Computer terminals are used more and more today for many different kinds of exams.
For an examination with very few applicants, you may be told to record your answers in the test booklet itself. Separate answer sheets are much more common. If this separate answer sheet is to be scored by machine – and this is often the case – it is highly important that you mark your answers correctly in order to get credit.
An electronic scoring machine is often used in civil service offices because of the speed with which papers can be scored. Machine-scored answer sheets must be marked with a pencil, which will be given to you. This pencil has a high graphite content which responds to the electronic scoring machine. As a matter of fact, stray dots may register as answers, so do not let your pencil rest on the answer sheet while you are pondering the correct answer. Also, if your pencil lead breaks or is otherwise defective, ask for another.

Since the answer sheet will be dropped in a slot in the scoring machine, be careful not to bend the corners or get the paper crumpled.

The answer sheet normally has five vertical columns of numbers, with 30 numbers to a column. These numbers correspond to the question numbers in your test booklet. After each number, going across the page are four or five pairs of dotted lines. These short dotted lines have small letters or numbers above them. The first two pairs may also have a "T" or "F" above the letters. This indicates that the first two pairs only are to be used if the questions are of the true-false type. If the questions are multiple choice, disregard the "T" and "F" and pay attention only to the small letters or numbers.

Answer your questions in the manner of the sample that follows:

32. The largest city in the United States is
    A. Washington, D.C.
    B. New York City
    C. Chicago
    D. Detroit
    E. San Francisco

1) Choose the answer you think is best. (New York City is the largest, so "B" is correct.)
2) Find the row of dotted lines numbered the same as the question you are answering. (Find row number 32)
3) Find the pair of dotted lines corresponding to the answer. (Find the pair of lines under the mark "B.")
4) Make a solid black mark between the dotted lines.

VI. BEFORE THE TEST

Common sense will help you find procedures to follow to get ready for an examination. Too many of us, however, overlook these sensible measures. Indeed, nervousness and fatigue have been found to be the most serious reasons why applicants fail to do their best on civil service tests. Here is a list of reminders:

- Begin your preparation early – Don't wait until the last minute to go scurrying around for books and materials or to find out what the position is all about.
- Prepare continuously – An hour a night for a week is better than an all-night cram session. This has been definitely established. What is more, a night a week for a month will return better dividends than crowding your study into a shorter period of time.
- Locate the place of the exam – You have been sent a notice telling you when and where to report for the examination. If the location is in a different town or otherwise unfamiliar to you, it would be well to inquire the best route and learn something about the building.
- Relax the night before the test – Allow your mind to rest. Do not study at all that night. Plan some mild recreation or diversion; then go to bed early and get a good night's sleep.
- Get up early enough to make a leisurely trip to the place for the test – This way unforeseen events, traffic snarls, unfamiliar buildings, etc. will not upset you.
- Dress comfortably – A written test is not a fashion show. You will be known by number and not by name, so wear something comfortable.

- Leave excess paraphernalia at home – Shopping bags and odd bundles will get in your way. You need bring only the items mentioned in the official notice you received; usually everything you need is provided. Do not bring reference books to the exam. They will only confuse those last minutes and be taken away from you when in the test room.
- Arrive somewhat ahead of time – If because of transportation schedules you must get there very early, bring a newspaper or magazine to take your mind off yourself while waiting.
- Locate the examination room – When you have found the proper room, you will be directed to the seat or part of the room where you will sit. Sometimes you are given a sheet of instructions to read while you are waiting. Do not fill out any forms until you are told to do so; just read them and be prepared.
- Relax and prepare to listen to the instructions
- If you have any physical problem that may keep you from doing your best, be sure to tell the test administrator. If you are sick or in poor health, you really cannot do your best on the exam. You can come back and take the test some other time.

VII. AT THE TEST

The day of the test is here and you have the test booklet in your hand. The temptation to get going is very strong. Caution! There is more to success than knowing the right answers. You must know how to identify your papers and understand variations in the type of short-answer question used in this particular examination. Follow these suggestions for maximum results from your efforts:

1) Cooperate with the monitor

The test administrator has a duty to create a situation in which you can be as much at ease as possible. He will give instructions, tell you when to begin, check to see that you are marking your answer sheet correctly, and so on. He is not there to guard you, although he will see that your competitors do not take unfair advantage. He wants to help you do your best.

2) Listen to all instructions

Don't jump the gun! Wait until you understand all directions. In most civil service tests you get more time than you need to answer the questions. So don't be in a hurry. Read each word of instructions until you clearly understand the meaning. Study the examples, listen to all announcements and follow directions. Ask questions if you do not understand what to do.

3) Identify your papers

Civil service exams are usually identified by number only. You will be assigned a number; you must not put your name on your test papers. Be sure to copy your number correctly. Since more than one exam may be given, copy your exact examination title.

4) Plan your time

Unless you are told that a test is a "speed" or "rate of work" test, speed itself is usually not important. Time enough to answer all the questions will be provided, but this does not mean that you have all day. An overall time limit has been set. Divide the total time (in minutes) by the number of questions to determine the approximate time you have for each question.

5) Do not linger over difficult questions

If you come across a difficult question, mark it with a paper clip (useful to have along) and come back to it when you have been through the booklet. One caution if you do this – be sure to skip a number on your answer sheet as well. Check often to be sure that you have not lost your place and that you are marking in the row numbered the same as the question you are answering.

6) Read the questions

Be sure you know what the question asks! Many capable people are unsuccessful because they failed to *read* the questions correctly.

7) Answer all questions

Unless you have been instructed that a penalty will be deducted for incorrect answers, it is better to guess than to omit a question.

8) Speed tests

It is often better NOT to guess on speed tests. It has been found that on timed tests people are tempted to spend the last few seconds before time is called in marking answers at random – without even reading them – in the hope of picking up a few extra points. To discourage this practice, the instructions may warn you that your score will be "corrected" for guessing. That is, a penalty will be applied. The incorrect answers will be deducted from the correct ones, or some other penalty formula will be used.

9) Review your answers

If you finish before time is called, go back to the questions you guessed or omitted to give them further thought. Review other answers if you have time.

10) Return your test materials

If you are ready to leave before others have finished or time is called, take ALL your materials to the monitor and leave quietly. Never take any test material with you. The monitor can discover whose papers are not complete, and taking a test booklet may be grounds for disqualification.

VIII. EXAMINATION TECHNIQUES

1) Read the general instructions carefully. These are usually printed on the first page of the exam booklet. As a rule, these instructions refer to the timing of the examination; the fact that you should not start work until the signal and must stop work at a signal, etc. If there are any *special* instructions, such as a choice of questions to be answered, make sure that you note this instruction carefully.

2) When you are ready to start work on the examination, that is as soon as the signal has been given, read the instructions to each question booklet, underline any key words or phrases, such as *least, best, outline, describe* and the like. In this way you will tend to answer as requested rather than discover on reviewing your paper that you *listed without describing*, that you selected the *worst* choice rather than the *best* choice, etc.

3) If the examination is of the objective or multiple-choice type – that is, each question will also give a series of possible answers: A, B, C or D, and you are called upon to select the best answer and write the letter next to that answer on your answer paper – it is advisable to start answering each question in turn. There may be anywhere from 50 to 100 such questions in the three or four hours allotted and you can see how much time would be taken if you read through all the questions before beginning to answer any. Furthermore, if you come across a question or group of questions which you know would be difficult to answer, it would undoubtedly affect your handling of all the other questions.

4) If the examination is of the essay type and contains but a few questions, it is a moot point as to whether you should read all the questions before starting to answer any one. Of course, if you are given a choice – say five out of seven and the like – then it is essential to read all the questions so you can eliminate the two that are most difficult. If, however, you are asked to answer all the questions, there may be danger in trying to answer the easiest one first because you may find that you will spend too much time on it. The best technique is to answer the first question, then proceed to the second, etc.

5) Time your answers. Before the exam begins, write down the time it started, then add the time allowed for the examination and write down the time it must be completed, then divide the time available somewhat as follows:
    - If 3-1/2 hours are allowed, that would be 210 minutes. If you have 80 objective-type questions, that would be an average of 2-1/2 minutes per question. Allow yourself no more than 2 minutes per question, or a total of 160 minutes, which will permit about 50 minutes to review.
    - If for the time allotment of 210 minutes there are 7 essay questions to answer, that would average about 30 minutes a question. Give yourself only 25 minutes per question so that you have about 35 minutes to review.

6) The most important instruction is to *read each question* and make sure you know what is wanted. The second most important instruction is to *time yourself properly* so that you answer every question. The third most important instruction is to *answer every question*. Guess if you have to but include something for each question. Remember that you will receive no credit for a blank and will probably receive some credit if you write something in answer to an essay question. If you guess a letter – say "B" for a multiple-choice question – you may have guessed right. If you leave a blank as an answer to a multiple-choice question, the examiners may respect your feelings but it will not add a point to your score. Some exams may penalize you for wrong answers, so in such cases *only*, you may not want to guess unless you have some basis for your answer.

7) Suggestions
    a. Objective-type questions
        1. Examine the question booklet for proper sequence of pages and questions
        2. Read all instructions carefully
        3. Skip any question which seems too difficult; return to it after all other questions have been answered
        4. Apportion your time properly; do not spend too much time on any single question or group of questions

5. Note and underline key words – *all, most, fewest, least, best, worst, same, opposite*, etc.
6. Pay particular attention to negatives
7. Note unusual option, e.g., unduly long, short, complex, different or similar in content to the body of the question
8. Observe the use of "hedging" words – *probably, may, most likely,* etc.
9. Make sure that your answer is put next to the same number as the question
10. Do not second-guess unless you have good reason to believe the second answer is definitely more correct
11. Cross out original answer if you decide another answer is more accurate; do not erase until you are ready to hand your paper in
12. Answer all questions; guess unless instructed otherwise
13. Leave time for review

b. Essay questions
1. Read each question carefully
2. Determine exactly what is wanted. Underline key words or phrases.
3. Decide on outline or paragraph answer
4. Include many different points and elements unless asked to develop any one or two points or elements
5. Show impartiality by giving pros and cons unless directed to select one side only
6. Make and write down any assumptions you find necessary to answer the questions
7. Watch your English, grammar, punctuation and choice of words
8. Time your answers; don't crowd material

8) Answering the essay question

Most essay questions can be answered by framing the specific response around several key words or ideas. Here are a few such key words or ideas:

M's: manpower, materials, methods, money, management
P's: purpose, program, policy, plan, procedure, practice, problems, pitfalls, personnel, public relations

a. Six basic steps in handling problems:
1. Preliminary plan and background development
2. Collect information, data and facts
3. Analyze and interpret information, data and facts
4. Analyze and develop solutions as well as make recommendations
5. Prepare report and sell recommendations
6. Install recommendations and follow up effectiveness

b. Pitfalls to avoid
1. *Taking things for granted* – A statement of the situation does not necessarily imply that each of the elements is necessarily true; for example, a complaint may be invalid and biased so that all that can be taken for granted is that a complaint has been registered

2. *Considering only one side of a situation* – Wherever possible, indicate several alternatives and then point out the reasons you selected the best one
3. *Failing to indicate follow up* – Whenever your answer indicates action on your part, make certain that you will take proper follow-up action to see how successful your recommendations, procedures or actions turn out to be
4. *Taking too long in answering any single question* – Remember to time your answers properly

IX. AFTER THE TEST

Scoring procedures differ in detail among civil service jurisdictions although the general principles are the same. Whether the papers are hand-scored or graded by machine we have described, they are nearly always graded by number. That is, the person who marks the paper knows only the number – never the name – of the applicant. Not until all the papers have been graded will they be matched with names. If other tests, such as training and experience or oral interview ratings have been given, scores will be combined. Different parts of the examination usually have different weights. For example, the written test might count 60 percent of the final grade, and a rating of training and experience 40 percent. In many jurisdictions, veterans will have a certain number of points added to their grades.

After the final grade has been determined, the names are placed in grade order and an eligible list is established. There are various methods for resolving ties between those who get the same final grade – probably the most common is to place first the name of the person whose application was received first. Job offers are made from the eligible list in the order the names appear on it. You will be notified of your grade and your rank as soon as all these computations have been made. This will be done as rapidly as possible.

People who are found to meet the requirements in the announcement are called "eligibles." Their names are put on a list of eligible candidates. An eligible's chances of getting a job depend on how high he stands on this list and how fast agencies are filling jobs from the list.

When a job is to be filled from a list of eligibles, the agency asks for the names of people on the list of eligibles for that job. When the civil service commission receives this request, it sends to the agency the names of the three people highest on this list. Or, if the job to be filled has specialized requirements, the office sends the agency the names of the top three persons who meet these requirements from the general list.

The appointing officer makes a choice from among the three people whose names were sent to him. If the selected person accepts the appointment, the names of the others are put back on the list to be considered for future openings.

That is the rule in hiring from all kinds of eligible lists, whether they are for typist, carpenter, chemist, or something else. For every vacancy, the appointing officer has his choice of any one of the top three eligibles on the list. This explains why the person whose name is on top of the list sometimes does not get an appointment when some of the persons lower on the list do. If the appointing officer chooses the second or third eligible, the No. 1 eligible does not get a job at once, but stays on the list until he is appointed or the list is terminated.

X. HOW TO PASS THE INTERVIEW TEST

The examination for which you applied requires an oral interview test. You have already taken the written test and you are now being called for the interview test – the final part of the formal examination.

You may think that it is not possible to prepare for an interview test and that there are no procedures to follow during an interview. Our purpose is to point out some things you can do in advance that will help you and some good rules to follow and pitfalls to avoid while you are being interviewed.

What is an interview supposed to test?

The written examination is designed to test the technical knowledge and competence of the candidate; the oral is designed to evaluate intangible qualities, not readily measured otherwise, and to establish a list showing the relative fitness of each candidate – as measured against his competitors – for the position sought. Scoring is not on the basis of "right" and "wrong," but on a sliding scale of values ranging from "not passable" to "outstanding." As a matter of fact, it is possible to achieve a relatively low score without a single "incorrect" answer because of evident weakness in the qualities being measured.

Occasionally, an examination may consist entirely of an oral test – either an individual or a group oral. In such cases, information is sought concerning the technical knowledges and abilities of the candidate, since there has been no written examination for this purpose. More commonly, however, an oral test is used to supplement a written examination.

Who conducts interviews?

The composition of oral boards varies among different jurisdictions. In nearly all, a representative of the personnel department serves as chairman. One of the members of the board may be a representative of the department in which the candidate would work. In some cases, "outside experts" are used, and, frequently, a businessman or some other representative of the general public is asked to serve. Labor and management or other special groups may be represented. The aim is to secure the services of experts in the appropriate field.

However the board is composed, it is a good idea (and not at all improper or unethical) to ascertain in advance of the interview who the members are and what groups they represent. When you are introduced to them, you will have some idea of their backgrounds and interests, and at least you will not stutter and stammer over their names.

What should be done before the interview?

While knowledge about the board members is useful and takes some of the surprise element out of the interview, there is other preparation which is more substantive. It *is* possible to prepare for an oral interview – in several ways:

1) Keep a copy of your application and review it carefully before the interview

This may be the only document before the oral board, and the starting point of the interview. Know what education and experience you have listed there, and the sequence and dates of all of it. Sometimes the board will ask you to review the highlights of your experience for them; you should not have to hem and haw doing it.

2) Study the class specification and the examination announcement

Usually, the oral board has one or both of these to guide them. The qualities, characteristics or knowledges required by the position sought are stated in these documents. They offer valuable clues as to the nature of the oral interview. For example, if the job involves supervisory responsibilities, the announcement will usually indicate that knowledge of modern supervisory methods and the qualifications of the candidate as a supervisor will be tested. If so, you can expect such questions, frequently in the form of a hypothetical situation which you are expected to solve. NEVER go into an oral without knowledge of the duties and responsibilities of the job you seek.

3) Think through each qualification required

Try to visualize the kind of questions you would ask if you were a board member. How well could you answer them? Try especially to appraise your own knowledge and background in each area, *measured against the job sought*, and identify any areas in which you are weak. Be critical and realistic – do not flatter yourself.

4) Do some general reading in areas in which you feel you may be weak

For example, if the job involves supervision and your past experience has NOT, some general reading in supervisory methods and practices, particularly in the field of human relations, might be useful. Do NOT study agency procedures or detailed manuals. The oral board will be testing your understanding and capacity, not your memory.

5) Get a good night's sleep and watch your general health and mental attitude

You will want a clear head at the interview. Take care of a cold or any other minor ailment, and of course, no hangovers.

What should be done on the day of the interview?

Now comes the day of the interview itself. Give yourself plenty of time to get there. Plan to arrive somewhat ahead of the scheduled time, particularly if your appointment is in the fore part of the day. If a previous candidate fails to appear, the board might be ready for you a bit early. By early afternoon an oral board is almost invariably behind schedule if there are many candidates, and you may have to wait. Take along a book or magazine to read, or your application to review, but leave any extraneous material in the waiting room when you go in for your interview. In any event, relax and compose yourself.

The matter of dress is important. The board is forming impressions about you – from your experience, your manners, your attitude, and your appearance. Give your personal appearance careful attention. Dress your best, but not your flashiest. Choose conservative, appropriate clothing, and be sure it is immaculate. This is a business interview, and your appearance should indicate that you regard it as such. Besides, being well groomed and properly dressed will help boost your confidence.

Sooner or later, someone will call your name and escort you into the interview room. *This is it.* From here on you are on your own. It is too late for any more preparation. But remember, you asked for this opportunity to prove your fitness, and you are here because your request was granted.

What happens when you go in?

The usual sequence of events will be as follows: The clerk (who is often the board stenographer) will introduce you to the chairman of the oral board, who will introduce you to the other members of the board. Acknowledge the introductions before you sit down. Do not be surprised if you find a microphone facing you or a stenotypist sitting by. Oral interviews are usually recorded in the event of an appeal or other review.

Usually the chairman of the board will open the interview by reviewing the highlights of your education and work experience from your application – primarily for the benefit of the other members of the board, as well as to get the material into the record. Do not interrupt or comment unless there is an error or significant misinterpretation; if that is the case, do not hesitate. But do not quibble about insignificant matters. Also, he will usually ask you some question about your education, experience or your present job – partly to get you to start talking and to establish the interviewing "rapport." He may start the actual questioning, or turn it over to one of the other members. Frequently, each member undertakes the questioning on a particular area, one in which he is perhaps most competent, so you can expect each member to participate in the examination. Because time is limited, you may also expect some rather abrupt switches in the direction the questioning takes, so do not be upset by it. Normally, a board member will not pursue a single line of questioning unless he discovers a particular strength or weakness.

After each member has participated, the chairman will usually ask whether any member has any further questions, then will ask you if you have anything you wish to add. Unless you are expecting this question, it may floor you. Worse, it may start you off on an extended, extemporaneous speech. The board is not usually seeking more information. The question is principally to offer you a last opportunity to present further qualifications or to indicate that you have nothing to add. So, if you feel that a significant qualification or characteristic has been overlooked, it is proper to point it out in a sentence or so. Do not compliment the board on the thoroughness of their examination – they have been sketchy, and you know it. If you wish, merely say, "No thank you, I have nothing further to add." This is a point where you can "talk yourself out" of a good impression or fail to present an important bit of information. Remember, *you close the interview yourself.*

The chairman will then say, "That is all, Mr. _____, thank you." Do not be startled; the interview is over, and quicker than you think. Thank him, gather your belongings and take your leave. Save your sigh of relief for the other side of the door.

How to put your best foot forward

Throughout this entire process, you may feel that the board individually and collectively is trying to pierce your defenses, seek out your hidden weaknesses and embarrass and confuse you. Actually, this is not true. They are obliged to make an appraisal of your qualifications for the job you are seeking, and they want to see you in your best light. Remember, they must interview all candidates and a non-cooperative candidate may become a failure in spite of their best efforts to bring out his qualifications. Here are 15 suggestions that will help you:

1) Be natural – Keep your attitude confident, not cocky

If you are not confident that you can do the job, do not expect the board to be. Do not apologize for your weaknesses, try to bring out your strong points. The board is interested in a positive, not negative, presentation. Cockiness will antagonize any board member and make him wonder if you are covering up a weakness by a false show of strength.

2) Get comfortable, but don't lounge or sprawl

Sit erectly but not stiffly. A careless posture may lead the board to conclude that you are careless in other things, or at least that you are not impressed by the importance of the occasion. Either conclusion is natural, even if incorrect. Do not fuss with your clothing, a pencil or an ashtray. Your hands may occasionally be useful to emphasize a point; do not let them become a point of distraction.

3) Do not wisecrack or make small talk

This is a serious situation, and your attitude should show that you consider it as such. Further, the time of the board is limited – they do not want to waste it, and neither should you.

4) Do not exaggerate your experience or abilities

In the first place, from information in the application or other interviews and sources, the board may know more about you than you think. Secondly, you probably will not get away with it. An experienced board is rather adept at spotting such a situation, so do not take the chance.

5) If you know a board member, do not make a point of it, yet do not hide it

Certainly you are not fooling him, and probably not the other members of the board. Do not try to take advantage of your acquaintanceship – it will probably do you little good.

6) Do not dominate the interview

Let the board do that. They will give you the clues – do not assume that you have to do all the talking. Realize that the board has a number of questions to ask you, and do not try to take up all the interview time by showing off your extensive knowledge of the answer to the first one.

7) Be attentive

You only have 20 minutes or so, and you should keep your attention at its sharpest throughout. When a member is addressing a problem or question to you, give him your undivided attention. Address your reply principally to him, but do not exclude the other board members.

8) Do not interrupt

A board member may be stating a problem for you to analyze. He will ask you a question when the time comes. Let him state the problem, and wait for the question.

9) Make sure you understand the question

Do not try to answer until you are sure what the question is. If it is not clear, restate it in your own words or ask the board member to clarify it for you. However, do not haggle about minor elements.

10) Reply promptly but not hastily

A common entry on oral board rating sheets is "candidate responded readily," or "candidate hesitated in replies." Respond as promptly and quickly as you can, but do not jump to a hasty, ill-considered answer.

11) Do not be peremptory in your answers

A brief answer is proper – but do not fire your answer back. That is a losing game from your point of view. The board member can probably ask questions much faster than you can answer them.

12) Do not try to create the answer you think the board member wants

He is interested in what kind of mind you have and how it works – not in playing games. Furthermore, he can usually spot this practice and will actually grade you down on it.

13) Do not switch sides in your reply merely to agree with a board member

Frequently, a member will take a contrary position merely to draw you out and to see if you are willing and able to defend your point of view. Do not start a debate, yet do not surrender a good position. If a position is worth taking, it is worth defending.

14) Do not be afraid to admit an error in judgment if you are shown to be wrong

The board knows that you are forced to reply without any opportunity for careful consideration. Your answer may be demonstrably wrong. If so, admit it and get on with the interview.

15) Do not dwell at length on your present job

The opening question may relate to your present assignment. Answer the question but do not go into an extended discussion. You are being examined for a *new* job, not your present one. As a matter of fact, try to phrase ALL your answers in terms of the job for which you are being examined.

Basis of Rating

Probably you will forget most of these "do's" and "don'ts" when you walk into the oral interview room. Even remembering them all will not ensure you a passing grade. Perhaps you did not have the qualifications in the first place. But remembering them will help you to put your best foot forward, without treading on the toes of the board members.

Rumor and popular opinion to the contrary notwithstanding, an oral board wants you to make the best appearance possible. They know you are under pressure – but they also want to see how you respond to it as a guide to what your reaction would be under the pressures of the job you seek. They will be influenced by the degree of poise you display, the personal traits you show and the manner in which you respond.

ABOUT THIS BOOK

This book contains tests divided into Examination Sections. Go through each test, answering every question in the margin. We have also attached a sample answer sheet at the back of the book that can be removed and used. At the end of each test look at the answer key and check your answers. On the ones you got wrong, look at the right answer choice and learn. Do not fill in the answers first. Do not memorize the questions and answers, but understand the answer and principles involved. On your test, the questions will likely be different from the samples. Questions are changed and new ones added. If you understand these past questions you should have success with any changes that arise. Tests may consist of several types of questions. We have additional books on each subject should more study be advisable or necessary for you. Finally, the more you study, the better prepared you will be. This book is intended to be the last thing you study before you walk into the examination room. Prior study of relevant texts is also recommended. NLC publishes some of these in our Fundamental Series. Knowledge and good sense are important factors in passing your exam. Good luck also helps. So now study this Passbook, absorb the material contained within and take that knowledge into the examination. Then do your best to pass that exam.

EXAMINATION SECTION

EXAMINATION SECTION
TEST 1

DIRECTIONS: Each question or incomplete statement is followed by several suggested answers or completions. Select the one that BEST answers the question or completes the statement. *PRINT THE LETTER OF THE CORRECT ANSWER IN THE SPACE AT THE RIGHT.*

1. _____ refers to a ranger's power or right to give commands, enforce obedience, take action and make decisions. 1.____

   A. Jurisdiction
   B. License
   C. Authority
   D. Sanction

2. The primary objective of most of a park ranger's enforcement actions is 2.____

   A. correction and punishment
   B. establishing authority and control
   C. education and information
   D. decreasing liability

3. Which of the following ranger services is LEAST likely to be provided through visitor contact? 3.____

   A. Interpretive
   B. Resource management
   C. Safety
   D. Search, rescue and recovery

4. A ranger comes upon a location that she believes to be a crime scene, but she has no training in criminal investigation. As the first park official on the scene, she should 4.____

   A. disperse everyone in the area
   B. record existing and relevant data in a notebook
   C. straighten or clean up the scene
   D. interview available witnesses

5. In most automobiles, the VIN plate is on the 5.____

   A. driver's side doorjamb
   B. driver's side windshield post
   C. driver's side dashboard
   D. passenger's side dashboard

6. A park's "situation map" should be marked on a surface of 6.____

   A. wood or plywood
   B. paper
   C. enamel or clear acetate
   D. canvas

7. The Rhomberg test is a field test most useful for indicating _____ intoxication. 7._____

   A. alcohol
   B. marijuana
   C. cocaine
   D. methamphetamine

8. A ranger on patrol should imagine his/her key responsibility to be 8._____

   A. conservation
   B. prevention
   C. surveillance
   D. observation

9. The form of federal jurisdiction that a park ranger will encounter most rarely is _____ jurisdiction, which means the federal government has been granted the right by a state to exercise certain state authorities. 9._____

   A. partial
   B. proprietary
   C. multiple
   D. concurrent

10. One of the actions within a park ranger's continuum of enforcement levels is the verbal warning. The key to issuing a verbal warning is for a park ranger to 10._____

    A. maintain a stern and authoritative tone of voice
    B. convince the offender of the seriousness of the offense
    C. convince the offender that the warning is really just a friendly chat
    D. be certain he has the authority to implement the consequences if it becomes necessary

11. For most park agencies, the most appropriate training vehicle for providing training to rangers who will have law enforcement authority includes a 11._____

    I.   basic agency-wide course of 40 to 80 hours
    II. 20- to 40-hour orientation course at the assigned park
    III. 3- to 6-month on-the-job training program at the assigned park
    IV. participation in special training courses as opportunities arise.

    A. I and II
    B. II and III
    C. II, III and IV
    D. I, II, III and IV

12. Generally, the use of vehicles for park patrol 12._____

    I.   greatly increases a ranger's ability to respond quickly to emergencies
    II. is the optimal method for increasing personal contact with visitors
    III. affords the ranger a degree of protection
    IV. offers the most efficient method of patrol with limited man power

    A. I, II and III
    B. I, III and IV
    C. II and III
    D. I, II, III and IV

13. Whenever a suitable wall surface isn't available for conducting a search of an offender, a kneeling search may be appropriate. In a standard kneeling search, the

    A. offender's knees should be together
    B. offender's feet should be spread apart
    C. offender's hand should be raised high above his head
    D. ranger should search from behind the offender

13.____

14. When initiating communication with visitors in an enforcement situation, the ranger's most immediate responsibility is to

    A. help the visitor understand the seriousness of the offense
    B. create a supportive rather than defensive climate
    C. make sure the visitor is aware of the ranger's authority to enforce
    D. ensure that the visitor is physically incapable of mounting an attack

14.____

15. Which of the following types of knots is used to attach a rope to the middle of another rope?

    A. Prusik
    B. Clove hitch
    C. Square lashing
    D. Shear lashing

15.____

16. Listening is usually thought of as being accomplished on four levels. The highest level involves

    A. listening with understanding of the speaker's point of view
    B. making sense out of sound
    C. critically evaluating what is said
    D. understanding the literal meaning of what is said

16.____

17. Which of the following structures may generally be entered unconditionally by a ranger in an enforcement situation?
    I. Park administrative building
    II. Public restrooms
    III. Visitor abodes
    IV. Concessionaire's leased building

    A. I and II
    B. I, II and III
    C. II and III
    D. I, II, III and IV

17.____

18. Which of the following is most likely to be a standard item for a mounted patrol?

    A. Animal noose
    B. Survival kit
    C. Flares
    D. Hydraulic jack

18.____

19. "Thumbnail" descriptions of persons include each of the following, EXCEPT

   A. Hair color
   B. Eyes
   C. Clothing
   D. Race

20. A ranger is reading a park map grid reference. On such maps, a four-digit grid reference number refers to the grid square located to the _____ the point of intersection of the lines relating to the grid numbers.

   A. right and above
   B. right and below
   C. left and above
   D. left and below

21. It is usually permissible to search an offender incidental to an arrest. Which of the following statements about such searches is TRUE?

   A. During a legal search, a ranger may seize items that are not only in actual possession, but within reach of the person at the time of the search.
   B. Evidence of a crime other than the one for which the ranger has an arrest warrant is generally not seizable.
   C. Stop-and-frisk searches are permitted under most situations.
   D. A legal search may usually be conducted by any ranger who has arrest powers.

22. A ranger is helping to compose the interpretive text for visitor center exhibits. The best text-on-background color combination in terms of legibility would be

   A. black on white
   B. green on white
   C. green on red
   D. blue on white

23. Before conducting a search, a park ranger should always obtain a search warrant if there is time, or whenever there is doubt as to whether one is necessary. Generally, a search warrant is required if

   A. exceptional circumstances create probable cause that contraband or other evidence will soon be destroyed
   B. the search is of a motor vehicle that is capable of being moved out of the ranger's control and there is probable cause to believe that someone in the vehicle has been involved in the commission of a crime
   C. the search is of a habitable dwelling on park grounds that is owned by the park, but occupied by the suspect as a camping abode
   D. the search is incidental to a lawful arrest and confined to the offender's person

24. A ranger should consider the primary objective of a park agency's interpretive services to be

   A. informing
   B. dispelling commonly held assumptions
   C. furthering an agenda
   D. inciting the visitor to some action or feeling

25. In certain circumstances, search of a person or premises may be appropriate even though legal grounds are weak or absent. Such searches may be conducted with consent. Which of the following statements concerning consent searches is TRUE?

    A. The person granting consent does not necessarily have to be aware of the right to refuse consent.
    B. A consent to enter premises implies a consent to search.
    C. A statement welcoming a search implies that a warrant is not demanded.
    D. Consent may be revoked at any time, but the revocation does not invalidate any evidence seized prior to the revocation.

25.____

KEY (CORRECT ANSWERS)

1.	C	11.	C
2.	C	12.	B
3.	B	13.	D
4.	B	14.	B
5.	C	15.	A
6.	C	16.	A
7.	A	17.	A
8.	D	18.	C
9.	A	19.	B
10.	D	20.	A

21.	A
22.	D
23.	C
24.	D
25.	D

TEST 2

DIRECTIONS: Each question or incomplete statement is followed by several suggested answers or completions. Select the one that BEST answers the question or completes the statement. *PRINT THE LETTER OF THE CORRECT ANSWER IN THE SPACE AT THE RIGHT.*

1. In most cases it is appropriate for a park ranger to think of visitors as
    I. not dependent on the ranger; it is the ranger who is dependent on them
    II. the most important people the ranger will come into contact with
    III. not an interruption of the ranger's work, but the main reason for it
    IV. outsiders who will alter the park, rather than an integral part of the environment

    A. I and II
    B. I, II and III
    C. II, III and IV
    D. I, II, III and IV

    1.____

2. Which of following legal terms is used to denote the proof that a crime has occurred?

    A. *Corpus delicti*
    B. *Habeus corpus*
    C. *Respondent superior*
    D. Probable cause

    2.____

3. In the continuum of a park ranger's enforcement priorities, "Priority 1" situations deal with

    A. the protection of visitors from each other
    B. situations in which neither the park nor its visitors are in any immediate danger
    C. the protection of the park's resources from the visitor
    D. the protection of visitors from hazardous conditions created by park resources

    3.____

4. The strongest ropes are generally made of

    A. polypropylene
    B. nylon
    C. manila
    D. Dacron

    4.____

5. A ranger is helping to compose the interpretive text for visitor center exhibits. For one exhibit, visitors will be about 15 feet from the text. The letters for this text should be at least _____ high.

    A. a half-inch
    B. an inch
    C. an inch-and-a-half
    D. two inches

    5.____

6. The primary purposes of patrol include
    I. providing resource protection
    II. making assistance available to visitors
    III. providing a deterrent for destructive behavior
    IV. observing the park and visitor behavior

    A. I and II
    B. II and IV
    C. II, III and IV
    D. I, II, III and IV

    6.____

7. A ranger is one of the first officials to arrive at the scene of a crime. Preliminary procedures that will ordinarily be undertaken by the investigating ranger include each of the following, EXCEPT

   A. safeguarding the area
   B. conducting a methodic crime scene search
   C. separating witnesses from bystanders and obtaining statements
   D. rendering assistance to the injured

8. In areas of _____ jurisdiction, only state law is considered to be in effect, meaning that federal officers may enforce rules and regulations only such as Title 36, CFR and other federal laws allow regardless of jurisdiction.

   A. partial
   B. proprietary
   C. concurrent
   D. exclusive

9. To be legal, a search warrant should specifically identify the
   I. property to be seized
   II. place to be searched
   III. limits of the search
   IV. probable cause upon which the search is based

   A. I and II
   B. II, III and IV
   C. III and IV
   D. I, II, III and IV

10. Which of the following is a guideline that should be followed in handling a domestic dispute on park property?

    A. If the situation seems to justify the intervention of a professional counselor, recommend counseling in a general way.
    B. Offer legal advice if either of the parties is considering legal action.
    C. Ask questions that will determine who is at fault or who began the altercation.
    D. Try to stay out of such disputes unless it becomes clear that someone is in danger of imminent physical harm.

11. Rangers are often brought into contact with groups who represent "subcultures"-groups of a similar age, race, occupation or other grouping characteristics that may lead to the development of a kind of dialect or language system all their own. In communicating with these groups—especially in enforcement situations—it is important for the ranger to

    A. acknowledge only standard grammatical English
    B. understand the "language" of the subculture, but not to use it
    C. try to communicate with these groups using their own dialect or jargon
    D. try to speak as little as possible

12. Rangers without law enforcement authority are empowered, in some situations, to   12._____
    I. issue citations
    II. detain visitors
    III. search visitors
    IV. seize property

    A. I only
    B. I and II
    C. I, II and III
    D. I, II, III and IV

13. Which of the following is a disadvantage associated with foot patrol?   13._____

    A. Ranger's presence is suggested, rather than seen or heard
    B. Restricted to extensive-use areas
    C. Direct contact with visitors is inhibited
    D. Limited ability to respond to situations outside the immediate area

14. Guidelines for search-and-rescue operations within a park include   14._____
    I. Radio-equipped searchers should be sent to danger or vantage points.
    II. If dogs are used, they should be on a leash.
    III. Searches should generally not be continued after dark unless a life-or-death situation exists.
    IV. Each searcher should periodically call out the name(s) of the lost person(s).

    A. I and II
    B. I, II and III
    C. IV only
    D. I, II, III and IV

15. The ability of park rangers to implement enforcement services is dependent upon a num-   15._____
    ber of factors. Which of the following is LEAST likely to be one of these factors?

    A. The park agency's policies
    B. The ranger's level of certainty about the appropriateness of enforcement
    C. The individual ranger's level of training and expertise
    D. The authority and jurisdiction authorized by law

16. Good listening skills for rangers include   16._____
    I. Forming judgements before listening to the speaker, based on appearance and demeanor
    II. Considering listening to be an active process
    III. Always taking notes while listening
    IV. Listening to how something is being said before concentrating on the actual content of the message

    A. I and II
    B. II only
    C. II, III and IV
    D. I, II, III and IV

17. Which of the following is NOT generally considered part of the standard frisk procedure?   17.____

    A. Offender's feet spread about two feet apart.
    B. Offender's hands extended above the head, with fingers spread.
    C. Ranger moves fingertips over all searchable areas, crushing clothing to locate concealed weapons.
    D. Offenders considered dangerous should be handcuffed prior to the frisk.

18. One of the signs that a person has overdosed on a stimulant is   18.____

    A. cold, clammy skin
    B. fatigue
    C. slurred speech
    D. convulsions

19. Which of the following is NOT a guideline that should usually be followed in conducting patrols?   19.____

    A. Patrols should always follow the same method, route, and schedule.
    B. Patrol rangers should periodically stop at "overview" points.
    C. Open patrol is, in most situations, preferred to hidden patrol.
    D. Whenever possible, patrols should be conducted by a team of two.

20. In relaying a description of an individual, the first detail given is usually   20.____

    A. sex   B. age   C. race   D. height

21. Normally, searches of vehicles by a park ranger require a search warrant. Exceptions include   21.____

    I.   whenever probable cause to search exists
    II. the search is incidental to an arrest
    III. items are in open view through the vehicle's window
    IV. the vehicle has stopped at an authorized roadblock

    A. I only
    B. I and II
    C. I, II and III
    D. I, II, III and IV

22. Which of the following is LEAST likely to be a standard item for a cycle patrol?   22.____

    A. Portable spotlight
    B. First aid kit
    C. Maps and brochures
    D. Folding shovel

23. A ranger must attempt to stop a moving vehicle to implement an enforcement action. While in motion, the ranger should stay within _____ feet of the vehicle.   23.____

    A. 15 and 20   B. 25 and 40   C. 50 and 75   D. 100 and 200

24. Research demonstrates that _____ percent of a ranger's duty time involves some form of communication.

    A. 55-65
    B. 65-75
    C. 75-85
    D. 85-95

25. A ranger is called on to approach an offender who is belligerent. Guidelines to follow during such an encounter include
    I. making sure that a weapon is visible and at the ready
    II. trying to bargain with the offender for better behavior
    III. if you do not have the authority to make an arrest, trying to give the impression that you do
    IV. regardless of the provocation, never exhibiting anger or impatience

    A. I only
    B. I and II
    C. IV only
    D. II, III and IV

KEY (CORRECT ANSWERS)

1. B		11. B
2. A		12. A
3. A		13. D
4. B		14. D
5. B		15. B
6. D		16. B
7. B		17. C
8. B		18. D
9. D		19. A
10. A		20. A

21. C
22. D
23. C
24. C
25. C

TEST 3

DIRECTIONS: Each question or incomplete statement is followed by several suggested answers or completions. Select the one that BEST answers the question or completes the statement. *PRINT THE LETTER OF THE CORRECT ANSWER IN THE SPACE AT THE RIGHT.*

1. A ranger is composing a sketch of an accident scene. He will need to discriminate between temporary, short-lived, and long-lived evidence. Which of the following would be considered short-lived evidence?

    A. Gasoline puddles
    B. Vehicle debris
    C. Skid marks
    D. Gouges in the pavement

    1.____

2. In most situations, the best attitude for the park ranger to adopt is one that is _____ oriented.

    A. service
    B. enterprise
    C. task
    D. staff

    2.____

3. In the park setting, courts have ruled that search-and-seizure laws apply to visitor abodes (motor homes, trailers, screen canopies, rented cabins), as well as the area surrounding the abode and normally considered a part thereof (campsite, trash can, storage shed, etc.). The legal term for this surrounding area is

    A. environs
    B. curtilage
    C. quadrangle
    D. milieu

    3.____

4. Which of the following is NOT a guideline that a park ranger should use in handling a complaint?

    A. Remember that some complaints should be taken more seriously than others
    B. Focus initially on the facts surrounding the situation or problem
    C. Always thank the complainant for his or her interest
    D. Notify the complainant when corrective action has been taken

    4.____

5. Guidelines for a park ranger's enforcement actions include
    I. the use of physical force should be limited to the minimum necessary to implement the action
    II. the vigor or severity of enforcement actions should be dependent on the attitude of the offender
    III. whenever a ranger is unable to secure cooperation, he should withdraw from the immediate area and seek appropriate assistance
    IV. whenever doubt exists as to whether a situation actually constitutes a violation, or whether the suspect is in fact the perpetrator, the ranger should rule in favor of the visitor and try to resolve the doubt

    A. I and II
    B. I, III and IV
    C. I and IV
    D. I, II, III and IV

    5.____

6. A park ranger should usually think of her primary duty as

   A. assuring each park visitor a quality experience
   B. enforcing the existing rules within park boundaries
   C. observing visitor behaviors and being prepared for any problems that might arise
   D. protecting the park's most important resources

7. Which of the following is NOT a principle that should guide the composition and delivery of interpretive services in a park?

   A. Interpretation should tell the whole story, rather than just a part of it.
   B. Interpretation should arouse curiosity in addition to giving facts.
   C. The best interpretation sticks to information within the "comfort zone" of visitors.
   D. The best interpretation occurs through person-to-person communication.

8. _____ patrol is the method that provides the greatest amount of visitor access, but usually prohibits extensive observation of visitor behavior and park conditions.

   A. Cycle
   B. Mounted
   C. Foot
   D. Vehicle

9. One of the signs that a person has overdosed on a depressant is

   A. hallucinations
   B. slow pulse
   C. cold, clammy skin
   D. constricted pupils

10. A ranger is conducting a field interview to determine the cause of an incident. The ranger should know that of all the behaviors that suggest an untruthful response, the one most commonly demonstrated by deceitful people is

    A. bringing the hand to the head
    B. interrupting the questioner
    C. hesitation
    D. crossing the arms over the chest

11. A ranger is conducting a field interview to record a visitor's perceptions of an event. In recording the visitor's account, the ranger should remember each of the following general truths about human perception EXCEPT that

    A. people tend to overestimate the length of verticals while underestimating the width of horizontals
    B. danger and stress cause people to underestimate duration and distance
    C. light-colored objects tend to be seen as heavier and nearer than dark objects of the same size and distance away
    D. people usually recall actions and events better than objects

12. If a DWI suspect refuses to submit to a chemical test, many jurisdictions accept this as an admission of intoxication resulting in the revocation of driving privileges for a period of time. This result, however, is predicated on several criteria. Which of the following is NOT one of these criteria?

    A. The ranger has probable cause to believe the suspect is DWI.
    B. The suspect has already completed a standard' field sobriety test.
    C. The ranger placed the suspect under arrest.
    D. The ranger specifically requested the suspect to submit to a chemical test.

13. A ranger is reading a park map grid reference. On this map, the numbers are read from

    A. left to right and top to bottom
    B. left to right and bottom to top
    C. right to left and top to bottom
    D. right to left and bottom to top

14. Defensive measures consist of several levels of defense. The level known as "defensive opposition" involves

    A. warding off blows with limbs or a baton
    B. the use of a firearm
    C. the use of chemical irritants
    D. simply ignoring verbal and visual abuse

15. Which of the following is NOT an element of the "legal scope" of a park ranger's jurisdiction?

    A. The park's physical boundaries
    B. Traffic codes
    C. Fish and game laws
    D. Criminal statutes

16. Which of the following is an example of a "transitional" interpretive experience?

    A. Slide presentation
    B. Visitor center exhibit
    C. Outdoor interpretive stations
    D. Automobile tour

17. A ranger is designing an interpretive activity for a group of elementary school children who are all about eight years old. For children at this age,

    A. ideas, rather than objects, are very important
    B. relations with others are based primarily on self-interest
    C. there is a strong desire for independence from adults
    D. peer relationships are very important

18. Which of the following is most likely to be a standard item for a foot patrol?

    A. Jumper cables
    B. Tranquilizer gun
    C. Folding stretcher
    D. Transceiver

19. In the continuum of a park ranger's enforcement priorities, "Priority 3" situations deal with

    A. the protection of visitors from hazardous conditions created by park resources
    B. the protection of the park's resources from the visitor
    C. the protection of visitors from each other
    D. situations in which neither the park nor its visitors are in any immediate danger

20. Recreational resources may be managed under the guidance of several viewpoints. The _____ viewpoint holds that resources should be used in an essentially "as is" manner, and that visitor use should blend with the resource base.

    A. preservationist
    B. landscape maintenance
    C. conservationist
    D. recreation activity

21. Which of the following is NOT a guideline that should be used for the conduct of station duty?

    A. Whenever rangers are in conversation with visitors, they should stand.
    B. Each question should be answered as if it were the first time the ranger has heard it.
    C. Rangers should remain sitting or standing behind a counter.
    D. Rangers should attempt to serve all visitors who need assistance.

22. Which of the following statements about search warrants is typically FALSE?

    A. Searchers may remain only a sufficient length of time as is "reasonably" necessary to search for and seize the property described in the search warrant.
    B. Generally, searchers may not seize items relating to criminal activity that are not specifically identified in the search warrant
    C. Search warrants for the premises do not permit a search of all persons present in the premises
    D. In most situations, real estate can be seized under a search warrant

23. A ranger's boundary maintenance responsibilities typically include each of the following functions EXCEPT

    A. physically locating the boundary line, either by previous marks or survey
    B. identifying trespass and/or encroachment
    C. marking and signing the boundary
    D. preventing erosion of coastal/shoreline boundaries

24. The park's public relations program must
    I. emphasize specific stages in a process, rather than ultimate goals
    II. solve the problems of others while solving the problems of the park
    III. focus on challenges and shortcomings that are in need of assistance or support
    IV. consist of actions that are coordinated and integrated

    A. I only
    B. I, II and III
    C. II and IV
    D. I, II, III and IV

25. Arrests can normally be made by park rangers 25.____
    I. on an arrest warrant
    II. on view of a felony being committed
    III. on reasonable suspicion of a felony
    IV. on reasonable suspicion of a misdemeanor

    A. I only
    B. I and II
    C. I, II and III
    D. I, II, III and IV

KEY (CORRECT ANSWERS)

1.	C	11.	B
2.	A	12.	B
3.	B	13.	B
4.	A	14.	A
5.	B	15.	A
6.	A	16.	D
7.	C	17.	D
8.	C	18.	D
9.	C	19.	B
10.	A	20.	C

21. C
22. D
23. D
24. C
25. C

EXAMINATION SECTION
TEST 1

DIRECTIONS: Each question or incomplete statement is followed by several suggested answers or completions. Select the one that BEST answers the question or completes the statement. *PRINT THE LETTER OF THE CORRECT ANSWER IN THE SPACE AT THE RIGHT.*

1. Which of the following is NOT an advantage to using classroom teachers as outdoor-education staff members?

    A. Most are trained in educational methodology.
    B. Most are knowledgeable about the outdoors.
    C. They are familiar with the participants from their own classrooms.
    D. They are generally efficient users of instructional time.

2. The MAIN difference between the objectives of an environmental education program and its purposes is that the objectives

    A. are specific, measurable changes in the participants of a program
    B. are designed to be more far-reaching
    C. are concerned primarily with the internal workings of a program
    D. often vary from program to program

3. Which of the following is NOT considered to be one of the basic components of an ecological system?

    A. Abiotic substances such as soil, water, and air
    B. Weather patterns
    C. Producers
    D. Decomposers

4. Making informed choices between essential and nonessential goods is an objective associated with the _____ domain of environmental education.

    A. ecological   B. political
    C. social   D. economic

5. Which of the following represents a lower-level activity in the environmental education hierarchy?

    A. Problem-solving processes
    B. Analogies
    C. Decision-making
    D. Ecological principles

6. In the United States, the main body of environmental information comes INITIALLY from

    A. government reports and studies
    B. privately-funded scientific periodicals
    C. the mainstream news media
    D. public-funded radio and television programs

17

7. Which of the following is normally a characteristic of camp-centered outdoor/environmental education?

   A. Experiences are planned in the classroom and applied in camp.
   B. The program is operated by a classroom teacher with the help of trained resource persons.
   C. Camping experiences are evaluated on their contribution to the work of the classroom.
   D. Experiences are not planned to bring out specific learnings, but valuable concepts are gained through incidental experience.

8. Which of the following is a concept associated with the economic aspect of environmental education?

   A. Public opinion constitutes a control over the use of conservation practices.
   B. Animal populations are renewable resources.
   C. Individuals tend to select short-term gains at the expense of long-term environmental benefits.
   D. Individual citizens should be stimulated to become involved in the political process.

9. The standard recommendation for an outdoor-education site's distance from a hospital is no more than _____ miles.

   A. 5-10   B. 15-20   C. 25-30   D. 50

10. In general, NOT considered to be an experience involved in the process of environmental education is

    A. environmental discovery and inquiry
    B. environmental evaluation and problem identification
    C. planned alteration of the environment
    D. problem-solving in the environment

11. A PRIMARY difference between the instructional and social living phases of environmental education is that during the instructional phase

    A. student groups are not mixed
    B. staff attempt to shape student attitudes
    C. students are taught to share responsibilities
    D. student progress is not evaluated

12. According to the conceptual framework for environmental education, _____ exemplifies the *macro* level of ecological analysis.

    A. the classroom or school
    B. political or legal institutions
    C. larger social structures
    D. the family and neighborhood of schools

13. In order to insure that sleeping arrangements in an outdoor education bunkhouse are both safe and efficient, it is IMPORTANT to arrange beds or sleepers so that

    A. there is a minimum of six feet of space between the sides of the beds
    B. there is at least 60 square feet of usable floor space for each sleeper

C. their heads are at least six feet apart
D. the bunks are tripled

14. Which of the following is NOT an explanation for why environmental education is usually described as a *human-centered* process?

    A. Humans are an indivisible part of world dynamics.
    B. All awareness and decision-making associated with education begins in the human mind.
    C. Humans alone have the conscious ability to alter the world's balances.
    D. Humans are generally the most important world species.

15. Which is usually NOT a subcategory of the environment for which measurable objectives are targeted in the early stages of an education program?

    A. Social   B. Biotic   C. Political   D. Physical

16. Which of the following is an evaluative activity for students that would be classified in the category of problem-solving?

    A. Compiling complete and accurate information in both written and graphic form
    B. Selecting and completing optional assignments related to the selected topic of study
    C. Identifying and defining issues and problems affecting the total environment
    D. Attempting to work harmoniously with others on a given task

17. Which of the following is a concept associated with the political aspect of environmental education?

    A. Modern humans affect the structure of their environment.
    B. Pollutants and contaminants are produced by natural and human-made processes.
    C. Humans have psychobiological and biosocial needs.
    D. As population increases, the freedom of individuals to use natural resources decreases.

18. The discipline that environmental education is designed PRIMARILY to influence in all individuals is

    A. art   B. history   C. living   D. science

19. Which of the following learning processes involves the MOST complex set of skills and behaviors?

    A. Experimenting   B. Observing
    C. Classifying   D. Inferring

20. In the global model for environmental interaction, humans exert influence on the environment by their output through the

    A. biosphere   B. ecosphere
    C. technosphere   D. geosphere

21. According to most environmental education models, which of the concepts below would be reserved for the latest stages of the education process?

    A. Philosophy of human/earth interaction
    B. Environmental sensitivity
    C. Factual knowledge
    D. Problem-solving skills

22. Usually, the BEST method of teaching decision-making skills in outdoor education is(are)

    A. researching the decisions made by public bodies in the past
    B. self-reliance survival exercises
    C. simulation games and hypothetical issues
    D. case studies

23. Which of these curricular disciplines is the one LEAST likely to be integrated into an environmental education program?

    A. Social science
    B. Mathematics
    C. Humanities
    D. Health

24. Which of the following is NOT a method for dealing with population growth that is supported by most recent research?

    A. Engaging people of all socioeconomic backgrounds in the decision-making process
    B. Concentration of birth control and family planning efforts on minority populations
    C. A program of incentives to adopt available children
    D. Ruling out any and all programs for mandatory sterilization

25. In an environmental education program, the objectives that are MOST easily and accurately measured are

    A. behavioral
    B. attitudinal
    C. emotional
    D. social

KEY (CORRECT ANSWERS)

1. B
2. A
3. B
4. D
5. B

6. A
7. D
8. C
9. B
10. C

11. A
12. B
13. C
14. D
15. C

16. D
17. D
18. C
19. A
20. C

21. A
22. C
23. B
24. B
25. A

TEST 2

DIRECTIONS: Each question or incomplete statement is followed by several suggested answers or completions. Select the one that BEST answers the question or completes the statement. *PRINT THE LETTER OF THE CORRECT ANSWER IN THE SPACE AT THE RIGHT.*

1. The collective term for the concepts and values through which humans recognize their interdependence with the environment, as well as their own responsibilities for maintaining it, is

    A. biotics   B. ecototics   C. ekistics   D. socioties

    1.____

2. Which of the following is NOT usually considered to be a guiding concept for outdoor/environmental education programs?

    A. The majority of young children access the physical universe through abstractions, rather than firsthand experience.
    B. Modern living has increased the need for outdoor/ environmental education.
    C. Outdoor/environmental education is not a separate discipline in itself.
    D. In outdoor/environmental education, learning is controlled by instructors who lead students to discover a set of prescribed educational goals.

    2.____

3. Which of the following would be an objective for the discovery-inquiry level of an environmental education program?

    A. Defining an environmental issue or problem
    B. Recognizing the living components of a single ecosystem
    C. Determining alternative solutions to an environmental problem
    D. Identifying opportunities for environmental improvement

    3.____

4. In the standard progression of outdoor-education activities, which courses would a program's participants engage in FIRST?

    A. Ecological principles
    B. Investigating environmental habitats
    C. Recognizing land-use problems
    D. Outdoor survival

    4.____

5. Most environmental education programs are structured around the belief that environmental problems are caused by

    A. the actions of a limited number of political bodies
    B. the way all civilized humans presently try to meet their personal and social needs
    C. industrial trends that begin primarily in the United States
    D. the geometric increase in the world's human population

    5.____

6. Environmental components that provide for human physical needs are related to each of the following characteristics EXCEPT

    A. social well-being and interaction
    B. durability or lastingness
    C. convenience and efficiency
    D. safety and health

    6.____

7. Which of the following is an affective component of the human attitude toward nature?

   A. Concern for the existing parts of natural systems
   B. Awareness of the interrelationship of parts of natural systems
   C. Appreciation of the need for stability in a healthy natural system
   D. Awareness of changes in the structure and function of natural systems

8. The human behavior that would be studied and evaluated at the more advanced stages of an environmental education program would USUALLY be

   A. residing
   B. working
   C. taking leisure
   D. obtaining goods

9. A concept associated with the socio-cultural aspect of environmental education is:

   A. An organism is the product of its heredity and environment
   B. Humans have a moral responsibility for their environmental decisions
   C. Conservation policies are often the result of group action
   D. Plants are renewable resources

10. In order to meet the accepted standard, a site for outdoor education must have an infirmary that will house at least _____ people for every 100 housed on the site.

    A. 1   B. 3   C. 10   D. 30

11. The *strand* approach to environmental education involves each of the following concepts EXCEPT

    A. patterns
    B. continuity and change
    C. interaction and interdependence
    D. manipulation

12. Which of the following would be an objective for the problem-solving level of an environmental education program?

    A. Evaluating the satisfaction of human needs by environmental processes
    B. Recognizing the structure of a natural ecosystem
    C. Determining alternative solutions to an environmental dilemma
    D. Investigating the natural cycles or processes of an individual ecosystem

13. Which of the events below would be MOST likely to take place in the social living phase of the environmental teaching progression?

    A. Courses in naturecraft
    B. Discovery activities such as nature walks
    C. Group courses in natural resource study areas
    D. Student preparation of morning meals

14. The ULTIMATE aim of most environmental education programs is to

    A. stimulate participants' interest and performance in scientific academic disciplines
    B. change attitudes and behavior patterns among its participants
    C. provide a constructive and instructive recreational outlet for its participants
    D. stimulate environmental awareness and sensitivity

15. In developing a curriculum for environmental education programs, which of the following is NOT considered to be an influential factor?

    A. Transferability
    B. Past experiences of students
    C. Socioeconomic status of students
    D. Economy of time

16. The production of art forms is an objective associated with the _____ conceptual domain of environmental education.

    A. ecological
    B. cultural
    C. familial
    D. psychological

17. In the standard environmental education hierarchy, which concept would students usually be required to learn FIRST?

    A. Patterns in the use of earth resources are affected by people's lifestyles.
    B. An unchecked increase in human populations will impede the maintenance of environmental quality.
    C. The earth is a closed and limited life-supporting system powered by the sun's energy.
    D. Environmental decisions are made by both private individuals and groups, and by public bodies or their agents.

18. Which of the following is NORMALLY a characteristic of school-centered outdoor/environmental education?

    A. The program concentrates on academic classes such as math and English, with recreational activities as a supplement to the learning experience.
    B. Camping experiences are not directly connected with classroom work.
    C. A trained staff in outdoor education operates the program with the pupils and teachers participating together.
    D. The majority of time is spent outdoors, with students learning how to cook and build shelter outdoors.

19. Of the duties listed below, the responsibility of a student who acts as a teaching technician is to

    A. assist students in working together on all tasks
    B. supervise work responsibilities such as cleanup and wood-gathering
    C. coordinate songs and activities at evening campfires
    D. assemble materials and equipment for field study areas

20. According to the conceptual framework for environmental education, which of the following exemplifies the *micro* level of ecological analysis?

    A. The classroom or school
    B. Political or legal institutions
    C. Larger social structures
    D. The family and neighborhood of schools

21. In the global model for environmental interaction, humans are MOST directly affected by input from the

    A. biosphere
    B. ecosphere
    C. technosphere
    D. geosphere

22. Which of the following is a cognitive component of the human attitude toward nature?

    A. Appreciation of the existing aspects of the natural environment
    B. Concern for the future aspects of the natural environment
    C. Awareness of the structure of a natural ecosystem
    D. Awareness of the human potential for improving the quality of any living system

23. A concept associated with the ecological aspect of environmental education is:

    A. The nonrenewable resource base is considered to be limited
    B. Natural resources are interdependent and will be affected by the use or misuse of their neighboring resources
    C. More efficient use of some resources is the result of technical and marketing improvements
    D. All living things, including man, are continually evolving

24. Which of the following would be an objective for the evaluation/problem identification level of an environmental education program?

    A. Investigating the processes in a living ecosystem
    B. Recognizing the total components of a single ecosystem
    C. Evaluating the consequences of possible solutions
    D. Identifying opportunities for environmental maintenance

25. Which of the following is NOT a characteristic of most environmental education programs? A(n)

    A. interdisciplinary approach to instruction
    B. target population that concentrates on a specific age and level of education
    C. continuous evaluation process
    D. problem-oriented instruction process

KEY (CORRECT ANSWERS)

1. C
2. D
3. B
4. A
5. B

6. A
7. A
8. D
9. B
10. B

11. D
12. C
13. D
14. B
15. C

16. D
17. C
18. A
19. D
20. A

21. A
22. C
23. B
24. D
25. B

———

EXAMINATION SECTION
TEST 1

DIRECTIONS: Each question or incomplete statement is followed by several suggested answers or completions. Select the one that BEST answers the question or completes the statement. *PRINT THE LETTER OF THE CORRECT ANSWER IN THE SPACE AT THE RIGHT.*

1. The officer who investigates accidents is always required to make a complete and accurate report.
   Of the following, the BEST reason for this procedure is to

   A. protect the operating agency against possible false claims
   B. provide a file of incidents which can be used as basic material for an accident prevention campaign
   C. provide the management with concrete evidence of violations of the rules by employees
   D. indicate what repairs need to be made

   1.____

2. It is suggested that an officer keep all persons away from the area of an accident until an investigation has been completed.
   This suggested procedure is

   A. *good;* witnesses will be more likely to agree on a single story
   B. *bad;* such action blocks traffic flow and causes congestion
   C. *good;* objects of possible use as evidence will be protected from damage or loss
   D. *bad;* the flow of normal pedestrian traffic provides an opportunity for an investigator to determine the cause of the accident

   2.____

3. A man having business with your agency is arguing with you and accuses you of being prejudiced against him. Although you explain to him that this is not so, he demands to see your supervisor.
   Of the following, the BEST course of action for you to take is to

   A. continue arguing with him until you have worn him out or convinced him
   B. take him to your supervisor
   C. ignore him and walk away from him to another part of the office
   D. escort him out of the office

   3.____

4. An officer receives instructions from his supervisor which he does not fully understand.
   For the officer to ask for a further explanation would be

   A. *good;* chiefly because his supervisor will be impressed with his interest in his work
   B. *poor;* chiefly because the time of the supervisor will be needlessly wasted
   C. *good;* chiefly because proper performance depends on full understanding of the work to be done
   D. *poor;* chiefly because officers should be able to think for themselves

   4.____

5. A person is making a complaint to an officer which seems unreasonable and of little importance.
   Of the following, the BEST action for the officer to take is to

   5.____

A. criticize the person making the complaint for taking up his valuable time
B. laugh over the matter to show that the complaint is minor and silly
C. tell the person that anyone responsible for his grievance will be prosecuted
D. listen to the person making the complaint and tell him that the matter will be investigated

6. A member of the department shall not indulge in intoxicating liquor while in uniform. A member of the department is not required to wear a uniform, and a uniformed member while out of uniform shall not indulge in intoxicants to an extent unfitting him for duty.
Of the following, the MOST correct interpretation of this rule is that a

A. member, off duty, not in uniform, may drink intoxicating liquor
B. member, not on duty, but in uniform, may drink intoxicating liquor
C. member, on duty, in uniform, may drink intoxicants
D. uniformed member, in civilian clothes, may not drink intoxicants

7. You have a suggestion for an important change which you believe will improve a certain procedure in your agency. Of the following, the next course of action for you to take is to

A. try it out yourself
B. submit the suggestion to your immediate supervisor
C. write a letter to the head of your agency asking for his approval
D. wait until you are asked for suggestions before submitting this one

8. An officer shall study maps and literature concerning his assigned area and the streets and points of interest nearby.
Of the following, the BEST reason for this rule is that

A. the officer will be better able to give correct information to persons desiring it
B. the officer will be better able to drive a vehicle in the area
C. the officer will not lose interest in his work
D. supervisors will not need to train the officers in this subject

9. In asking a witness to a crime to identify a suspect, it is a common practice to place the suspect with a group of persons and ask the witness to pick out the person in question.
Of the following, the BEST reason for this practice is that it will

A. make the identification more reliable than if the witness were shown the suspect alone
B. protect the witness against reprisals
C. make sure that the witness is telling the truth
D. help select other participants in the crime at the same time

10. It is most important for all officers to obey the "Rules and Regulations" of their agency.
Of the following, the BEST reason for this statement is that

A. supervisors will not need to train their new officers
B. officers will never have to use their own judgment
C. uniform procedures will be followed
D. officers will not need to ask their supervisors for assistance

Questions 11-13.

DIRECTIONS: Answer questions 11 to 13 SOLELY on the basis of the following paragraph.

All members of the police force must recognize that the people, through their representatives, hire and pay the police and that, as in any other employment, there must exist a proper employer-employee relationship. The police officer must understand that the essence of a correct police attitude is a willingness to serve, but at the same time, he should distinguish between service and servility, and between courtesy and softness. He must be firm but also courteous, avoiding even an appearance of rudeness. He should develop a position that is friendly and unbiased, pleasant and sympathetic, in his relations with the general public, but firm and impersonal on occasions calling for regulation and control. A police officer should understand that his primary purpose is to prevent violations, not to arrest people. He should recognize the line of demarcation between a police function and passing judgment which is a court function. On the other side, a public that cooperates with the police, that supports them in their efforts and that observes laws and regulations, may be said to have a desirable attitude.

11. In accordance with this paragraph, the PROPER attitude for a police officer to take is to   11._____

    A. be pleasant and sympathetic at all times
    B. be friendly, firm, and impartial
    C. be stern and severe in meting out justice to all
    D. avoid being rude, except in those cases where the public is uncooperative

12. Assume that an officer is assigned by his superior officer to a busy traffic intersection and is warned to be on the lookout for motorists who skip the light or who are speeding. According to this paragraph, it would be proper for the officer in this assignment to   12._____

    A. give a summons to every motorist whose ear was crossing when the light changed
    B. hide behind a truck and wait for drivers who violate traffic laws
    C. select at random motorists who seem to be impatient and lecture them sternly on traffic safety
    D. stand on post in order to deter violations and give offenders a summons or a warning as required

13. According to this paragraph, a police officer must realize that the primary purpose of police work is to   13._____

    A. provide proper police service in a courteous manner
    B. decide whether those who violate the law should be punished
    C. arrest those who violate laws
    D. establish a proper employer-employee relationship

Questions 14-15.

DIRECTIONS: Answer questions 14 and 15 SOLELY on the basis of the following paragraph.

If a motor vehicle fails to pass inspection, the owner will be given a rejection notice by the inspection station. Repairs must be made within ten days after this notice is issued. It is not necessary to have the required adjustment or repairs made at the station where the inspection occurred. The vehicle may be taken to any other garage. Re-inspection after repairs may be made at any official inspection station, not necessarily the same station which made the initial inspection. The registration of any motor vehicle for which an inspection sticker has not been obtained as required, or which is not repaired and inspected within ten days after inspection indicates defects, is subject to suspension. A vehicle cannot be used on public highways while its registration is under suspension.

14. According to the above paragraph, the owner of a car which does NOT pass inspection must 14._____

    A. have repairs made at the same station which rejected his car
    B. take the car to another station and have it re-inspected
    C. have repairs made anywhere and then have the car re-inspected
    D. not use the car on a public highway until the necessary repairs have been made

15. According to the above paragraph, the one of the following which may be cause for suspension of the registration of a vehicle is that 15._____

    A. an inspection sticker was issued before the rejection notice had been in force for ten days
    B. it was not re-inspected by the station that rejected it originally
    C. it was not re-inspected either by the station that rejected it originally or by the garage which made the repairs
    D. it has not had defective parts repaired within ten days after inspection

Questions 16-20.

DIRECTIONS: Answer questions 16 to 20 SOLELY on the basis of the following paragraph.

If we are to study crime in its widest social setting, we will find a variety of conduct which, although criminal in the legal sense, is not offensive to the moral conscience of a considerable number of persons. Traffic violations, for example, do not brand the offender as guilty of moral offense. In fact, the recipient of a traffic ticket is usually simply the subject of some good-natured joking by his friends. Although there may be indignation among certain groups of citizens against gambling and liquor law violations, these activities are often tolerated, if not openly supported, by the more numerous residents of the community. Indeed, certain social and service clubs regularly conduct gambling games and lotteries for the purpose of raising funds. Some communities regard violations involving the sale of liquor with little concern in order to profit from increased license fees and taxes paid by dealers. The thousand and one forms of political graft and corruption which infest our urban centers only occasionally arouse public condemnation and official action.

16. According to the paragraph, all types of illegal conduct are 16._____

    A. condemned by all elements of the community
    B. considered a moral offense, although some are tolerated by a few citizens
    C. violations of the law, but some are acceptable to certain elements of the community
    D. found in a social setting which is not punishable by law

17. According to the paragraph, traffic violations are generally considered by society as 17._____

    A. crimes requiring the maximum penalty set by the law
    B. more serious than violations of the liquor laws

C. offenses against the morals of the community
D. relatively minor offenses requiring minimum punishment

18. According to the paragraph, a lottery conducted for the purpose of raising funds for a church   18._____

    A. is considered a serious violation of law
    B. may be tolerated by a community which has laws against gambling
    C. may be conducted under special laws demanded by the more numerous residents of a community
    D. arouses indignation in most communities

19. On the basis of the paragraph, the MOST likely reaction in the community to a police raid on a gambling casino would be   19._____

    A. more an attitude of indifference than interest in the raid
    B. general approval of the raid
    C. condemnation of the raid by most people
    D. demand for further action since this raid is not sufficient to end gambling activities

20. The one of the following which BEST describes the central thought of this paragraph and would be MOST suitable as a title for it is   20._____

    A. CRIME AND THE POLICE
    B. PUBLIC CONDEMNATION OF GRAFT AND CORRUPTION
    C. GAMBLING IS NOT ALWAYS A VICIOUS BUSINESS
    D. PUBLIC ATTITUDE TOWARD LAW VIOLATIONS

Questions 21-23.

DIRECTIONS: Answer questions 21 to 23 SOLELY on the basis of the following paragraph.

The law enforcement agency is one of the most important agencies in the field of juvenile delinquency prevention. This is so not because of the social work connected with this problem, however, for this is not a police matter, but because the officers are usually the first to come in contact with the delinquent. The manner of arrest and detention makes a deep impression upon him and affects his life-long attitude toward society and the law. The juvenile court is perhaps the most important agency in this work. Contrary to the general opinion, however, it is not primarily concerned with putting children into correctional schools. The main purpose of the juvenile court is to save the child and to develop his emotional make-up in order that he can grow up to be a decent and well-balanced citizen. The system of probation is the means whereby the court seeks to accomplish these goals.

21. According to this paragraph, police work is an important part of a program to prevent juvenile delinquency because   21._____

    A. social work is no longer considered important in juvenile delinquency prevention
    B. police officers are the first to have contact with the delinquent
    C. police officers jail the offender in order to be able to change his attitude toward society and the law
    D. it is the first step in placing the delinquent in jail

22. According to this paragraph, the CHIEF purpose of the juvenile court is to   22.____

    A. punish the child for his offense
    B. select a suitable correctional school for the delinquent
    C. use available means to help the delinquent become a better person
    D. provide psychiatric care for the delinquent

23. According to this paragraph, the juvenile court directs the development of delinquents   23.____
    under its care CHIEFLY by

    A. placing the child under probation
    B. sending the child to a correctional school
    C. keeping the delinquent in prison
    D. returning the child to his home

Questions 24-27.

DIRECTIONS: Answer questions 24 to 27 SOLELY on the basis of the following paragraph.

When a vehicle has been disabled in the tunnel, the officer on patrol in this zone shall press the EMERGENCY TRUCK light button. In the fast lane, red lights will go on throughout the tunnel; in the slow lane, amber lights will go on throughout the tunnel. The yellow zone light will go on at each signal control station throughout the tunnel and will flash the number of the zone in which the stoppage has occurred. A red flashing pilot light will appear only at the signal control station at which the EMERGENCY TRUCK button was pressed. The emergency garage will receive an audible and visual signal indicating the signal control station at which the EMERGENCY TRUCK button was pressed. The garage officer shall acknowledge receipt of the signal by pressing the acknowledgment button. This will cause the pilot light at the operated signal control station in the tunnel to cease flashing and to remain steady. It is an answer to the officer at the operated signal control station that the emergency truck is responding to the call.

24. According to this paragraph, when the EMERGENCY TRUCK light button is pressed,   24.____

    A. amber lights will go on in every lane throughout the tunnel
    B. emergency signal lights will go on only in the lane in which the disabled vehicle happens to be
    C. red lights will go on in the fast lane throughout the tunnel
    D. pilot lights at all signal control stations will turn amber

25. According to this paragraph, the number of the zone in which the stoppage has occurred   25.____
    is flashed

    A. immediately after all the lights in the tunnel turn red
    B. by the yellow zone light at each signal control station
    C. by the emergency truck at the point of stoppage
    D. by the emergency garage

26. According to this paragraph, an officer near the disabled vehicle will know that the emer-   26.____
    gency tow truck is coming when

    A. the pilot light at the operated signal control station appears and flashes red
    B. an audible signal is heard in the tunnel

C. the zone light at the operated signal control station turns red
D. the pilot light at the operated signal control station becomes steady

27. Under the system described in the paragraph, it would be CORRECT to come to the conclusion that

    A. officers at all signal control stations are expected to acknowledge that they have received the stoppage signal
    B. officers at all signal control stations will know where the stoppage has occurred
    C. all traffic in both lanes of that side of the tunnel in which the stoppage has occurred must stop until the emergency truck has arrived
    D. there are two emergency garages, each able to respond to stoppages in traffic going in one particular direction

Questions 28-30.

DIRECTIONS: Answer questions 28 to 30 SOLELY on the basis of the following paragraphs.

In cases of accident, it is most important for an officer to obtain the name, age, residence, occupation, and a full description of the person injured, names and addresses of witnesses. He shall also obtain a statement of the attendant circumstances. He shall carefully note contributory conditions, if any, such as broken pavement, excavation, tights not burning, snow and ice on the roadway, etc. He shall enter all facts in his memorandum book and on Form 17 or Form 18 and promptly transmit the original of the form to his superior officer and the duplicate to headquarters.

An officer shall render reasonable assistance to sick or injured persons. If the circumstances appear to require the services of a physician, he shall summon a physician by telephoning the superior officer on duty and notifying him of the apparent nature of the illness or accident and the location where the physician will be required. He may summon other officers to assist if circumstances warrant.

In case of an accident or where a person is sick on city property, an officer shall obtain the information necessary to fill out card Form 18 and record this in his memorandum book and promptly telephone the facts to his superior officer. He shall deliver the original card at the expiration of his tour to his superior officer and transmit the duplicate to headquarters.

28. According to this quotation, the MOST important consideration in any report on a case of accident or injury is to

    A. obtain all the facts
    B. telephone his superior officer at once
    C. obtain a statement of the attendant circumstances
    D. determine ownership of the property on which the accident occurred

29. According to this quotation, in the case of an accident on city property, the officer should always

    A. summon a physician before filling out any forms or making any entries in his memorandum book
    B. give his superior officer on duty a prompt report by telephone

C. immediately bring the original of Form 18 to his superior officer on duty
D. call at least one other officer to the scene to witness conditions

30. If the procedures stated in this quotation were followed for all accidents in the city, an impartial survey of accidents occurring during any period of time in this city may be MOST easily made by

    A. asking a typical officer to show you his memorandum book
    B. having a superior officer investigate whether contributory conditions mentioned by witnesses actually exist
    C. checking all the records of all superior officers
    D. checking the duplicate card files at headquarters

Questions 31-55.

DIRECTIONS: In each of questions 31 to 55, select the lettered word or phrase which means MOST NEARLY the same as the first word in the row.

31. RENDEZVOUS
    A. parade   B. neighborhood
    C. meeting place   D. wander about

32. EMINENT
    A. noted   B. rich   C. rounded   D. nearby

33. CAUSTIC
    A. cheap   B. sweet   C. evil   D. sharp

34. BARTER
    A. annoy   B. trade   C. argue   D. cheat

35. APTITUDE
    A. friendliness   B. talent
    C. conceit   D. generosity

36. PROTRUDE
    A. project   B. defend   C. choke   D. boast

37. FORTITUDE
    A. disposition   B. restlessness
    C. courage   D. poverty

38. PRELUDE
    A. introduction   B. meaning
    C. prayer   D. secret

39. SECLUSION
    A. primitive   B. influence
    C. imagination   D. privacy

40. RECTIFY
    - A. correct
    - B. construct
    - C. divide
    - D. scold

41. TRAVERSE
    - A. rotate
    - B. compose
    - C. train
    - D. cross

42. ALLEGE
    - A. raise
    - B. convict
    - C. declare
    - D. chase

43. MENIAL
    - A. pleasant
    - B. unselfish
    - C. humble
    - D. stupid

44. DEPLETE
    - A. exhaust
    - B. gather
    - C. repay
    - D. close

45. ERADICATE
    - A. construct
    - B. advise
    - C. destroy
    - D. exclaim

46. CAPITULATE
    - A. cover
    - B. surrender
    - C. receive
    - D. execute

47. RESTRAIN
    - A. restore
    - B. drive
    - C. review
    - D. limit

48. AMALGAMATE
    - A. join
    - B. force
    - C. correct
    - D. clash

49. DEJECTED
    - A. beaten
    - B. speechless
    - C. weak
    - D. low-spirited

50. DETAIN
    - A. hide
    - B. accuse
    - C. hold
    - D. mislead

KEY (CORRECT ANSWERS)

1. A	11. B	21. B	31. C	41. D
2. C	12. D	22. C	32. A	42. C
3. B	13. A	23. A	33. D	43. C
4. C	14. C	24. C	34. B	44. A
5. D	15. D	25. B	35. B	45. C
6. A	16. C	26. D	36. A	46. B
7. B	17. D	27. B	37. C	47. D
8. A	18. B	28. A	38. A	48. A
9. A	19. A	29. B	39. D	49. D
10. C	20. D	30. D	40. A	50. C

TEST 2

DIRECTIONS: Each question or incomplete statement is followed by several suggested answers or completions. Select the one that BEST answers the question or completes the statement. *PRINT THE LETTER OF THE CORRECT ANSWER IN THE SPACE AT THE RIGHT.*

1. AMPLE

    A. necessary   B. plentiful   C. protected   D. tasty

2. EXPEDITE

    A. sue   B. omit   C. hasten   D. verify

3. FRAGMENT

    A. simple tool   B. broken part
    C. basic outline   D. weakness

4. ADVERSARY

    A. thief   B. partner   C. loser   D. foe

5. ACHIEVE

    A. accomplish   B. begin   C. develop   D. urge

Questions 6-10.

DIRECTIONS: Answer Questions 6 to 10 on the basis of the information given in the table on the following page. The numbers which have been omitted from the table can be calculated from the other numbers which are given.

NUMBER OF DWELLING UNITS CONSTRUCTED

Year	Private one-family houses	In private apt. houses	In public housing	Total dwelling units
1996	4,500	500	600	5,600
1997	9,200	5,300	2,800	17,300
1998	8,900	12,800	6,800	28,500
1999	12,100	15,500	7,100	34,700
2000	?	12,200	14,100	39,200
2001	10,200	26,000	8,600	44,800
2002	10,300	17,900	7,400	35,600
2003	11,800	18,900	7,700	38,400
2004	12,700	22,100	8,400	43,200
2005	13,300	24,300	8,100	45,700
TOTALS	105,900	?	?	?

6. According to this table, the average number of public housing units constructed yearly during the period 1996 through 2005 was

    A. 7,160   B. 6,180   C. 7,610   D. 6,810

7. Of the following, the two years in which the number of private one-family homes constructed was GREATEST for the two years together is

    A. 1998 and 1999   B. 1997 and 2003
    C. 1998 and 2004   D. 2001 and 2002

8. For the entire period of 1996 through 2005, the total of all private one-family houses constructed exceeded the total of all public housing units constructed by

    A. 34,300   B. 45,700   C. 50,000   D. 83,900

9. Of the total number of private apartment house dwelling units constructed in the ten years given in the table, the percentage which was constructed in 2002 was MOST NEARLY

    A. 5%   B. 11%   C. 16%   D. 21%

10. Considering dwelling units of all types, the average number constructed annually in the period from 2001 through 2005 was GREATER than the average number constructed annually in the period from 1996 through 2000 by

    A. 16,480   B. 33,320   C. 79,300   D. 82,400

11. A car speeds through the toll entrance of a 2 1/4 mile long bridge without paying the toll and reaches the other end of the bridge 1 minute and 30 seconds later. The car was traveling MOST NEARLY at a rate of _____ miles per hour.

    A. 60   B. 70   C. 80   D. 90

12. During one week, 21,500 vehicles passed through the toll booths of a certain bridge. Of these, 550 were buses, 2,230 were trucks, and the rest were passenger cars. The toll charges were $3.50 for a passenger car, $7 for a truck and $14 for a bus. The total income for the week was

    A. $80,850   B. $88,830   C. $102,550   D. $109,550

13. A bullet fired from a revolver travels 100 feet the first second, and each succeeding second it travels a distance 10% less than during the immediately preceding second. The number of feet the bullet will have traveled at the end of the fourth second is MOST NEARLY

    A. 272   B. 320   C. 344   D. 360

14. An officer receives a uniform allowance of $500 a year in a lump sum. Of this amount, he spends $180 for a winter jacket and 40% of the remainder for two pairs of trousers. The officer now wishes to buy a winter overcoat which costs $240.
The percentage of the purchase price of the overcoat by which he will be short is

    A. 20%   B. 25%   C. 48%   D. 60%

15. It has been suggested that small light cars can be used for certain kinds of police work. These light vehicles can run 30 miles per gallon of gasoline as contrasted with standard cars which run only 15 miles per gallon. Assume gasoline costs the city $3.75 per gallon. During 9,000 miles of travel, use of the small light car in preference to the standard car would result in a saving in gasoline costs of MOST NEARLY

    A. $1,125   B. $1,500   C. $1,875   D. $2,250

16. Out of a total of 34,750 felony complaints in 2006, 14,200 involved burglary. In 2005, there was a total of 32,300 felony complaints of which 12,800 were burglary.
    Of the increase in felonies from 2005 to 2006, the increase in burglaries comprised APPROXIMATELY

    A. 27%   B. 37%   C. 47%   D. 57%

    16.____

17. A certain city department has two offices which issue permits, one office handling twice as many applicants as the other. The smaller office grants permits to 40% of its applicants. The larger office handling twice as many applicants grants permits to 60% of its applicants.
    If there were 900 applicants at both offices together on a given day, the total number of permits granted by both offices would be MOST NEARLY

    A. 420   B. 450   C. 480   D. 510

    17.____

18. If a co-worker is not breathing after receiving an electric shock but is no longer in contact with the electricity, it is MOST important for you to

    A. avoid moving him
    B. wrap the victim in a blanket
    C. start artificial respiration promptly
    D. force him to take hot liquids

    18.____

19. Employees using supplies from one of the first-aid kits available throughout the building are required to submit an immediate report of the occurrence.
    Logical reasoning shows that the MOST important reason for this report is so that the

    A. supplies used will be sure to be replaced
    B. first-aid kit can be properly sealed again
    C. employee will be credited for his action
    D. record of first-aid supplies will be up-to-date

    19.____

20. The BEST IMMEDIATE first-aid treatment for a scraped knee is to

    A. apply plain vaseline   B. wash it with soap and water
    C. apply heat   D. use a knee splint

    20.____

21. Artificial respiration after a severe electrical shock is ALWAYS necessary when the shock results in

    A. unconsciousness   B. stoppage of breathing
    C. bleeding   D. a burn

    21.____

22. The authority gives some of its maintenance employees instruction in first aid.
    The MOST likely reason for doing this is to

    A. eliminate the need for calling a doctor in case of accident
    B. provide temporary emergency treatment in case of accident
    C. lower the cost of accidents to the authority
    D. reduce the number of accidents

    22.____

23. The BEST IMMEDIATE first aid if a chemical solution splashes into the eyes is to

    A. protect the eyes from the light by bandaging
    B. rub the eyes dry with a towel

    23.____

- C. cause tears to flow by staring at a bright light
- D. flush the eyes with large quantities of clean water

24. If you had to telephone for an ambulance because of an accident, the MOST important information for you to give the person who answered the telephone would be the

    A. exact time of the accident
    B. cause of the accident
    C. place where the ambulance is needed
    D. names and addresses of those injured

25. If a person has a deep puncture wound in his finger caused by a sharp nail, the BEST IMMEDIATE first aid procedure would be to

    A. encourage bleeding by exerting pressure around the injured area
    B. stop all bleeding
    C. prevent air from reaching the wound
    D. probe the wound for steel particles

26. In addition to cases of submersion, artificial respiration is a recommended first aid procedure for

    A. sunstroke   B. electrical shock   C. chemical poisoning   D. apoplexy

27. Assume that you are called on to render first aid to a man injured in an accident. You find he is bleeding profusely, is unconscious, and has a broken arm. There is a strong odor of alcohol about him.
    The FIRST thing for which you should treat him is the

    A. bleeding   B. unconsciousness   C. broken arm   D. alcoholism

28. In applying first aid for removal of a foreign body in the eye, an important precaution to be observed is NOT to

    A. attempt to wash out the foreign body
    B. bring the upper eyelid down over the lower
    C. rub the eye
    D. touch or attempt to remove a speck on the lower lid

29. The one of the following symptoms which is LEAST likely to indicate that a person involved in an accident requires first aid for shock is that

    A. he has fainted twice
    B. his face is red and flushed
    C. his skin is wet with sweat
    D. his pulse is rapid

30. When giving first aid to a person suffering from shock as a result of an auto accident, it is MOST important to

    A. massage him in order to aid blood circulation
    B. have him sip whiskey
    C. prop him up in a sitting position
    D. cover the person and keep him warm

Questions 31-34.

DIRECTIONS: Answer questions 31 to 34 SOLELY on the basis of the following paragraph.

Assume that you are an officer assigned to one large office which issues and receives applications for various permits and licenses. The office consists of one section where the necessary forms are issued; another section where fees are paid to a cashier; and desks where applicants are interviewed and their forms reviewed and completed. There is also a section containing tables and chairs where persons may sit and fill out their applications before being interviewed or paying the fees. your duties consist of answering simple questions, directing the public to the correct section of the office, and maintaining order.

31. A man who speaks English poorly asks you for assistance in obtaining and filling out an application for a permit. You should 31.____

    A. send him to an interviewer who can assist him
    B. try to determine what permit he wants and fill out the form for him
    C. refer the man to the office supervisor
    D. ask another applicant to help this person

32. The office becomes noisy and crowded, with people milling around waiting for service at the various sections. 32.____
    Of the following, the BEST action for you to take is to

    A. stand in a prominent place and in a loud voice request the people to be quiet
    B. direct all the people not being served to wait at the unoccupied tables until you call them
    C. line up the people in front of each section and keep the lines in good order
    D. tell the people to form a single line outside the office and let in a few at a time

33. A man who has just been denied a permit becomes angry and shouts that if he "knew the right people" he too could get a permit. His behavior is disturbing the office. 33.____
    Of the following, the BEST action for you to take is to

    A. order the man to leave at once since his business is done
    B. tell the man to be quiet and file another application
    C. suggest to the supervisor that a pamphlet be prepared explaining the requirements for permits in simple language
    D. ask an interviewer to explain the requirements for his permit to the person and his right of appeal

34. Just before the close of business, a man rushes in and insists on being interviewed for a permit because his present one expires that night. 34.____
    Of the following, the BEST action for you to take is to

    A. tell the man that the office is closed
    B. tell the man that there will be no penalty if he returns early the next morning
    C. inquire if an interviewer is still available to take care of him and send him to that desk
    D. tell the cashier to collect the fee and tell the man to return the next morning for an interview

35. Fingerprints are often taken of applicants for licenses. Of the following, the MOST valid reason for this procedure is that

    A. the license of someone who commits a crime can be more readily revoked
    B. applicants can be checked for possible criminal records
    C. it helps to make sure that the proper license fee is paid
    D. a complete employment record of the applicant is obtained

36. Assume that an officer is on patrol at 2 A.M. He notices that the night light inside one of the stores in a public building is out. The store is locked.
    Of the following, the FIRST action for him to take at this time is to

    A. continue on his patrol since the light probably burned out
    B. enter the store by any means possible so he can check it
    C. report the matter to his superior
    D. shine his flashlight through the window to look for anything unusual

37. In questioning a man suspected of having committed a theft, the BEST procedure for an officer to follow is to

    A. induce the man to express his feelings about the police, the courts, and his home environment
    B. threaten him with beatings when he refuses to answer your questions
    C. make any promises necessary to get him to confess
    D. remain calm and objective

38. As an officer, you are on duty in one of the offices of a large public building. A woman who has just finished her business with this office comes to you and reports that her son who was with her is missing.
    The one of the following which is the BEST action for you to take FIRST is to

    A. tell the mother that the child is probably all right and ask her to go to the local police station for help in finding the boy
    B. suggest that the mother wait in the office until the child turns up
    C. check nearby offices in an attempt to locate the child
    D. telephone the local police station and ask if any reports fitting the description of the child have been received

39. An officer assigned to patrol inside a public building at night has observed two men standing outside the doorway. Of the following, the MOST appropriate action for the officer to take FIRST is to

    A. approach the two men and ask them why they are standing there
    B. hide and wait for the two men to take some action
    C. phone the local police station and ask for help since these men may be planning criminal action
    D. check all the entrance doors of the building to make sure that they are locked

40. It is standard practice for special officers to inspect the restrooms in public buildings. This is done at regular intervals while on patrol.
    Of the following, the BEST reason for this practice is to

    A. inspect sanitary conditions
    B. discourage loiterers and potential criminals

C. check the ventilation
D. determine if all the equipment and plumbing is working properly

41. While on duty in the evening as an officer assigned to a public building, you receive a report that a card game is going on in one of the offices. Gambling is forbidden on government property.
Of the following, the BEST course of action for you to take is to

    A. go to the office and order the card players to leave
    B. ignore the complaint since this is probably just harmless social card playing
    C. report the matter to the building manager the next day
    D. go to the office and, if warranted, issue an appropriate warning

41.____

42. It has been suggested that special officers establish good working relationships with the local police officers of the police department on duty in the neighborhood.
Of the following, the MOST valid reason for this practice is that

    A. a spirit of good feeling and high morale will be created among members of the police department
    B. local police officers will probably cooperate more readily with the special officer
    C. local police officers can take over the building patrol duties of the special officer in case he is absent
    D. special officers have an even stronger obligation than ordinary citizens to cooperate with the police

42.____

43. It has been proposed that an officer assigned to a public building at night remain at one location in the building, instead of walking on patrol through the building.
This proposal is

    A. *bad;* chiefly because the officer would probably sit instead of stand at the proper location
    B. *good;* chiefly because the officer could do a better job of watching the entire building from one point
    C. *bad;* chiefly because anyone seeking to enter the building for illegal purposes might be able to do so at a point other than where the special officer is on duty
    D. *good;* chiefly because his supervisors would know exactly where to find him

43.____

44. In a busy office, an officer has been assigned the duty of making sure that the public is served in the order of their arrival at the office and that some employee is always taking care of a person desiring help.
Of the following, the BEST method for the officer to follow is to

    A. line up the persons in the waiting room
    B. give a numbered ticket to each person waiting and call out the numbers, in order, when an employee becomes available
    C. loudly announce "next" when an employee is available to serve someone
    D. seat one person next to each employee's desk and let the others wait for the first vacant seat

44.____

45. Two men have broken into and entered a building at night. The officer on duty at this building sees them, chases them out, and then observes them in the adjoining building. Of the following, the BEST course of action for the officer to take is to

   A. notify the local police station and be ready to aid the police
   B. enter the adjoining building to find the men
   C. notify the manager of his own building
   D. continue on duty since these men have left the building for which he is responsible

46. While an officer is on duty in a crowded waiting room, he finds a woman's purse on the floor.
   Of the following, the FIRST course of action for him to take is to

   A. hold it up in the air, ask who owns it, and give it to whoever claims it
   B. keep the purse until someone claims it
   C. immediately deliver the purse to the "lost and found" desk
   D. ask the lady who is nearest to him if she lost a purse

47. Special officers often have the power of arrest.
   Of the following, the BEST reason for this practice is to

   A. have the officer always arrest any person who refuses to obey his orders
   B. aid in maintaining order in places where he is assigned
   C. promote good public relations
   D. aid in preventing illegal use of public buildings by tenants or employees

48. An officer has told a mother that he found her son writing on the walls of the building with chalk. The mother tells the officer that he should be more concerned with "crooks" than with children's minor pranks.
   Of the following, the BEST answer for the officer to make to this woman is that

   A. children should be taught good conduct by their parents
   B. damage to public property means higher taxes
   C. serious criminals often begin their careers with minor violations
   D. it is his duty to enforce all rules and regulations

49. A man asks you, a special officer, where to get a certain kind of license not issued in your office. You don't know where such licenses are issued.
   Of the following, the BEST procedure for you to follow is to

   A. refer him to the manager of the office
   B. get the information if you can and give it to the man
   C. tell the man to inquire at any police station house
   D. tell the man that you just do not know

50. Special officers are not permitted to ask private citizens to buy tickets for dances or other such social functions, not even when such functions are operated by charitable organizations. Of the following, the BEST reason for this rule is that

   A. private citizens are under no obligation to buy any such tickets
   B. not all groups are allowed equal opportunity in the sale of their tickets
   C. private citizens might complain to officials
   D. private citizens might feel they would not get proper service unless they bought such tickets

KEY (CORRECT ANSWERS)

1. B	11. D	21. B	31. A	41. D
2. C	12. B	22. B	32. C	42. B
3. B	13. C	23. D	33. D	43. C
4. D	14. A	24. C	34. C	44. B
5. A	15. A	25. A	35. B	45. A
6. A	16. D	26. B	36. D	46. C
7. C	17. C	27. A	37. D	47. B
8. A	18. C	28. C	38. C	48. D
9. B	19. A	29. B	39. D	49. B
10. A	20. B	30. D	40. B	50. D

SOLUTIONS TO ARITHMETIC PROBLEMS

11. $2\frac{1}{4}$ miles are completed in 1 1/2 minutes (1 minute and 30 seconds)

$$\therefore 2\frac{1}{4} \div 1\frac{1}{2} = \text{rate per minute}$$

$$= \frac{9}{4} \div 1\frac{1}{2}$$

$$= \frac{9}{4} \div \frac{3}{2}$$

$$= \frac{9}{4} \times \frac{2}{3}$$

$$= \frac{3}{2} \text{ miles per minute}$$

$\therefore \frac{3}{2} \times 60$ (minutes in an hour) = rate per hour = 90 miles per hour

(Ans. D)

12. 550 + 2230 = 2780; 21,500 - 2780 = 18,720 passengers

550 buses at $14.00	=	$ 7,700
2230 trucks at $7.00	=	15,610
18720 passengers at $3.50	=	65,520
		$88,830

(Ans. B)

13. Given: speed = 100 feet the first second

100 - 10 (10% of 100)	=	90 feet - the second second
90 - 9 (10% of 90)	=	81 feet - the third second
81 - 8.1 (10% of 81)	=	72.9 feet - the fourth second
		343.9 (total at end of the fourth second)

(Ans. C)

14. Given: 500 = uniform allowance

$500 - 180	=	$320	(amount left after buying winter jacket)
$320 x 40%	=	$128	(amount spent for two pairs of trousers)
$320 - 128	=	$192	(amount now left)

Since the winter overcoat costs $240, he is now short $48 ($240 - 192) or 20% of the purchase price of the overcoat. (48/240 = $\frac{1}{5}$ = 20%)

46

(Ans. A)

15. Light care: 9000(miles)÷30(miles per gallon)×3.75(per gallon)

$$= \frac{9000}{30} \times 3.75$$
$$= 300 \times 3.75$$
$$= \$1,125 \text{ (total gasoline cost)}$$

Standard cars: 9000 (miles) ÷ 15 (miles per gallon) x 3.75

$$= \frac{9000}{15} \times 3.75$$
$$= 600 \times 3.75$$
$$= \$2,250 \text{ (total gasoline cost)}$$

∴ use of light car would result in a saving in gasoline costs of $1,125 ($2,250 - $1,125).

(Ans. A)

16. 2006: 14,200 (burglary)
     2005: 12,800 (burglary)
           1,400 (increase in burglaries)

     2006: 34,750 (felony)
     2005: 32,300 (felony)
           2,450 (increase in felonies

$$\therefore 1400 \div 2450 = \frac{1400}{2450} = .57$$

WORK

```
        .57
2450)1400.0
     1225.0
      175.00
      171.50
```

(Ans. D)

17. Given: smaller office: grants permits to 40% of 1/3 of the total number of applicants (900)

    larger office: grants permits to 60% of 2/3 of the total number of applicants (900)

    Solving: smaller office: $.40 \times \frac{1}{3} \times 900 = 120$ permits

    larger office: $.60 \times \frac{2}{3} \times 900 = \underline{360}$ permits

    480 permits (total)

(Ans. C)

EXAMINATION SECTION
TEST 1

DIRECTIONS: Each question or incomplete statement is followed by several suggested answers or completions. Select the one that BEST answers the question or completes the statement. *PRINT THE LETTER OF THE CORRECT ANSWER IN THE SPACE AT THE RIGHT.*

1. As an officer, you should know that, of the following, the one which is LEAST likely to be followed by an increase in crime is   1.____

    A. war
    B. depression
    C. poor housing
    D. prosperity

2. As an officer interested in the promotion of traffic safety, you should know that according to recent statistics, the one group which has the highest number of deaths as a result of being struck in traffic is   2.____

    A. adults over 55 years of age
    B. adults between 36 and 55 years of age
    C. adults between 22 and 35 years of age
    D. children up to 4 years old

3. As an officer having a knowledge of the various types of crimes, you should know that in recent years, the age group 16 through 25 showed the greatest number of arrests for   3.____

    A. grand larceny from highways and vehicles
    B. burglary
    C. rape
    D. homicide

4. Of the following groups, the GREATEST number of arrests made and summonses served is for   4.____

    A. offenses against property rights
    B. general criminality
    C. bestial criminality
    D. offenses against public health and safety

5. As an officer interested in the reduction of unnecessary traffic accidents, you should know that two of the chief sources of such accidents to pedestrians in recent years were for crossing a street   5.____

    A. against the light, and crossing past a parked car
    B. at a point other than the crossing, and crossing against the light
    C. at a point other than the crossing, and running off the sidewalk
    D. against the light, and failing to observe whether cars were making right or left turns

6. A "modus operandi" file will be MOST valuable to an officer as a means of showing the   6.____

    A. methods used by criminals
    B. various bureaus and divisions of the police department
    C. number and nature of vehicular accidents
    D. forms used by the police department

49

7. An officer is frequently advised to lie down before returning fire, if a person is shooting at him.
   This is *primarily* for the reason that

   A. a smaller target will thus be presented to the assailant
   B. he can return fire more quickly while in the prone position
   C. the assailant will think he has struck the officer and cease firing
   D. it will indicate that the officer is not the aggressor

8. In making arrests during a large riot, it is the practice of the police to take the ringleaders into custody as soon as possible.
   This is *primarily* because

   A. the police can obtain valuable information from them
   B. they deserve punishment more than the other rioters
   C. rioters need leadership and, without it, will disperse more quickly
   D. arrests of wrongdoers should always be in order of their importance

9. You observe two men running toward a parked automobile in which a driver is seated. You question the three men and you note the license number.
   You should

   A. let them go if you see nothing suspicious
   B. warn them not to be caught litering again
   C. arrest them because they have probably committed a crime
   D. take them back with you to the place from which the two men came

10. You find a flashlight and a screw-driver lying near a closed bar and grill. You notice further some jimmy marks on the door.
    You should

    A. note in your memorandum book what you have seen
    B. arrest any persons standing in the vicinity
    C. try to enter the bar and grill to investigate whether it has been robbed
    D. telephone the owner of the bar and grill to inform him of what you have seen outside the door

11. While you are patrolling your post, you notice that a peddler is vending merchandise. As you approach, he gathers up his wares and begins to run.
    You should

    A. shoot at him as he is a violator of the law
    B. blow your whistle to summon other patrolmen in order to apprehend him
    C. remain for some time at this place so as to be certain that he does not return
    D. disregard him and continue patrolling your post

12. You have been assigned to a patrol post in a park during winter months. You hear the cries of a boy who has fallen through the ice.
    The FIRST thing you should do is to

    A. rush to the nearest call telephone and summon paramedics
    B. call upon passersby to summon additional patrolmen

C. rush to the spot from which the cries came and try to save the boy
D. rush to the spot from which the cries came and question the boy concerning his identity so that you can summon his parents

13. You have been summoned about a robbery in a train station. Three men are grappling with each other. Two of the men are plainclothesmen, but their identity is not known to you.
The FIRST thing you should do is to

   A. advance with your nightstick and be ready to use it as soon as you know which one is the thief
   B. order the men to stop fighting
   C. ask any bystanders to identify the thief before you use your gun
   D. shoot the one who is most likely to be the thief, letting yourself be guided by your own experience as to the thief's identity

14. Assume that you are a police officer. A woman has complained to you about a man's indecent exposure in front of a house. As you approach the house, the man begins to run.
You should

   A. shoot to kill as the man may be a dangerous maniac
   B. fire a warning shot to try to halt the man
   C. summon other officers in order to apprehend him
   D. question the woman regarding the man's identity

15. You are patrolling a parkway in a radio car with another officer. A maroon car coming from the opposite direction signals you to stop and the driver informs you that he was robbed by three men speeding ahead of him in a black sedan. Your radio car cannot cross the center abutment.
Your should

   A. request the driver to make a report to the nearest precinct as your car cannot cross over to the other side
   B. make a U turn in your radio car and give chase on the wrong side of the parkway
   C. fire warning shots in the air to summon other patrolmen
   D. flash headquarters over your radio system

16. You are on patrol duty in a crowded part of the city.
You hear the traffic patrolman fire four shots in the air and cry, "Get out of his way. He's got a gun." You see a man tearing along the street dodging traffic.
You should

   A. fire several shots in the air to alert other patrolmen
   B. give chase to the man and shoot as it is possible that one of your shots may hit him
   C. wait for an opening in the crowds and then shoot at the man from one knee
   D. disperse the crowds and then shout at the man to stop

17. Assume that you have been assigned to a traffic post at a busy intersection. A car bearing out-of-town license plates is about to turn into a one-way street going in the opposite direction. You blow your whistle and stop the car.
You should then

A. hand out a summons to the driver in order to make an example of him, since out-of-town drivers notoriously disregard our traffic regulations
B. pay no attention to him and let him continue in the proper direction
C. ask him to pull over to the curb and advise him to drive to the nearest precinct to get a copy of the latest traffic regulations
D. call his attention to the fact that he was violating a traffic regulation and permit him to continue in the proper direction

18. A storekeeper has complained to you that every day at noon several peddlers congregate outside his store in order to sell their merchandise.
You should

    A. inform him that such complaints must be made directly to the Police Commissioner
    B. inform him that peddlers have a right to earn their living too
    C. make it your business to patrol that part of your post around noon
    D. pay no attention to him as this storekeeper is probably a crank inasmuch as nobody else has complained

19. You notice that a man is limping hurriedly, leaving a trail of blood behind him. You question him and his explanation is that he was hurt accidentally while he was watching a man clean a gun.
You should

    A. let him go as you have no proof that his story is not true
    B. have him sent to the nearest city hospital under police escort
    C. ask him whether the man had a license for his gun
    D. ask him to lead you to the man who cleaned his gun so that you may question him further about the accident

20. There have been a series of burglaries in a certain residential area consisting of one-family houses. You have been assigned to select a house in this area in which detectives can wait secretly for the attempt to burglarize that house so that the burglars can be apprehended in the act.
Which of the following would be the BEST house to select for this purpose?

    A. The house was recently burglarized and several thousand dollars worth of clothing and personal property were taken.
    B. The house whose owner reports that several times the telephone has rung but the person making the call hung up as soon as the telephone was answered.
    C. The house is smaller and looks much less pretentious than other houses in the same area.
    D. The house is occupied by a widower who works long hours but who lives with an invalid mother requiring constant nursing service.

21. The two detectives noticed the man climb a ladder to the roof of a loft building. The detectives followed the same route. They saw him break a skylight and lower himself into the building. Through the broken skylight, one of the detectives covered the man with his gun and told him to throw up his hands.
The action of the detectives in this situation was FAULTY *chiefly* because

    A. one of the detectives should have remained on the ladder
    B. criminals should be caught red-handed

C. the detectives should have made sure of the identity of the man before following him
D. the possibility of another means of escape from the building should have been foreseen

22. Suppose that, while you are patrolling your post, a middle-aged woman informs you that three men are holding up a nearby express office. You rush immediately to the scene of the holdup. While you are still about 75 feet away, you see the three men, revolvers in their hands, emerge from the office and make for what is apparently their getaway car, which is pointed in the opposite direction.
Of the following, your FIRST consideration in this situation should be to

    A. enter the express office in order to find out what the men have taken
    B. maneuver quickly so as to get the getaway car between you and the express office
    C. make a mental note of the descriptions of the escaping men for immediate alarm
    D. attempt to disable the car in which the holdup men seek to escape

23. Which of the following situations, if observed by you while on patrol, should you consider MOST suspicious and deserving of further investigation?

    A. A shabbily dressed youth is driving a new Buick.
    B. An old battered car has been parked without lights outside an apartment house for several hours.
    C. A light is on in the rear of a one-family, luxurious residence.
    D. Two well-dressed men are standing at a bus stop at 2 A.M. and arguing heatedly.

24. Suppose that, while on patrol late at night, you find a woman lying in the street, apparently the victim of a hit-and-run driver. She seems to be injured seriously but you wish to ask her one or two questions in order to help apprehend the hit-and-run car.
Of the following, the BEST question to ask is:

    A. In what direction did the car go?
    B. What time did it happen?
    C. What kind of car was it?
    D. How many persons were in the car?

25. Assume that you are driving a police car, equipped with a two-way radio, along an isolated section of the parkway at 3 A.M. You note that the headlights of a car are blinking rapidly. When you stop to investigate, the driver of the car informs you that he was just forded to the side of the road by two men in a green convertible, who robbed him of a large amount of cash and jewelry at the point of a gun and then sped away.
Your FIRST consideration in this situation should be to

    A. drive rapidly along the parkway in the direction taken by the criminals in an effort to apprehend them before they escape
    B. question the driver carefully, looking for inconsistencies indicating that he made up the whole story
    C. obtain a complete listing and identification of all materials lost
    D. notify your superior to have the parkway exits watched for a car answering the description of the getaway car

26. Suppose that you have been assigned to check the story of a witness in a holdup case. The witness states that, while sitting at her window, she observed the suspect loitering outside a cigar store. As she watched, the suspect entered a nearby liquor store. He remained there only a minute or two. Then she saw him walk out rapidly, hurry to the corner and hail a cab. Assume that Figure 1 is a scale drawing of the scene. All four corners of the intersection are occupied by tall buildings. W indicates the window at which the witness sat, C indicates the cigar store and L indicates the liquor store.
On the basis of this sketch, the BEST reason for doubting the truthfulness of the witness is that
   A. the window is far removed from the cigar store
   B. the cigar store and the window are not on the same street
   C. distances may be distorted by a high angle of observation
   D. the liquor store cannot be seen from the window

FIGURE 1

27. Assume that you are investigating a case of reported suicide. You find the deceased sitting in a chair, sprawled over his desk, a revolver still clutched in his right hand. In your examination of the room, you find that the window is partly open. Only one bullet has been fired from the revolver. The bullet has lodged in the wall. Assume that Figure 2 is a scale drawing of the scene. D indicates the desk, C indicates the chair, W indicates the window and B indicates the bullet. The one of the following features which indicates *most strongly* that the deceased did NOT commit suicide is the
   A. distance between the desk and the bullet hole
   B. relative position of the bullet hole and the chair
   C. fact that the window was partly open
   D. relative position of the desk and the window

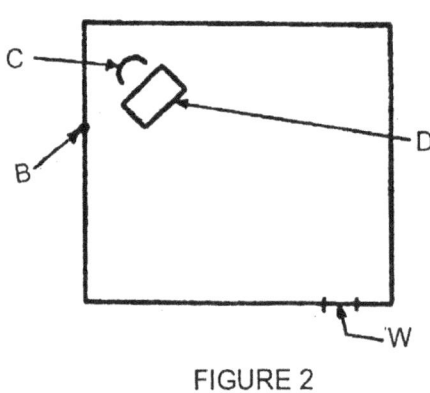

FIGURE 2

28. "Driver 1 claimed that the collision occurred because, as he approached the intersection, Driver 2 started to make a left turn suddenly and at high speed, even though the light had been red against him for 15 or 20 seconds." Suppose that you have been assigned to make a report on this accident. The position of the vehicles after the accident is indicated in Figure 3, the point in each case indicating the front of the vehicle. On the basis of this sketch, the BEST reason for concluding that Driver 1's statement is *false* is that Driver

    A. 2's car is beyond the center of the intersection
    B. 2's car is making the turn on the proper side of the road
    C. 1's car is beyond the sidewalk line
    D. 1's car is on the right hand side of the road

    FIGURE 3

29. Suppose that, while you are on patrol, a teen-age boy dashes out of a dry cleaning store, his clothes afire.
    The BEST action for you to take in this situation is to

    A. stop the boy and roll him in a coat to smother the flames
    B. lead the boy quickly to the nearest store and douse him with large quantities of water
    C. remove all burning articles of clothing from the boy as quickly as possible
    D. take the boy back into the dry cleaning store, where a fire extinguisher will almost certainly be available to extinguish the flames quickly

30. A woman comes running towards you crying that her child was bitten by their pet dog.
    The FIRST action you should take is to

    A. summon a doctor so that he may treat the wounds
    B. shoot the dog to prevent it from biting others
    C. have the child put to bed
    D. apply ice packs to the wounds until the pain subsides

31. You are called to an apartment house to stop a quarrel between a husband and wife. When you arrive there, you find that the husband has left and that the woman is lying unconscious on the floor. In the meantime, a neighbor has telephoned for an ambulance. You note that the room temperature is about 50 degrees.
    The FIRST action you should take is to

    A. rub the hands of the woman to keep her blood circulating
    B. make her drink hot tea or coffee to try to revive her
    C. place a hot water bottle under her feet to keep them warm
    D. place one blanket underneath her and another one over her

32. As an officer who is well-informed in the fundamentals of giving first aid, you should know that the "Schaefer Method" is MOST helpful for

    A. stopping bleeding
    B. transporting injured persons

C. promoting respiration
D. stopping the spread of infection

33. While you are on traffic duty, a middle-aged man crossing the street cries out with pain, presses his hand to his chest and stands perfectly still. You suspect that he may have suffered a heart attack. You should FIRST

    A. ask him to cross the street quickly in order to prevent his being hit by moving traffic
    B. permit him to lie down flat in the street while you divert the traffic
    C. ask him for the name of his doctor so that you can summon him
    D. request a cab to take him to the nearest hospital for immediate treatment

34. A misdemeanor is

    A. any crime not punishable by death or imprisonment in a state prison
    B. only such offense as is so defined in the Penal Law
    C. any violation of a state law or municipal ordinance which does not amount to a crime
    D. an act for which no penalty is imposed by the Penal Law

35. A writing in which a grand jury charges a person with the commission of a crime is called

    A. a pleading   B. a talesman
    C. a complaint   D. an indictment

36. A statute of limitations is a law

    A. limiting the time within which a criminal prosecution or civil action must be commenced
    B. prohibiting a second prosecution for a crime for which a person has once been tried
    C. regulating the descent and distribution of the property of a person dying intestate
    D. limiting the sentence that may be imposed upon conviction for a particular crime

37. Strengthening or confirming evidence given in support of the truth of facts testified to by another witness is most accurately termed

    A. hearsay evidence
    B. corroborative evidence
    C. circumstantial evidence
    D. conclusive evidence

38. A writ or order directed to a person and requiring his attendance at a particular time and place to testify as a witness is properly termed a

    A. summons   B. subpoena
    C. warrant   D. mandamus

39. If A is accused of having caused the death of B, of the following, the factor which will weigh most heavily in determining whether A should be indicted for murder or manslaughter is

    A. his age
    B. his intent in committing the homicide

C. the nature of the weapon used
D. the existence of a corpus delicti

QUESTIONS 40-42.

Items 40-42 consist of four words each. One word in each item is incorrectly pronounced. The stress in each word is indicated in capital letters while the spelling is indicated in parentheses. For each item, print the letter preceding the word which is incorrectly pronounced in the space at the right.

40. A. vee-HIK-yoo-ler (vehicular)
    B. phe-DESS-tree-an (pedestrian)
    C. myoo-nih-SIH-p'1 (municipal)
    D. rih-SEET (receipt)

    40.____

41. A. DEF (deaf)
    B. eye-TAL-yun (Italian)
    C. in-KLEM-'nt (inclement)
    D. awg-ZIL-yu-ree (auxiliary)

    41.____

42. A. kog-NEYE-z'ns (cognizance)
    B. MAYN-tuh-nunss (maintenance)
    C. FEB-roo-er-ee (February)
    D. ROSS-ter (roster)

    42.____

43. A section of the Penal Law provides, in part, that "whenever the punishment or penalty for an offense is mitigated by any provision of this chapter, such provision may be applied to any sentence or judgment imposed for the offense." The word "mitigated" as used in this statute means *most nearly*

    43.____

    A. removed
    C. changed
    B. augmented
    D. decreased

44. A section of the Penal Law states that "a morbid propensity to commit prohibited acts....forms no defense to a prosecution therefor." The word "propensity" as used in this statute means *most nearly*

    44.____

    A. capacity
    C. tendency
    B. ability
    D. aptitude

45. A police department rule provides that "a Chaplain shall have the assimilated rank of Inspector." The word "assimilated" as used in this rule means *most nearly*

    45.____

    A. false
    C. comparable
    B. superior
    D. presumed

46. A police department rule provides that, "Pushcarts and derelict automobiles shall be delivered to the Bureau of Incumbrances." The word "derelict" as used in this rule means *most nearly*

    46.____

    A. dilapidated
    C. delinquent
    B. abandoned
    D. contraband

47. A police department rule provides that "when the exigencies of the service shall so require, a captain may assign a patrolman from the outgoing platoon to house duty." The word "exigencies" as used in this rule means *most nearly*

    A. needs
    B. conveniences
    C. changes
    D. increases

48. A police department rule provides for the award of a Medal for Merit "for an act of outstanding bravery, performed in the line of duty, at imminent personal hazard of life." The word "imminent" as used in this rule means *most nearly*

    A. impending
    B. inherent
    C. certain
    D. great

49. A police department rule provides that "the Police Commissioner shall have cognizance and control of the government, administration, disposition and discipline of the Police Department." The word "cognizance" as used in this rule means *most nearly*

    A. responsibility for
    B. jurisdiction over
    C. knowledge of
    D. ability for

50. A police department rule provides that a member of the department shall not communicate with a railroad company "for the purpose of expediting the issue of a transportation pass." The word "expediting" as used in this rule means *most nearly*

    A. extorting
    B. procuring
    C. demanding
    D. hastening

51. A Police Department Manual of Procedure provides that a member of the force who comes into possession of a document containing scurrilous matter will take precautions to safeguard fingerprints thereon. The word "scurrilous" as used in this regulation means *most nearly*

    A. irrelevant
    B. offensive
    C. defamatory
    D. evidentiary

52. Under cases of "Mendicancy" should be listed cases of

    A. loitering
    B. begging
    C. carrying of weapons
    D. injury to property

53. A police department rule states that the Department Medal of Honor may be awarded to a member of the Force who distinguishes himself by an act of gallantry and intrepidity. The word "intrepidity" as used in this rule means *most nearly*

    A. chivalry
    B. virility
    C. fear
    D. courage

54. A person who, without lawful excuse, omits to perform a duty to furnish food, clothing, shelter or medical or surgical attendance to a minor, or to make such payments towards the maintenance of a minor as may have been required by a court, is guilty of a misdemeanor according to Section 482 of the Penal Law. In this sentence the word which is *misspelled s*

    A. lawful
    B. omits
    C. attendance
    D. maintenence

55. A section of the Penal Law provides that "a conviction under this article cannot be had on the uncorraborated testimony of the person with whom the offense is charged to have been committed." In this sentence the word which is *misspelled* is

    A. conviction
    B. uncorraborated
    C. offense
    D. committed

56. A section of the Penal Law provides, in part, that "a person who wilfully.... inflicts grievous bodily harm upon another is punishable by imprisonment in a penitentiary for a term not exceeding five years." In this sentence the word which is *misspelled* is

    A. wilfully
    B. grievous
    C. punishible
    D. exceeding

57. An article of the Penal Law provides that "moneys received by the Department of State persuant to this article may, within three months of the receipt thereof, be refunded to the person entitled thereto, on satisfactory proof that the applicant for the license has pre-deceased its issuance." In this sentence the word which is *misspelled* is

    A. persuant
    B. issuance
    C. satisfactory
    D. predeceased

58. "The Deputy Commissioner in charge is authorized to exercise all of the powers and duties of the Police Commissioner in connection with the granting, renewing, revoking, suspending, cancelling and transferring of the miscelaneous licenses and permits issued by the Division."
    In this sentence the word which is *misspelled* is

    A. authorized
    B. cancelling
    C. transferring
    D. miscelaneous

59. A police department rule states that "a commanding officer is responsible for properly preparing, transmitting, filing, using and preserving official records, returns, forms and correspondance originating in or forwarded to his command." In this sentence the word which is *misspelled* is

    A. responsible
    B. transmitting
    C. filing
    D. correspondance

QUESTIONS 60-67.

The sentences numbered 60-67 deal with some phase of police activity. They may be classified most appropriately under one of the following four categories:

    A. Faulty because of incorrect grammar
    B. Faulty because of incorrect punctuation
    C. Faulty because of incorrect use of a word
    D. Correct

Examine each sentence carefully. Then, in the space at the right, print the capital letter preceding the option which is the BEST of the four suggested above. All incorrect sentences contain only one type of error. Consider a sentence correct if it contains none of the types of errors mentioned, even though there may be other correct ways of expressing the same thought.

60. The Department Medal of Honor is awarded to a member of the Police Force who distin- 60.____
guishes himself inconspicuously in the line of police duty by the performance of an act
of gallantry.

61. Members of the Detective Division are charged with the prevention of crime, the detec- 61.____
tion and arrest of criminals and the recovery of lost or stolen property.

62. Detectives are selected from the uniformed patrol forces after they have indicated by 62.____
conduct, aptitude and performance that they are qualified for the more intricate duties of
a detective.

63. The patrolman, pursuing his assailant, exchanged shots with the gunman and immortaly 63.____
wounded him as he fled into a nearby building.

64. The members of the Traffic Division has to enforce the Vehicle and Traffic Law, the Traffic 64.____
Regulations and ordinances relating to vehicular and pedestrian traffic.

65. After firing a shot at the gunman, the crowd dispersed from the patrolman's line of fire. 65.____

66. The efficiency of the Missing Persons Bureau is maintained with a maximum of public 66.____
personnel due to the specialized training given to its members.

67. Records of persons arrested for violations of Vehicle and Traffic Regulations are trans- 67.____
mitted upon request to precincts, courts and other authorized agencies.

68. Assume that in 2008 there were 21,580 vehicular highway accidents resulting in 713 68.____
deaths. This represents a 17% decrease over the year 2001. If the year 2009 indicates a
6.5% decrease over 2001, the number of highway accidents taking place in 2009 is *most
nearly*

    A. 23,846   B. 24,817   C. 24,310   D. 22,983

69. Of 35 police officers assigned to Precinct P, 69.____
    5 have 2 years of service,
    5 have 4 years of service,
    9 have 6 years of service,
    4 have 8 years of service,
    7 have 12 years of service and
    5 have 16 years of service.
The average number of years of service in the Police Department for the 35 police officers
is *most nearly*

    A. 6   B. 8   C. 7   D. 9

70. An officer purchases a two-family house for $318,000 and immediately rents one apart- 70.____
ment to a tenant for $1500 a month. At the end of two years, he sells the house for
$352,000. Taxes, repairs, insurance, interest and other expenses cost him $31,840. His
total gain from renting and selling, based on his original investment, is *most nearly*

    A. 6%   B. 8%   C. 10%   D. 12%

71. Precincts S, T, W and Y are located in the county. The total number of officers assigned to these precincts is 430.
Precinct S has 7 officers more than Precinct Y;
Precinct T has 7 officers less than Precinct Y;
Precinct W has twice as many patrolmen as Precinct Y. The number of officers assigned to Precinct Y is *most nearly*

   A. 82   B. 86   C. 92   D. 96

72. Two radio patrol cars, coming from different directions, are rushing to the scene of a crime. The first car proceeds at the rate of 45 miles an hour and arrives there in 4 minutes. Although the second car travels over a route which is longer by 3/4 of a mile, it arrives only 1/2 minute later.
The speed of the second patrol car, expressed in miles per hour, is *most nearly*.

   A. 50   B. 55   C. 60   D. 65

73. A police department rule reads as follows: A Deputy Commissioner acting as Police Commissioner shall carry out the orders of the Police Commissioner, previously given, and such orders shall not, except in cases of extreme emergency, be countermanded.
This means *most nearly* that, except in case of extreme emergency,

   A. the orders given by a Deputy Commissioner acting as Police Commissioner may not be revoked
   B. a Deputy Commissioner acting as Police Commissioner should not revoke orders previously given by the Police Commissioner
   C. A Deputy Commissioner acting as Police Commissioner is vested with the same authority to issue orders as the Police Commissioner himself
   D. only a Deputy Commissioner acting as Police Commissioner may issue orders in the absence of the Police Commissioner himself

QUESTIONS 74-75.

Questions 74-75 pertain to the following section of the Penal Law:

A person who, after having been three times convicted within this state, of feronies or attempts to commit felonies, or under the law of any other state, government or country, of crimes which if committed within this state would be felonious, commits a felony, other than murder, first or second degree, or treason, within this state, shall be sentenced upon conviction of such fourth, or subsequent offense to imprisonment in a state prison for an indeterminate term the minimum of which shall be not less than the maximum term provided for first offenders for the crime for which the individual has been convicted, but, in any event, the minimum term upon conviction for a felony as the fourth or subsequent offense, shall be not less than fifteen years, and the maximum thereof shall be his natural life.

74. Under the terms of the above quoted portion of the section of the Penal Law, a person must receive the increased punishment therein provided, if

   A. he is convicted of a felony and has been three times previously convicted of felonies
   B. he has been three times previously convicted of felonies, regardless of the nature of his present conviction

C. his fourth conviction is for murder, first or second degree, or treason
D. he has previously been convicted three times of murder, first or second degree, or treason

75. Under the terms of the above quoted portion of the section of the Penal Law, a person convicted of a felony for which the penalty is imprisonment for a term not to exceed ten years, and who has been three times previously convicted of felonies in the state, shall be sentenced to a term the MINIMUM of which shall be

A. ten years
B. fifteen years
C. indeterminate
D. his natural life

QUESTIONS 76-80.
In answering questions 76-80, the following definitions of crime should be applied, bearing in mind that ALL elements contained in the definition must be present in order to charge a person with that crime:

BURGLARY is the breaking and entering a building with intent to commit some crime therein.
EXTORTION is the obtaining of property from another, with his consent, induced by a wrongful use of force or fear, or under color of official right.
LARCENY is the taking and carrying away of the personal property of another with intent to deprive or defraud the owner of the use and benefit of such property.
ROBBERY is the unlawful taking of the personal property of another from his person or his presence, by force or violence or by putting him in fear of injury, immediate or future, to his person or property.

76. If A entered B's store during business hours, tied B to a chair and then helped himself to the contents of B's cash register, A, upon arrest, should be charged with

A. burglary   B. extortion   C. larceny   D. robbery

77. If A broke the pane of glass in the window of B's store, stepped in and removed some merchandise from the window, he should, upon arrest, be charged with

A. burglary   B. extortion   C. larceny   D. robbery

78. If A, after B had left for the day, found the door of B's store open, walked in, took some merchandise and then left through the same open door, he should, upon arrest, be charged with

A. burglary   B. extortion   C. larceny   D. robbery

79. If A, by threatening to report B for failure to pay to the city the full amount of sales tax he had collected from various customers, induced B to give him the contents of his cash register, A should, upon arrest, be charged with

A. burglary   B. extortion   C. larceny   D. robbery

80. If A, in a crowded hockey game, put his hand into B's pocket and removed B's wallet without his knowledge, A should, upon arrest, be charged with

A. burglary   B. extortion   C. larceny   D. robbery

KEY (CORRECT ANSWERS)

1. D	16. D	31. D	46. B	61. B	76. D
2. A	17. D	32. C	47. A	62. D	77. A
3. B	18. C	33. B	48. A	63. C	78. C
4. D	19. B	34. A	49. C	64. A	79. B
5. B	20. B	35. D	50. D	65. A	80. C
6. A	21. D	36. A	51. B	66. C	
7. A	22. D	37. B	52. B	67. D	
8. C	23. D	38. B	53. D	68. C	
9. A	24. C	39. B	54. D	69. B	
10. C	25. D	40. C	55. B	70. D	
11. D	26. D	41. B	56. C	71. B	
12. C	27. B	42. A	57. A	72. A	
13. B	28. C	43. D	58. D	73. B	
14. D	29. A	44. C	59. D	74. A	
15. D	30. A	45. C	60. C	75. B	

EVALUATING INFORMATION AND EVIDENCE
EXAMINATION SECTION
TEST 1

DIRECTIONS: Each question or incomplete statement is followed by several suggested answers or completions. Select the one that BEST answers the question or completes the statement. *PRINT THE LETTER OF THE CORRECT ANSWER IN THE SPACE AT THE RIGHT.*

Questions 1-9.

DIRECTIONS: Questions 1 through 9 measure your ability to (1) determine whether statements from witnesses say essentially the same thing and (2) determine the evidence needed to make it reasonably certain that a particular conclusion is true.

1. Which of the following pairs of statements say essentially the same thing in two different ways?
    I. If you get your feet wet, you will catch a cold.
       If you catch a cold, you must have gotten your feet wet.
    II. If I am nominated, I will run for office.
        I will run for office only if I am nominated.
    The CORRECT answer is:
    A. I only   B. I and II   C. II only   D. Neither I nor II

    1.____

2. Which of the following pairs of statements say essentially the same thing in two different ways?
    I. The enzyme Rhopsin cannot be present if the bacterium Trilox is absent.
       Rhopsin and Trilox always appear together.
    II. A member of PENSA has an IQ of at least 175.
        A person with an IQ of less than 175 is not a member of PENSA
    The CORRECT answer is;
    A. I only   B. I and II   C. II only   D. Neither I nor II

    2.____

3. Which of the following pairs of statements say essentially the same thing in two different ways?
    I. None of Finer High School's sophomores will be going to the prom.
       No student at Finer High School who is going to the prom is a sophomore.
    II. If you have 20/20 vision, you may carry a firearm.
        You may not carry a firearm unless you have 20/20 vision.
    The CORRECT answer is:
    A. I only   B. I and II   C. II only   D. Neither I nor II

    3.____

4. Which of the following pairs of statements say essentially the same thing in two different ways?
   I. If the family doesn't pay the ransom, they will never see their son again.
      It is necessary for the family to pay the ransom in order for them to see their son again.
   II. If it is raining, I am carrying an umbrella.
       If I am carrying an umbrella, it is raining.
   The CORRECT answer is:
   A. I only   B. I and II   C. II only   D. Neither I nor II

5. Summary of Evidence Collected to Date:
   In the county's maternity wards, over the past year, only one baby was born who did not share a birthday with any other baby.
   Prematurely Drawn Conclusion: At least one baby was born on the same day as another baby in the county's maternity wards.
   Which of the following pieces of evidence, if any, would make it reasonably certain that the conclusion drawn is true?
   A. More than 365 babies were born in the county's maternity wards over the past year.
   B. No pairs of twins were born over the past year in the county's maternity wards.
   C. More than one baby was born in the county's maternity wards over the past year.
   D. None of the above

6. Summary of Evidence Collected to Date:
   Every claims adjustor for MetroLife drives only a Ford sedan when on the job.
   Prematurely Drawn Conclusion: A person who works for MetroLife and drives a Ford sedan is a claims adjustor.
   Which of the following pieces of evidence, if any, would make it reasonably certain that the conclusion drawn is true?
   A. Most people who work for MetroLife are claims adjustors.
   B. Some people who work for MetroLife are not claims adjustors.
   C. Most people who work for MetroLife drive Ford sedans
   D. None of the above

7. Summary of Evidence Collected to Date:
   Mason will speak to Zisk if Zisk will speak to Ronaldson.
   Prematurely Drawn Conclusion: Jones will not speak to Zisk if Zisk will speak to Ronaldson.
   Which of the following pieces of evidence, if any, would make it reasonably certain that the conclusion drawn is true?
   A. If Zisk will speak to Mason, then Ronaldson will not speak to Jones.
   B. If Mason will speak to Zisk, then Jones will not speak to Zisk.
   C. If Ronaldson will speak to Jones, then Jones will speak to Ronaldson.
   D. None of the above

8. Summary of Evidence Collected to Date:
No blue lights on the machine are indicators for the belt drive status.
Prematurely Drawn Conclusion: Some of the lights on the lower panel are not indicators for the belt drive status.
Which of the following pieces of evidence, if any, would make it reasonably certain that the conclusion drawn is true?
   A. No lights on the machine's lower panel are blue.
   B. An indicator light for the machine's belt drive status is either green or red.
   C. Some lights on the machine's lower panel are blue.
   D. None of the above

8.____

9. Summary of Evidence Collected to Date:
Of the four Sweeney sisters, two are married, three have brown eyes, and three are doctors.
Prematurely Drawn Conclusion: Two of the Sweeney sisters are brown-eyed, married doctors.
Which of the following pieces of evidence, if any, would make it reasonably certain that the conclusion is true?
   A. The sister who does not have brown eyes is married.
   B. The sister who does not have brown eyes is not a doctor, and one who is not married is not a doctor.
   C. Every Sweeney sister with brown eyes is a doctor.
   D. None of the above

9.____

Questions 10-14.

DIRECTIONS: Questions 10 through 14 refer to Map #5 and measure your ability to orient yourself within a given section of town, neighborhood or particular area. Each of the questions describes a starting point and a destination. Assume that you are driving a car in the area shown on the map accompanying the questions. Use the map as a basis for the shortest way to get from one point to another without breaking the law.

On the map, a street marked by arrows, or by arrows and the words "One Way," indicates one-way travel and should be assumed to be one-way for the entire length, even when there are breaks or jogs in the street. EXCEPTION: A street that does not have the same name over the full length.

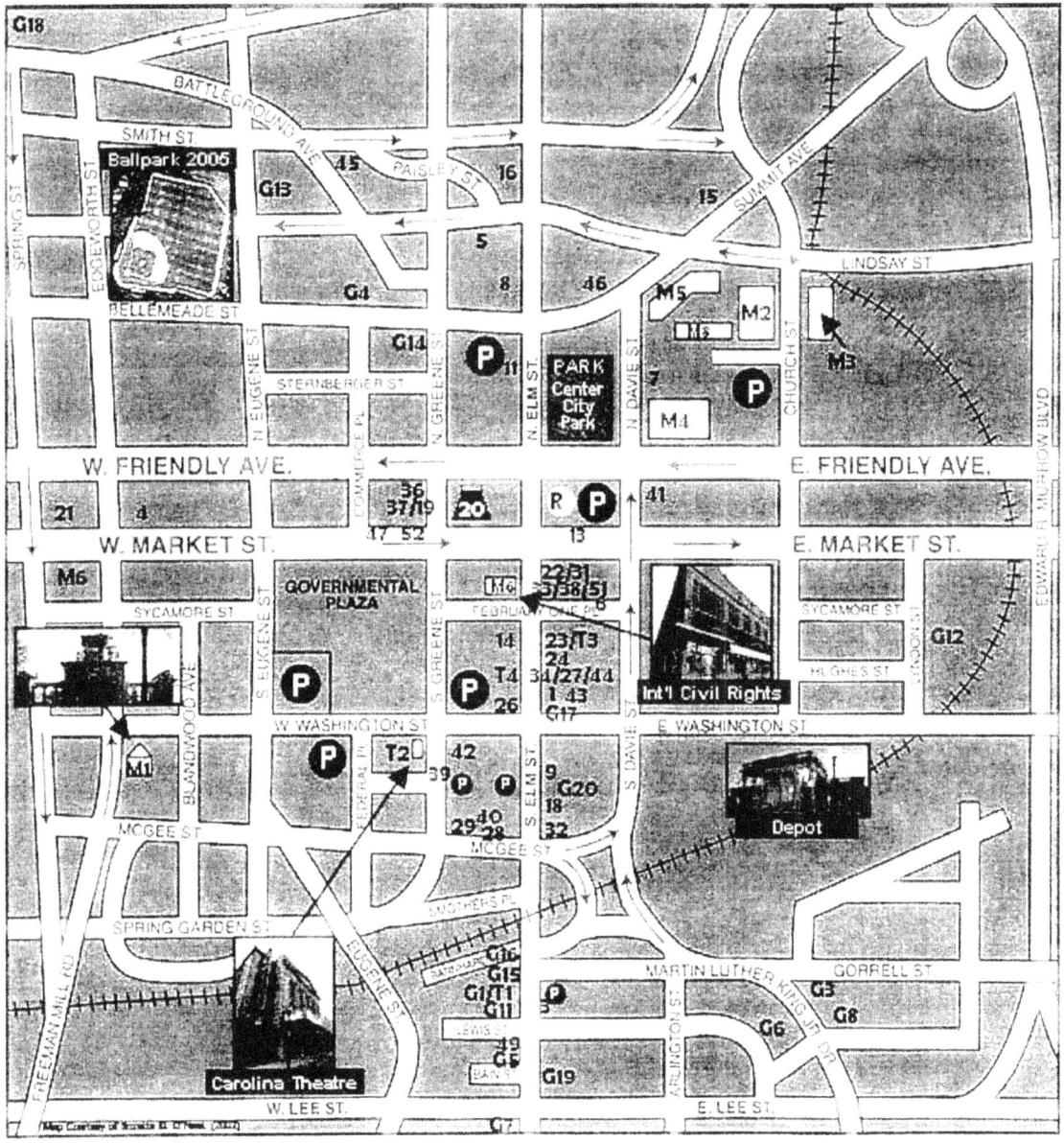

Map #5

10. The SHORTEST legal way from the depot to Center City Park is 10.____
    A. north on Church, west on Market, north on Elm
    B. east on Washington, north on Edward R. Murrow Blvd., west on Friendly Ave.
    C. west on Washington, north on Greene, east on Market, north on Davie
    D. north on Church, west on Friendly Ave.

11. The SHORTEST legal way from the Governmental Plaza to the Ballpark is 11._____
    A. west on Market, north on Edgeworth
    B. west on Market, north on Eugene
    C. north on Greene, west on Lindsay
    D. north on Commerce Place, west on Bellemeade

12. The SHORTEST legal way from the International Civil Rights Building to the building marked "M3" on the map is 12._____
    A. east on February One Place, north on Davie, east on Friendly Ave., north on Church
    B. south on Elm, west on Washington, north on Greene, east on Market, north on Church
    C. north on Elm, east on Market, north on Church
    D. north on Elm, east on Lindsay, south on Church

13. The SHORTEST legal way from the Ballpark to the Carolina Theatre is 13._____
    A. east on Lindsay, south on Greene
    B. south on Edgeworth, east on Friendly Ave., south on Greene
    C. east on Bellemeade, south on Elm, west on Washington

14. A car traveling north or south on Church Street may NOT go 14._____
    A. west onto Friendly Ave.   B. west onto Lindsay
    C. east onto Market   D. west onto Smith

Questions 15-19.

DIRECTIONS: Questions 15 through 19 refer to Figure #3, on the following page, and measure your ability to understand written descriptions of events. Each question presents a description of an accident or event and asks you which of the following five drawings in Figure #3 BEST represents it.
In the drawings, the following symbols are used:
Moving vehicle ◊   Non-moving vehicle ♦
Pedestrian or bicyclist •
The path and direction of travel of a vehicle or pedestrian is indicated by a solid line
The path and direction of travel of each vehicle or pedestrian directly involved in a collision from the point of impact is indicated by a dotted line.

6 (#1)

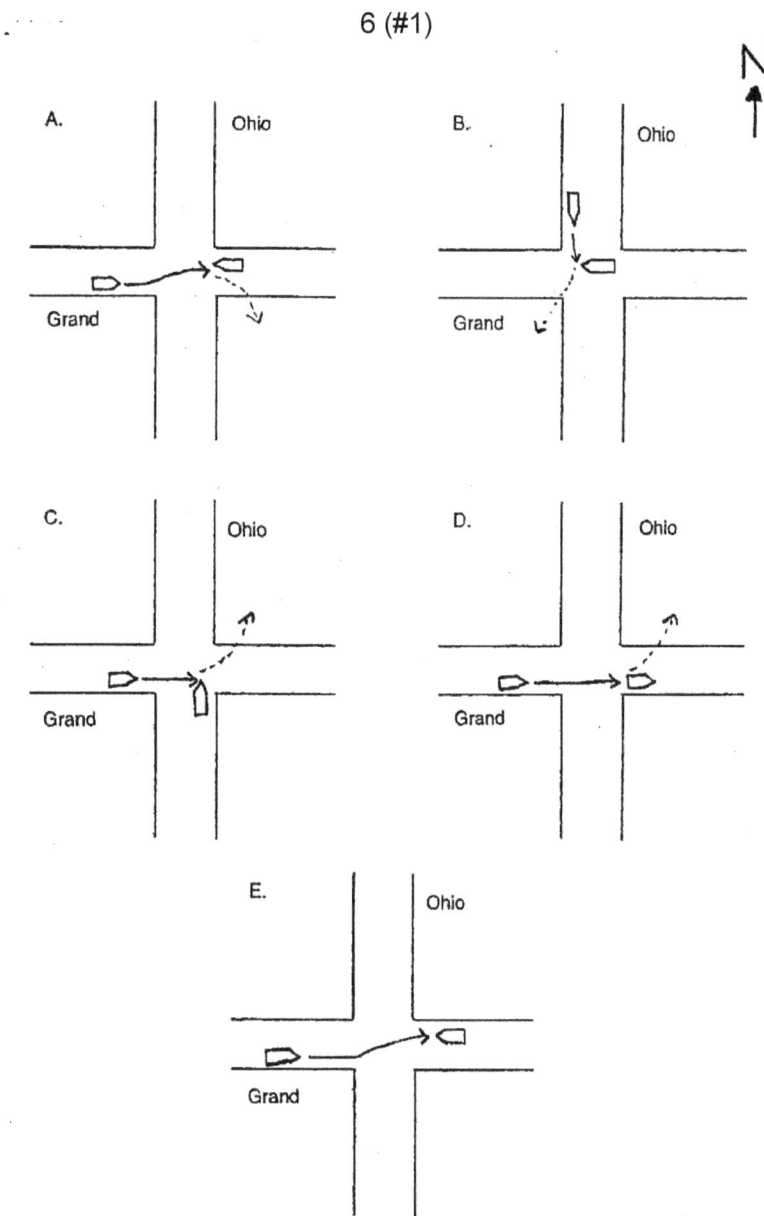

In the space at the right, print the letter of the drawing that BEST fit the descriptions written below.

15. A driver headed south on Ohio runs a red light and strikes the front of a car headed west on Grand. He glances off and leaves the roadway at the southwest corner of Grand and Ohio.

15._____

16. A driver heading east on Grand drifts into the oncoming lane as it travels through the intersection of Grand and Ohio, and strikes an oncoming car head-on

16._____

17. A driver heading east on Grand veers into the oncoming lane, sideswipes a westbound car and overcorrects as he swerves back into his lane. He leaves the roadway near the southeast corner of Grand and Ohio.

17._____

18. A driver heading east on Grand strikes the front of a car that is traveling north on Ohio and has run a red light. After striking the front of the northbound car, the driver veers left and leaves the roadway at the northeast corner of Grand and Ohio.

18._____

19. A driver heading east on Grand is traveling above the speed limit and clips the rear end of another eastbound car. The driver then veers to the left and leaves the roadway at the northeast corner of Grand and Ohio.

19._____

Questions 20-22.

DIRECTIONS: In Questions 20 through 22, choose the word or phrase CLOSEST in meaning to the word or phrase printed in capital letters.

20. PETITION
    A. appeal   B. law   C. oath   D. opposition

20._____

21. MALPRACTICE
    A. commission   B. mayhem   C. error   D. misconduct

21._____

22. EXONERATE
    A. incriminate   B. accuse   C. lengthen   D. acquit

22._____

Questions 23-25.

DIRECTIONS: Questions 23 through 25 measure your ability to do fieldwork-related arithmetic. Each question presents a separate arithmetic problem for you to solve.

23. Officers Lane and Bryant visited another city as part of an investigation. Because each is from a different precinct, they agree to split all expenses. With her credit card, Lane paid $70 for food and $150 for lodging. Bryant wrote checks for gas ($50) and entertainment ($40).
    How much does Bryant owe Lane?
    A. $65   B. $90   C. $155   D. $210

23._____

24. In a remote mountain pass, two search-and-rescue teams, one from Silverton and one from Durango, combine to look for a family that disappeared in a recent snowstorm. The combined team is composed of 20 members.
    Which of the following statements could NOT be true?
    A. The Durango team has a dozen members.
    B. The Silverton team has only one member.
    C. The Durango team has two more members than the Silverton team.
    D. The Silverton team has one more member than the Durango team.

24._____

25. Three people in the department share a vehicle for a period of one year. The average number of miles traveled per month by each person is 150. How many miles will be added to the car's odometer at the end of the year? 25._____
   A. 1,800   B. 2,400   C. 3,600   D. 5,400

KEY (CORRECT ANSWERS)

1.	D		11.	D
2.	C		12.	C
3.	A		13.	D
4.	A		14.	D
5.	A		15.	B
6.	A		16.	E
7.	B		17.	A
8.	C		18.	C
9.	B		19.	D
10.	D		20.	A

21. D
22. D
23. A
24. D
25. D

SOLUTIONS TO QUESTIONS 1-9

P implies Q = original statement

Not Q implies not P = contrapositive of the original statement. A statement and its contrapositive are logically equivalent.

Q implies P = converse of the original statement

Not P implies not Q = inverse of the original statement. The converse and inverse of an original statement are logically equivalent.

P implies Q = Not P or Q.

1. The CORRECT answer is D.
   In items I and II, each statement is the converses of the other. A converse of a statement is not equivalent to its original statement.

2. The CORRECT answer is C.
   In item I, the first statement is equivalent to "If Trilox is absent, then Rhopsin is also absent." But this does NOT imply that if Trilox is present, so too must Rhopsin be present. In item II, each statement is the contrapositive of the other. Thus, they are equivalent.

3. The CORRECT answer is A.
   In item I, the first sentence tells us that if a student is a sophomore, he/she will not go the prom. The second statement is equivalent to "If a student does attend the prom, he/she is not a sophomore." This is the contrapositive of the first statement, (so it is equivalent to it).

4. The CORRECT answer is A.
   In item I, the second statement can be written as "If the family sees their son again, then they must have paid the ransom." This is the contrapositive of the first statement. In item II, these statements are converses of each other; thus, they are not equivalent.

5. The CORRECT answer is A.
   If more than 365 babies were born in the county in one year, then at least two babies must share the same birthday.

6. The CORRECT answer is A.
   Given that most people who work for MetroLife are claims adjustors, plus the fact that all claims adjustors drive only a Ford sedan, it is a reasonable conclusion that any person who drives a Ford sedan and works for MetroLife is a claims adjustor.

7. The CORRECT answer is B.
   Jones will not speak to Zisk if Zisk will speak to Ronaldson, which will happen if Mason will speak to Zisk.

8. The CORRECT answer is C.
We are given that blue lights are never an indicator for the drive belt status. If some of the lights on the lower panel of the machine are blue, then it is reasonable to conclude that some of the lights on the lower panel are not indicators for the drive belt status.

9. The CORRECT answer is B.
There is only one sister that does not have brown eyes and only one sister that is not a doctor, and if the information in answer B is correct, then we learn that the same sister is a non-doctor without brown eyes. We also learn that this same non-doctor is not married. Since this all describes the same sister, we can conclude that two of the other sisters must be married doctors with brown eyes.

TEST 2

DIRECTIONS: Each question or incomplete statement is followed by several suggested answers or completions. Select the one that BEST answers the question or completes the statement. *PRINT THE LETTER OF THE CORRECT ANSWER IN THE SPACE AT THE RIGHT.*

Questions 1-9.

DIRECTIONS: Questions 1 through 9 measure your ability to (1) determine whether statements from witnesses say essentially the same thing and (2) determine the evidence needed to make it reasonably certain that a particular conclusion is true.
To do well on this part of the test, you do NOT have to have a working knowledge of police procedures and techniques. Nor do you have to have any more familiarity with criminals and criminal behavior than that acquired from reading newspapers, listening to radio or watching TV. To do well in this part, you must read and reason carefully.

1. Which of the following pairs of statements say essentially the same thing in two different ways?
   I. If there is life on Mars, we should fund NASA.
      Either there is life on Mars, or we should not fund NASA.
   II. All Eagle Scouts are teenage boys.
      All teenage boy are Eagle Scouts.
   The CORRECT answer is:
   A. I only   B. I and II   C. II only   D. Neither I nor II

   1.____

2. Which of the following pairs of statements say essentially the same thing in two different ways?
   I. If that notebook is missing its front cover, it definitely belongs to Carter.
      Carter's notebook is the only one missing its front cover.
   II. If it's hot, the pool is open.
      The pool is open if it's hot.
   The CORRECT answer is:
   A. I only   B. I and II   C. II only   D. Neither I nor II

   2.____

3 Which of the following pairs of statements say essentially the same thing in two different ways?
   I. Nobody who works at the mill is without benefits.
      Everyone who works at the mill has benefits.
   II. We will fund the program only if at least 100 people sign the petition.
      Either we will fund the program or at least 100 people will sign the petition.
   The CORRECT answer is:
   A. I only   B. I and II   C. II only   D. Neither I nor II

   3.____

75

4. Which of the following pairs of statements say essentially the same thing in two different ways?
   I. If the new parts arrive, Mr. Luther's request has been answered.
      Mr. Luther requested new parts to arrive.
   II. The machine's test cycle will not run unless the operation cycle is not running.
      The machine's test cycle must be running in order for the operation cycle to run.
   The CORRECT answer is:
   A. I only   B. I and II   C. II only   D. Neither I nor II

5. Summary of Evidence Collected to Date:
   I. To become a member of the East Side Crips, a kid must be either "jumped in" or steal a squad car without getting caught.
   II. Sid, a kid on the East Side, was caught stealing a squad car.
   Prematurely Drawn Conclusion: Sid did not become a member of the East Side Crips.
   Which of the following pieces of evidence, if any, would make it reasonably certain that the conclusion drawn is true?
   A. "Jumping in" is not allowed in prison.
   B. Sid was not "jumped in."
   C. Sid's stealing the squad car had nothing to do with wanting to join the East Side Crips.
   D. None of the above

6. Summary of Evidence Collected to Date:
   I. Jones, a Precinct 8 officer, has more arrests than Smith.
   II. Smith and Watson have exactly the same number of arrests.
   Prematurely Drawn Conclusion: Watson is not a Precinct 8 officer.
   Which of the following pieces of evidence, if any, would make it reasonably certain that the conclusion drawn is true?
   A. All the officers in Precinct 8 have more arrests than Watson.
   B. All the officers in Precinct 8 have fewer arrests than Watson.
   C. Watson has fewer arrests than Jones.
   D. None of the above

7. Summary of Evidence Collected to Date:
   I. Twenty one-dollar bills are divided among Frances, Kerry, and Brian.
   II. If Kerry gives her dollar bills to Frances, then Frances will have more money than Brian.
   Prematurely Drawn Conclusion: Frances has twelve dollars.
   Which of the following pieces of evidence, if any, would make it reasonably certain that the conclusion drawn is true?
   A. If Brian gives his dollars to Kerry, then Kerry will have more money than Frances.
   B. Brian has two dollars.
   C. If Kerry gives her dollars to Brian, Brian will still have less money than Frances.
   D. None of the above

8. Summary of Evidence Collected to Date:
   I. The street sweepers will be here at noon today.
   II. Residents on the west side of the street should move their cars before noon.
   Prematurely Drawn Conclusion: Today is Wednesday.
   Which of the following pieces of evidence, if any, would make it reasonably certain that the conclusion drawn is true?
   A. The street sweepers never sweep the east side of the street on Wednesday.
   B. The street sweepers arrive at noon every other day.
   C. There is no parking allowed on the west side of the street on Wednesday.
   D. None of the above

9. Summary of Evidence Collected to Date:
   The only time the warning light comes on is when there is a power surge.
   Prematurely Drawn Conclusion: The warning light does not come on if the air conditioner is not running.
   Which of the following pieces of evidence, if any, would make it reasonably certain that the conclusion drawn is true?
   A. The air conditioner does not turn on if the warning light is on.
   B. Sometimes a power surge is caused by the dishwasher.
   C. There is only a power surge when the air conditioner turns on.
   D. None of the above

Questions 10-14.

DIRECTIONS: Questions 10 through 14 refer to Map #3 and measure your ability to orient yourself within a given section of town, neighborhood or particular area. Each of the questions describes a starting point and a destination. Assume that you are driving a car in the area shown on the map accompanying the questions. Use the map as a basis for the shortest way to get from one point to another without breaking the law.
On the map, a street marked by arrows, or by arrows and the words "One Way," indicates one-way travel and should be assumed to be one-way for the entire length, even when there are breaks or jogs in the street. EXCEPTION: A street that does not have the same name over the full length.

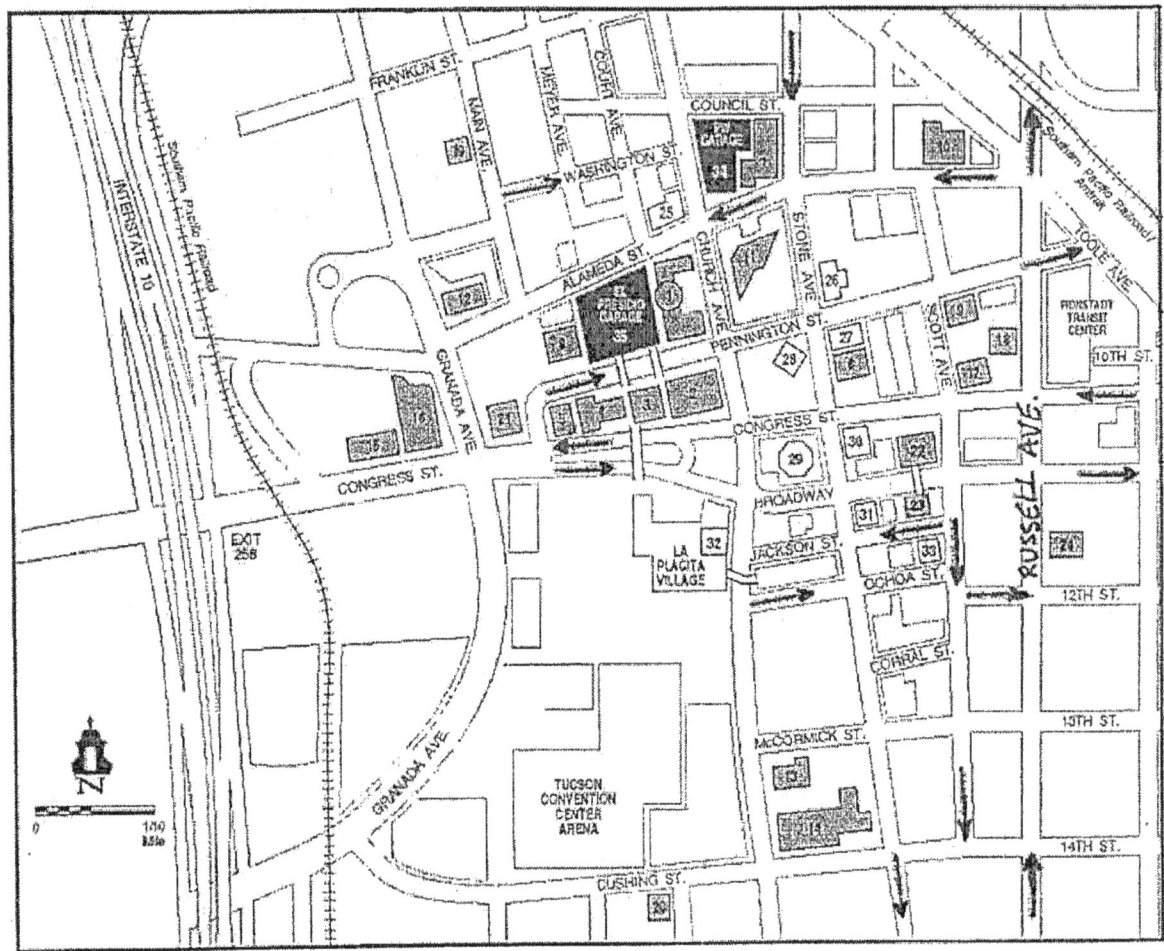

PIMA COUNTY
1. Old Courthouse
2. Superior Court Building
3. Administration Building
4. Health and Welfare Building
5. Mechanical Building
0. Legal Services Building
7. County/City Public Works Center

CITY OF TUCSON
8. City Hall
9. City Hall Annex
10. Alameda Plaza City Court Building
11. Public Library – Main Branch
12. Tucson Water Building
13. Fire Department Headquarters
14. Police Department Building

10. The SHORTEST legal way from the Public Library to the Alameda Plaza City Court Building is
    A. north on Stone Ave., east of Alameda
    B. south on Stone Ave., east on Congress, north on Russell Ave., west on Alameda
    C. south on Stone Ave., east on Pennington, north on Russell Ave., west on Alameda
    D. south on Church Ave., east on Pennington, north on Russell Ave., west on Alameda

10.____

5 (#2)

11. The SHORTEST legal way from City Hall to the Police Department is 11._____
    A. east on Congress, south on Scott Ave., west on 14th
    B. east on Pennington, south on Stone Ave.
    C. east on Congress, south on Stone Ave.
    D. east on Pennington, south on Church Ave.

12. The SHORTEST legal way from the Tucson Water Building to the Legal Service 12._____
    Building is
    A. south on Granada Ave., east on Congress, north to east on Pennington, south on Stone Ave.
    B. east on Alameda, south on Church Ave., east on Pennington, south on Stone Ave.
    C. north on Granada Ave., east on Washington, south on Church Ave., east on Pennington, south on Stone Ave.
    D. south on Granada Ave., east on Cushing, north on Stone Ave.

13. The SHORTEST legal way from the Tucson Convention Center Arena to the 13._____
    City Hall Annex is
    A. west on Cushing, north on Granada Ave., east on Congress east on Broadway
    B. east on Cushing, north on Church Ave., east on Pennington
    C. east on Cushing, north on Russel Ave., west on Pennington
    D. east on Cushing, north on Stone Ave., east on Pennington

14. The SHORTEST legal way from Ronstadt Transit Center to the Fire Department 14._____
    is
    A. west on Pennington, south on Stone Ave., west on McCormick
    B. west on Congress, south on Russell Ave., west on 13th
    C. west on Congress, south on Church Ave.
    D. west on Pennington, south on Church Ave.

Questions 15-19.

DIRECTIONS: Questions 15 through 19 refer to Figure #3, on the following page, and measure your ability to understand written descriptions of events. Each question presents a description of an accident or event and asks you which of the following five drawings in Figure #3 BEST represents it.
In the drawings, the following symbols are used:
Moving vehicle ⌂   Non-moving vehicle ▲
Pedestrian or bicyclist •
The path and direction of travel of a vehicle or pedestrian is indicated by a solid line.
The path and direction of travel of each vehicle or pedestrian directly involved in a collision from the point of impact is indicated by a dotted line.

In the space at the right, print the letter of the drawing that BEST fit the descriptions written below.

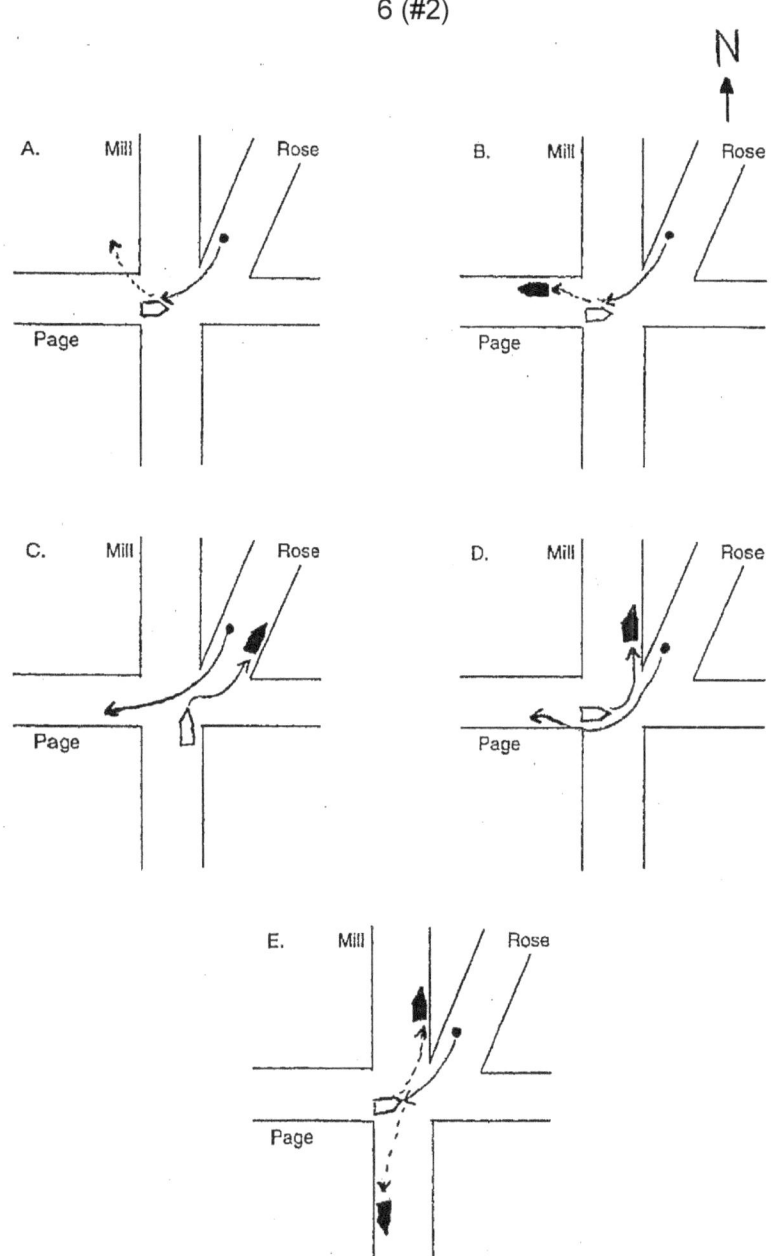

15. A bicyclist heading southwest on Rose travels into the intersection, sideswipes a car that is heading east on Page, and veers right, leaving the roadway at the northwest corner of Page and Mill.   15.____

16. A driver traveling north on Mill swerves right to avoid a bicyclist that is traveling southwest on Rose. The driver strikes the rear end of a car parked on Rose. The bicyclist continues through the intersection and travels west on Page.   16.____

17. A bicyclist heading southwest on Rose travels into the intersection, sideswipes a car that is heading east on Page, and veers right, striking the rear end of a car parked in the westbound lane on Page.   17.____

18. A driver traveling east on Page swerves left to avoid a bicyclist that is traveling southwest on Rose. The driver strikes the rear end of a car parked on Mill. The bicyclist continues through the intersection and travels west on Page.

18._____

19. A bicyclist heading southwest on Rose enters the intersection and sideswipes a car that is swerving left to avoid her. The bicyclist veers left and collides with a car parked in the southbound lane on Mill. The driver of the car veers left and collides with a car parked in the northbound lane on Mill.

19._____

Questions 20-22.

DIRECTIONS: In Questions 20 through 22, choose the word or phrase CLOSEST in meaning to the word or phrase printed in capital letters.

20. WAIVE
    A. cease   B. surrender   C. prevent   D. die

20._____

21. DEPOSITION
    A. settlement   B. deterioration   C. testimony   D. character

21._____

22. IMMUNITY
    A. exposure   B. accusation   C. protection   D. exchange

22._____

Questions 23-25.

DIRECTIONS: Questions 23 through 25 measure your ability to do fieldwork-related arithmetic. Each question presents a separate arithmetic problem for you to solve.

23. Dean, a claims investigator, is reading a 445-page case record in his spare time at work. He has already read 157 pages.
    If Dean reads 24 pages a day, he should finish reading the rest of the record in _____ days.
    A. 7   B. 12   C. 19   D. 24

23._____

24. The Fire Department owns four cars. The Department of Sanitation owns twice as many cars as the Fire Department. The Department of Parks and Recreation owns one fewer car than the Department of Sanitation. The Department of Parks and Recreation is buying new tires for each of its cars. Each tire costs $100.
    How much is the Department of Parks and Recreation going to spend on tires?
    A. $400   B. $2,800   C. $3,200   D. $4,900

24._____

25. A dance hall is about 5,000 square feet. The local ordinance does not allow more than 50 people per every 100 square feet of commercial space.
    The maximum capacity of the hall is
    A. 500   B. 2,500   C. 5,000   D. 25,000

25._____

KEY (CORRECT ANSWERS)

1.	D	11.	D
2.	B	12.	A
3.	A	13.	B
4.	D	14.	C
5.	B	15.	A
6.	D	16.	C
7.	D	17.	B
8.	A	18.	D
9.	C	19.	E
10.	C	20.	B

21.	C
22.	C
23.	B
24.	B
25.	B

SOLUTIONS TO QUESTIONS 1-9

P implies Q = original statement

Not Q implies not P = contrapositive of the original statement. A statement and its contrapositive are logically equivalent.

Q implies P = converse of the original statement

Not P implies not Q = inverse of the original statement. The converse and inverse of an original statement are logically equivalent.

P implies Q = Not P or Q.

1. The CORRECT answer is D.
   For item I, the second statement should be "Either there is no life on Mars or we should fund NASA" in order to be logically equivalent to the first statement. For item II, the statements are converses of each other; thus, they are not equivalent.

2. The CORRECT answer is B.
   In item I, this is an example of P implies Q and Q implies P. In this case, P = the notebook is missing its cover and Q = the notebook belongs to Carter. In item II, the ordering of the words is changed, but the If P then Q is exactly the same. P = it is hot and Q = the pool is open.

3. The CORRECT answer is A.
   For item I, if nobody is without benefits, then everybody has benefits. For item II, the second equivalent statement should be "either we will not fund the program or at least 100 people will sign the petition."

4. The CORRECT answer is D.
   For item I, the first statement is an implication, whereas the second statement mentions only one part of the implication (new parts are requested) and says nothing about the other part. For item II, the first statement is equivalent to "if the operating cycle is not running, then the test cycle will run." The second statement is equivalent to "if the operating cycle is running, then the test cycle will run." So, these statements in item II are not equivalent.

5. The CORRECT answer is B.
   Since Sid did not steal a car and avoid getting caught, the only other way he could become a Crips member would be "jumped in." Choice B tells us that Sid was not "jumped in," so we conclude that he did not become a member of the Crips.

6. The CORRECT answer is D.
   Since Smith and Watson have the same number of arrests, Watson must have fewer arrests than Jones. This means that each of choices A and B is impossible. Choice C would also not reveal whether or not Watson is a Precinct 8 officer.

7. The CORRECT answer is D.
Exact dollar amounts still cannot be ascertained by using any of the other choices.

8. The CORRECT answer is A.
The street sweepers never sweep on the east side of the street on Wednesday; however, they will be here at noon today. This implies that they will sweep on the west side of the street. Since the residents should move their cars before noon, we can conclude that today is Wednesday.

9. The CORRECT answer is C.
We start with W implies P, where W = warning light comes on and P = power surge. Choice C would read as P implies A, where A = air conditioning is running. Combining these statements leads to W implies A. The conclusion can be read as: Not A implies Not W, which is equivalent to W implies A.

MAP READING
EXAMINATION SECTION
TEST 1

DIRECTIONS: Each question or incomplete statement is followed by several suggested answers or completions. Select the one that BEST answers the question or completes the Statement. *PRINT THE LETTER OF THE CORRECT ANSWER IN THE SPACE AT THE RIGHT.*

Questions 1-5.

DIRECTIONS: Questions 1 through 5 are to be answered SOLELY on the basis of the following information and map.

An employee may be required to assist civilians who seek travel directions or referral to city agencies and facilities.

The following is a map of part of a city, where several public offices and other institutions are located. Each of the squares represents one city block. Street names are as shown. If there is an arrow next to the street name, it means the street is one-way only in the direction of the arrow. If there is no arrow next to the street name, two-way traffic is allowed.

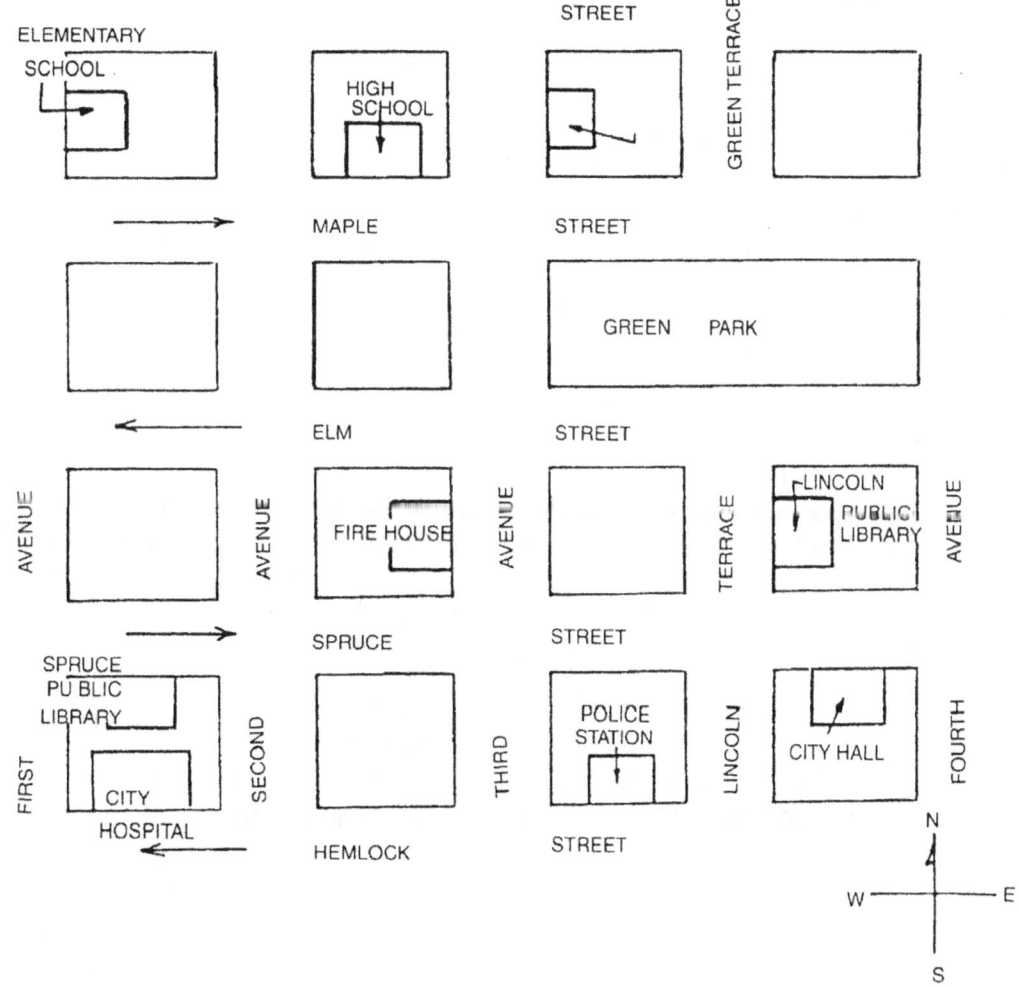

1. A woman whose handbag was stolen from her in Green Park asks a firefighter at the firehouse where to go to report the crime.
   The firefighter should tell the woman to go to the

   A. police station on Spruce Street
   B. police station on Hemlock Street
   C. city hall on Spruce Street
   D. city hall on Hemlock Street

1._____

2. A disabled senior citizen who lives on Green Terrace telephones the firehouse to ask which library is closest to her home.
   The firefighter should tell the senior citizen it is the

   A. Spruce Public Library on Lincoln Terrace
   B. Lincoln Public Library on Spruce Street
   C. Spruce Public Library on Spruce Street
   D. Lincoln Public Library on Lincoln Terrace

2._____

3. A woman calls the firehouse to ask for the exact location of City Hall.
   She should be told that it is on

   A. Hemlock Street, between Lincoln Terrace and Fourth Avenue
   B. Spruce Street, between Lincoln Terrace and Fourth Avenue
   C. Lincoln Terrace, between Spruce Street and Elm Street
   D. Green Terrace, between Maple Street and Pine Street

3._____

4. A delivery truck driver is having trouble finding the high school to make a delivery. The driver parks the truck across from the firehouse on Third Avenue facing north and goes into the firehouse to ask directions.
   In giving directions, the firefighter should tell the driver to go _____ to the school.

   A. north on Third Avenue to Pine Street and then make a right
   B. south on Third Avenue, make a left on Hemlock Street, and then make a right on Second Avenue
   C. north on Third Avenue, turn left on Elm Street, make a right on Second Avenue and go to Maple Street, then make another right
   D. north on Third Avenue to Maple Street, and then make a left

4._____

5. A man comes to the firehouse accompanied by his son and daughter. He wants to register his son in the high school and his daughter in the elementary school. He asks a firefighter which school is closest for him to walk to from the firehouse.
   The firefighter should tell the man that the

   A. high school is closer than the elementary school
   B. elementary school is closer than the high school
   C. elementary school and high school are the same distance away
   D. elementary school and high school are in opposite directions

5._____

Questions 6-8.

DIRECTIONS: Questions 6 through 8 are to be answered SOLELY on the basis of the following map and information. The flow of traffic is indicated by the arrows. If there is only one arrow shown, then traffic flows in the direction indicated by the arrow. If there are two arrows, then traffic flows in both directions. You must follow the flow of traffic

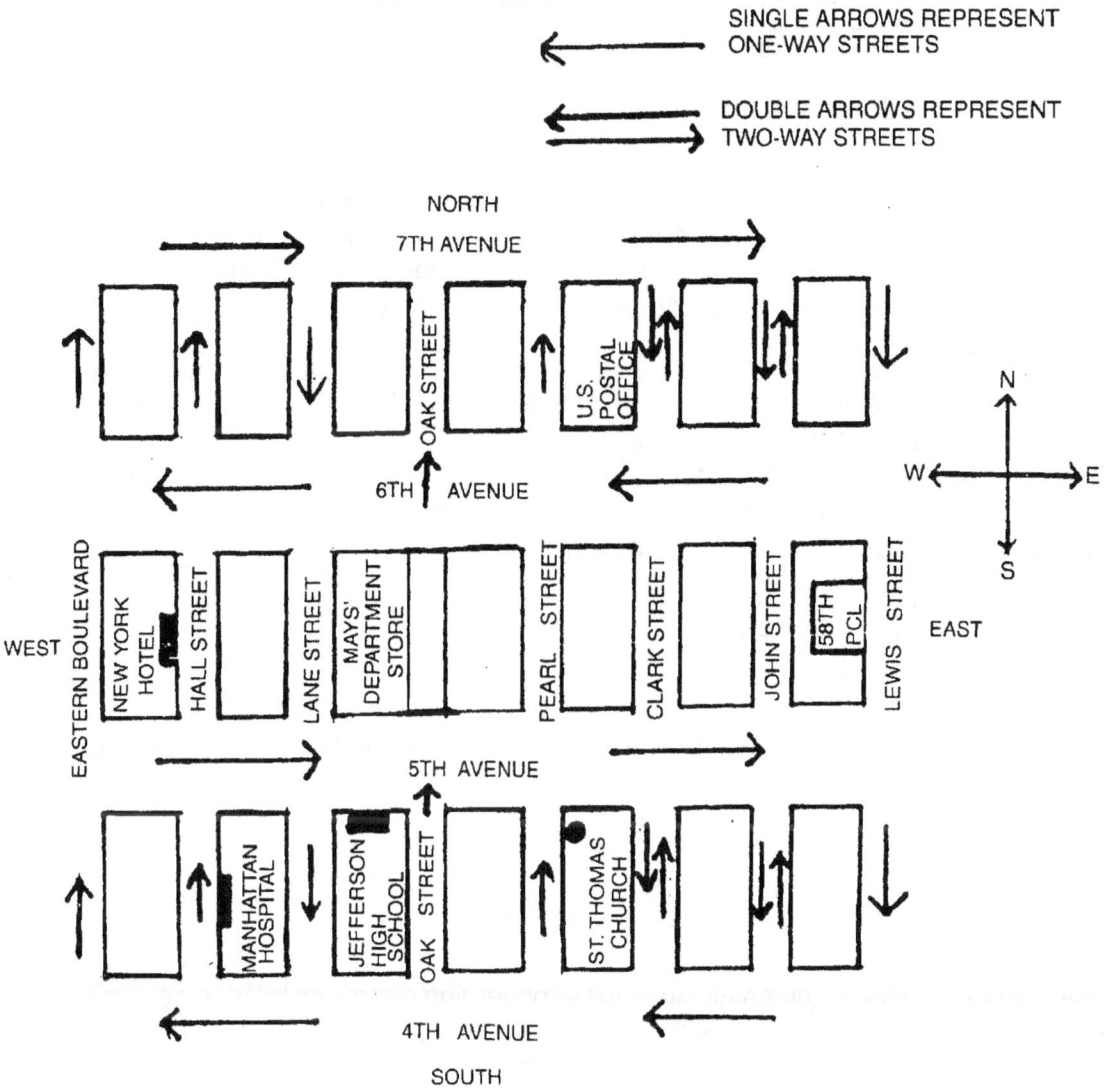

6. Traffic Enforcement Agent Fox was on foot patrol at John Street between 6th and 7th Avenues when a motorist driving southbound asked her for directions to the New York Hotel, which is located on Hall Street between 5th and 6th Avenues. Which one of the following is the SHORTEST route for Agent Fox to direct the motorist to take, making sure to obey all traffic regulations?
Travel _____ to the New York Hotel.

   A. north on John Street, then east on 7th Avenue, then north on Lewis Street, then west on 4th Avenue, then north on Eastern Boulevard, then east on 5th Avenue, then north on Hall Street
   B. south on John Street, then west on 6th Avenue, then south on Eastern Boulevard, then east on 5th Avenue, then north on Hall Street

6.____

C. south on John Street, then west on 6th Avenue, then south on Clark Street, then east on 4th Avenue, then north on Eastern Boulevard, then east on 5th Avenue, then north on Hall Street
D. south on John Street, then west on 4th Avenue, then north on Hall Street

7. Traffic Enforcement Agent Murphy is on motorized patrol on 7th Avenue between Oak Street and Pearl Street when Lt. Robertson radios him to go to Jefferson High School, located on 5th Avenue between Lane Street and Oak Street. Which one of the following is the SHORTEST route for Agent Murphy to take, making sure to obey all the traffic regulations?
Travel east on 7th Avenue, then south on _____, then east on 5th Avenue to Jefferson High School.

    A. Clark Street, then west on 4th Avenue, then north on Hall Street
    B. Pearl Street, then west on 4th Avenue, then north on Lane Street
    C. Lewis Street, then west on 6th Avenue, then south on Hall Street
    D. Lewis Street, then west on 4th Avenue, then north on Oak Street

7.____

8. Traffic Enforcement Agent Vasquez was on 4th Avenue and Eastern Boulevard when a motorist asked him for directions to the 58th Police Precinct, which is located on Lewis Street between 5th and 6th Avenues.
Which one of the following is the SHORTEST route for Agent Vasquez to direct the motorist to take, making sure to obey all traffic regulations.
Travel north on Eastern Boulevard, then east on _____ on Lewis Street to the 58th Police Precinct.

    A. 5th Avenue, then north
    B. 7th Avenue, then south
    C. 6th Avenue, then north on Pearl Street, then east on 7th Avenue, then south
    D. 5th Avenue, then north on Clark Street, then east on 6th Avenue, then south

8.____

Questions 9-13.

DIRECTIONS: Questions 9 through 13 are to be answered SOLELY on the basis of the following map and the following information.

Toll collectors answer motorists' questions concerning directions by reading a map of the metropolitan area. Although many alternate routes leading to destinations exist on the following map, you are to choose the MOST direct route of those given.

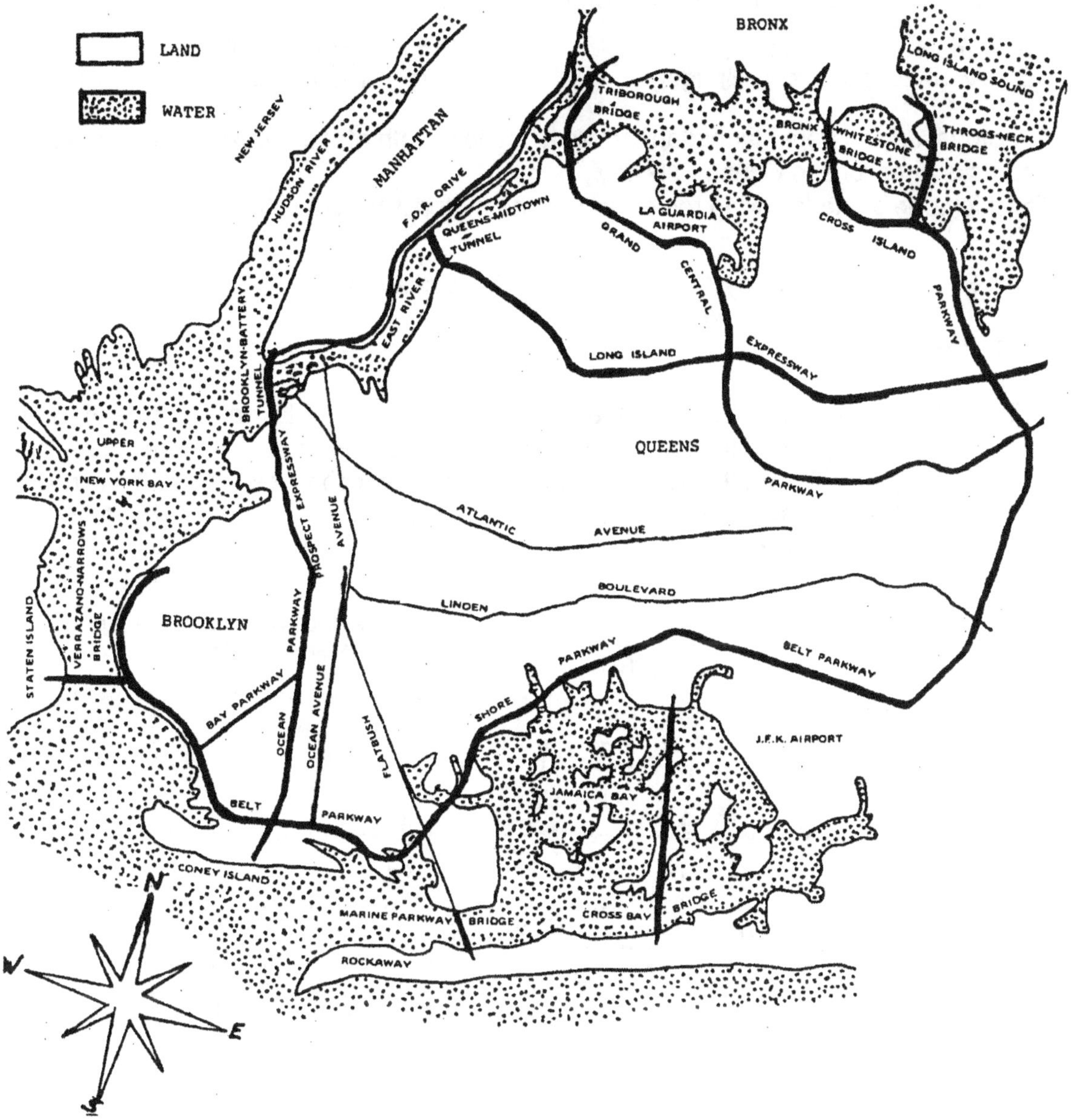

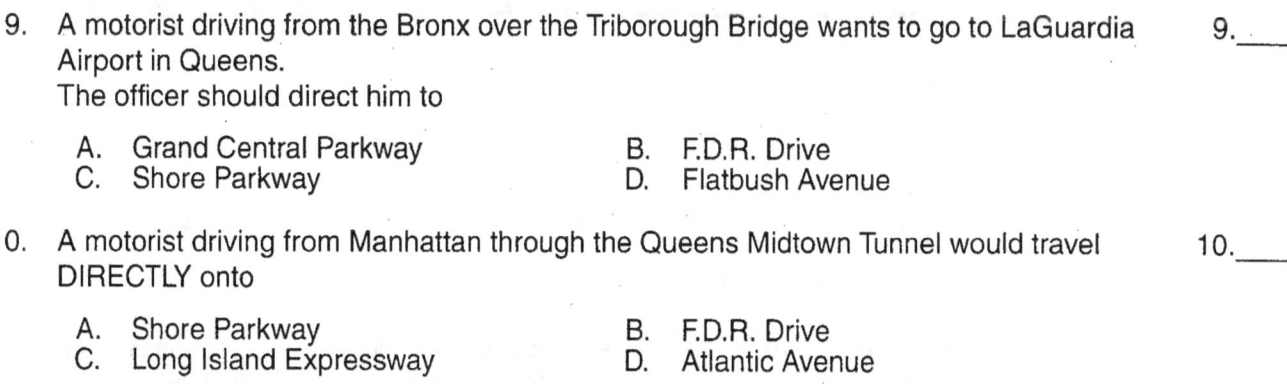

9. A motorist driving from the Bronx over the Triborough Bridge wants to go to LaGuardia Airport in Queens.
   The officer should direct him to

   A. Grand Central Parkway
   B. F.D.R. Drive
   C. Shore Parkway
   D. Flatbush Avenue

10. A motorist driving from Manhattan through the Queens Midtown Tunnel would travel DIRECTLY onto

    A. Shore Parkway
    B. F.D.R. Drive
    C. Long Island Expressway
    D. Atlantic Avenue

11. A motorist traveling north over the Marine Parkway Bridge should take which route to reach Coney Island?

    A. Shore Parkway East
    B. Belt Parkway West
    C. Linden Boulevard
    D. Ocean Parkway

12. Which facility does NOT connect the Bronx and Queens? 12.____

    A. Triborough Bridge   B. Bronx-Whitestone Bridge
    C. Verrazano-Narrows Bridge   D. Throgs-Neck Bridge

13. A motorist driving from Manhattan arrives at the toll booth of the Brooklyn-Battery Tunnel 13.____
    and asks directions to Ocean Parkway.
    To which one of the following routes should the motorist FIRST be directed?

    A. Atlantic Avenue   B. Bay Parkway
    C. Prospect Expressway   D. Ocean Avenue

Questions 14-16.

DIRECTIONS: Questions 14 through 16 are to be answered SOLELY on the basis of the following map. The flow of traffic is indicated by the arrows. If there is only one arrow shown, then traffic flows only in the direction indicated by the arrow. If there are two arrows, then traffic flows in both directions. You must follow the flow of traffic.

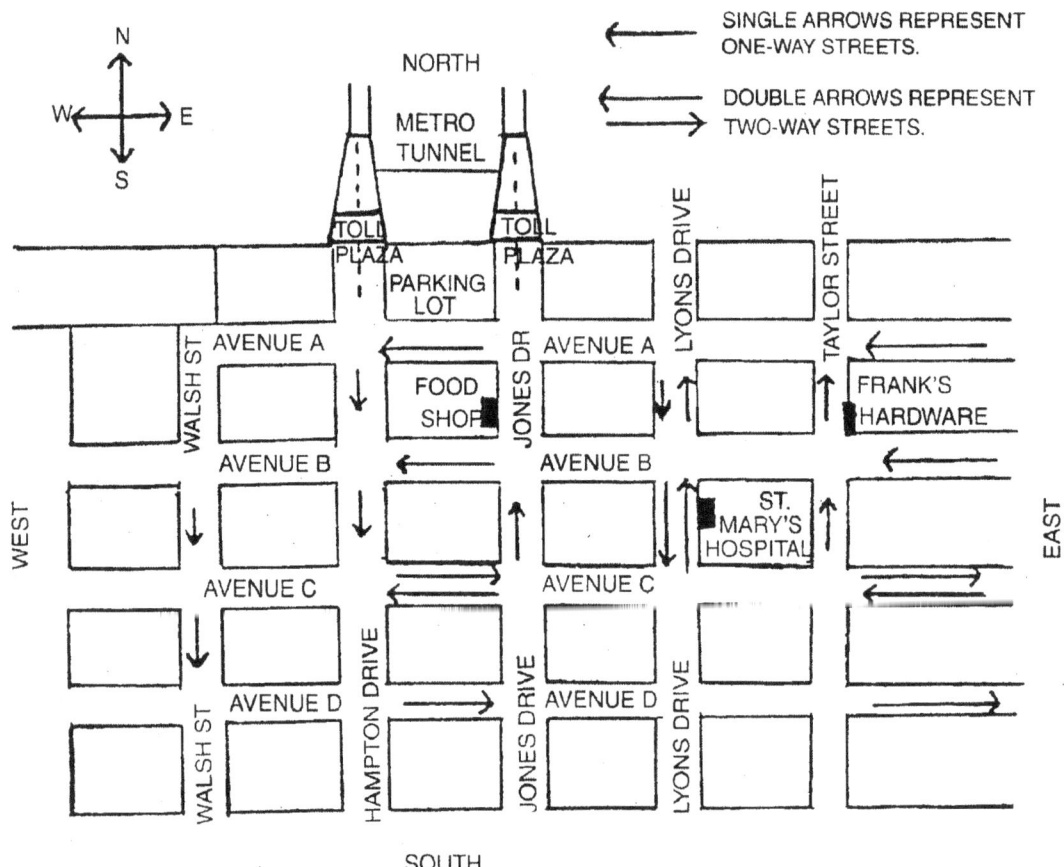

14. A motorist is exiting the Metro Tunnel and approaches the bridge and tunnel officer at the 14.____
    toll plaza. He asks the officer how to get to the food shop on Jones Drive. Which one of the following is the SHORTEST route for the motorist to take, making sure to obey all traffic regulations?
    Travel south on Hampton Drive, then left on _____ on Jones Drive to the food shop.

A. Avenue A, then right	B. Avenue B, then right
C. Avenue D, then left	D. Avenue C, then left

15. A motorist heading south pulls up to a toll booth at the exit of the Metro Tunnel and asks 15.____
Bridge and Tunnel Officer Evans how to get to Frank's Hardware Store on Taylor Street.
Which one of the following is the SHORTEST route for the motorist to take, making
sure to obey all traffic regulations?
Travel south on Hampton Drive, then east on

   A. Avenue B to Taylor Street
   B. Avenue D, then north on Taylor Street to Avenue B
   C. Avenue C, then north on Taylor Street to Avenue B
   D. Avenue C, then north on Lyons Drive, then east on Avenue B to Taylor Street

16. A motorist is exiting the Metro Tunnel and approaches the toll plaza. She asks Bridge 16.____
and Tunnel Officer Owens for directions to St. Mary's Hospital.
Which one of the following is the SHORTEST route for the motorist to take, making
sure to obey all traffic regulations?
Travel south on Hampton Drive, then _____ on Lyons Drive to St. Mary's Hospital.

   A. left on Avenue D, then left
   B. right on Avenue A, then left on Walsh Street, then left on Avenue D, then left
   C. left on Avenue C, then left
   D. left on Avenue B, then right

Questions 17-18.

DIRECTIONS: Questions 17 and 18 are to be answered SOLELY on the basis of the map which appears on the following page. The flow of traffic is indicated by the arrows. If there is only one arrow shown, then traffic flows only in the direction indicated by the arrow. If there are two arrows shown, then traffic flows in both directions. You must follow the flow of traffic.

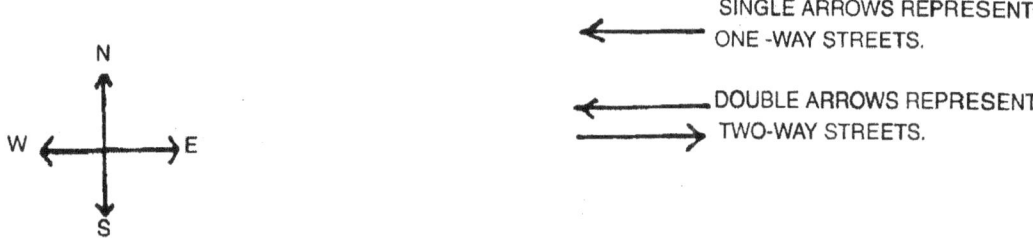

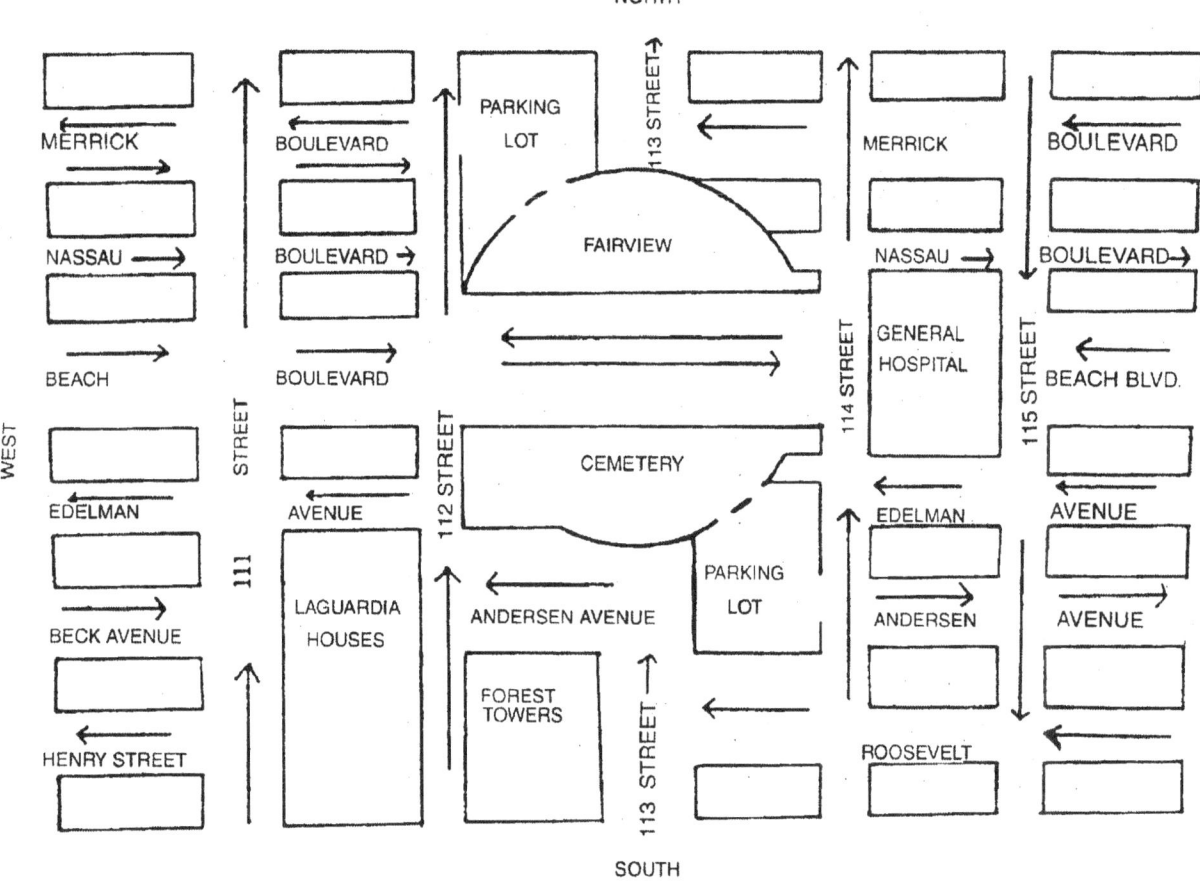

17. Police Officers Glenn and Albertson are on 111th Street at Henry Street when they are dispatched to a past robbery at Beach Boulevard and 115th Street.
Which one of the following is the SHORTEST route for the officers to follow in their patrol car, making sure to obey all traffic regulations?
Travel north on 111th Street, then east on _____ south on 115th Street.

  A. Edelman Avenue, then north on 112th Street, then east on Beach Boulevard, then north on 114th Street, then east on Nassau Boulevard, then one block
  B. Beach Boulevard, then north on 114th Street, then east on Nassau Boulevard, then one block
  C. Merrick Boulevard, then two blocks
  D. Nassau Boulevard, then south on 112th Street, then east on Beach Boulevard, then north on 114th Street, then east on Nassau Boulevard, then one block

17._____

9 (#1)

18. Later in their tour, Officers Glenn and Albertson are driving on 114th Street. If they make a left turn to enter the parking lot at Andersen Avenue, and then make a u-turn, in what direction would they now be headed?

    A. North   B. South   C. East   D. West

18.____

Questions 19-20.

DIRECTIONS: Questions 19 and 20 are to be answered SOLELY on the basis of the following map. The flow of traffic is indicated by the arrows. If there is only one arrow shown, then traffic flows only in the direction indicated by the arrow. If there are two arrows shown, then traffic flows in both directions. You must follow the flow of traffic.

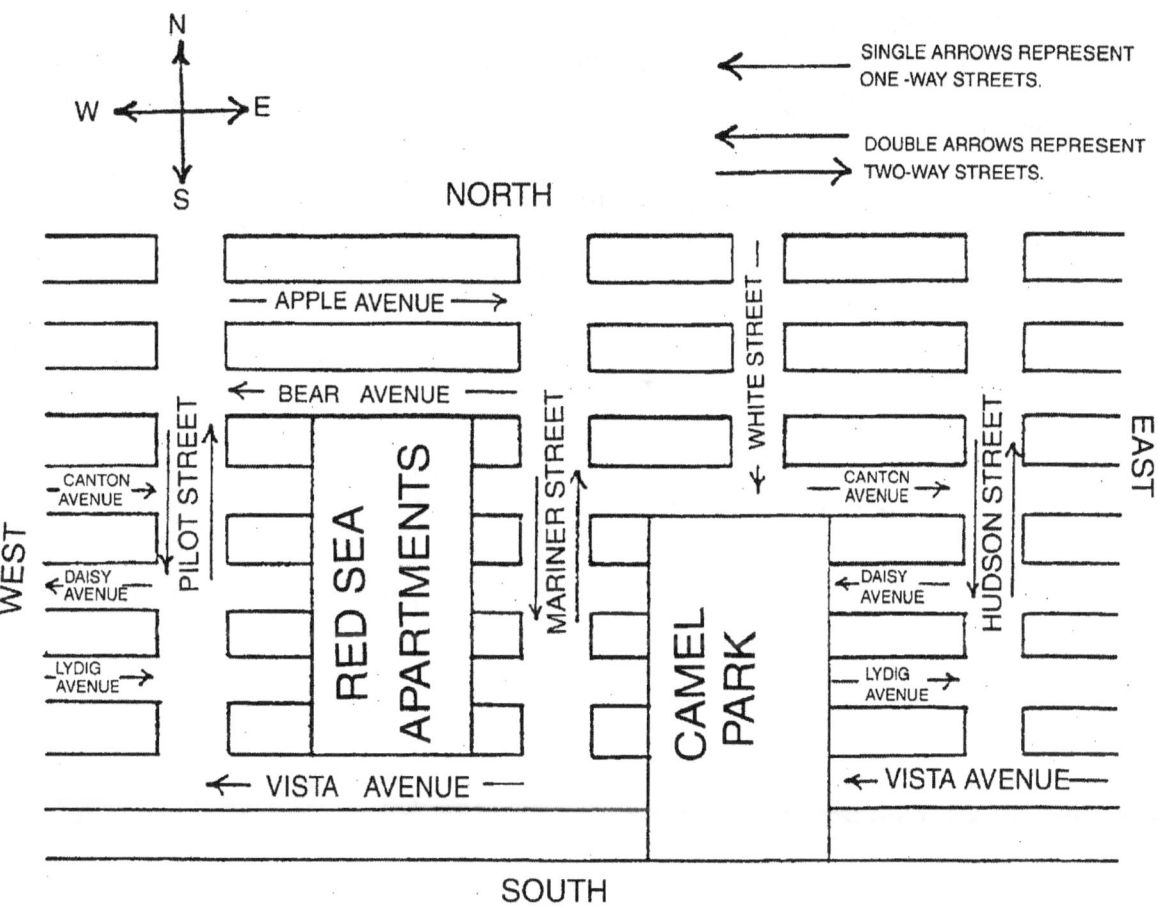

19. You are located at Apple Avenue and White Street. You receive a call to respond to the corner of Lydig Avenue and Pilot Street.
Which one of the following is the MOST direct route for you to take in your patrol car, making sure to obey all traffic regulations?
Travel _____ on Pilot Street.

19.____

   A. two blocks south on White Street, then one block east on Canton Avenue, then one block north on Hudson Street, then three blocks west on Bear Avenue, then three blocks south
   B. one block south on White Street, then two blocks west on Bear Avenue, then three blocks south

C. two blocks west on Apple Avenue, then four blocks south
D. two blocks south on White Street, then one block west on Canton Avenue, then three blocks south on Mariner Street, then one block west on Vista Avenue, then one block north

20. You are located at Canton Avenue and Pilot Street. You receive a call of a crime in progress at the intersection of Canton Avenue and Hudson Street.
Which one of the following is the MOST direct route for you to take in your patrol car, making sure to obey all traffic regulations?
Travel

   A. two blocks north on Pilot Street, then two blocks east on Apple Avenue, then one block south on White Street, then one block east on Bear Avenue, then one block south on Hudson Street
   B. three blocks south on Pilot Street, then travel one block east on Vista Avenue, then travel three blocks north on Mariner Street, then travel two blocks east on Canton Avenue
   C. one block north on Pilot Street, then travel three blocks east on Bear Avenue, then travel one block south on Hudson Street
   D. two blocks north on Pilot Street, then travel three blocks east on Apple Avenue, then travel two blocks south on Hudson Street

20.____

KEY (CORRECT ANSWERS)

1.	B	11.	B/D
2.	D	12.	C
3.	B	13.	C
4.	C	14.	D
5.	A	15.	C
6.	D	16.	C
7.	A	17.	B
8.	B	18.	C
9.	A	19.	B
10.	C	20.	D

READING COMPREHENSION
UNDERSTANDING AND INTERPRETING WRITTEN MATERIAL
EXAMINATION SECTION
TEST 1

DIRECTIONS: All questions are to be answered SOLELY on the basis of the information contained in the passage. Each question or incomplete statement is followed by several suggested answers or completions. Select the one that BEST answers the question or completes the statement. *PRINT THE LETTER OF THE CORRECT ANSWER IN THE SPACE AT THE RIGHT.*

Questions 1-7.

Snow-covered roads spell trouble for motorists all winter long. Clearing highways of snow and ice to keep millions of motor vehicles moving freely is a tremendous task. Highway departments now rely, to a great extent, on chemical de-icers to get the big job done. Sodium chloride, in the form of commercial salt, is the de-icer most frequently used.

There is no reliable evidence to prove that salt reduces highway accidents. But available statistics are impressive. For example, before Massachusetts used chemical de-icers, it had a yearly average of 21 fatal accidents and 1,635 injuries attributed to cars skidding on snow or ice. Beginning in 1990, the state began fighting hazardous driving conditions with chemical de-icers. During the period 1990-2000, there was a yearly average of only seven deaths and 736 injuries as a result of skids.

Economical and effective in a moderately low temperature range, salt is increasingly popular with highway departments, but not so popular with individual car owners. Salty slush eats away at metal, including auto bodies. It also sprinkles windshields with a fine-grained spray which dries on contact, severely reducing visibility. However, drivers who are hindered or immobilized by heavy winter weather favor the liberal use of products such as sodium chloride. When snow blankets roads, these drivers feel that the quickest way to get back to the safety of driving on bare pavement is through use of de-icing salts.

1. The MAIN reason given by the above passage for the use of sodium chloride as a de-icer is that it
   A. has no harmful effects
   B. is economical
   C. is popular among car owners
   D. reduces highway accidents

   1._____

2. The above passage may BEST be described as a(n)
   A. argument against the use of sodium chloride as a de-icer
   B. discussion of some advantages and disadvantages of sodium chloride as a de-icer
   C. recommendation to use sodium chloride as a de-icer
   D. technical account of the uses and effects of sodium chloride as a de-icer

   2._____

3. Based on the above passage, the use of salt on snow-covered roadways will eventually
   A. decrease the efficiency of the automobile fuel
   B. cause tires to deteriorate
   C. damage the surface of the roadway
   D. cause holes in the sides of cars

3.____

4. The average number of persons killed yearly in Massachusetts in car accidents caused by skidding on snow or ice, before chemical de-icers were used there, was
   A. 9   B. 12   C. 21   D. 30

4.____

5. According to the above passage, it would be advisable to use salt as a de-icer when
   A. outdoor temperatures are somewhat below freezing
   B. residues on highway surfaces are deemed to be undesirable
   C. snow and ice have low absorbency characteristics
   D. the use of a substance is desired which dries on contact

5.____

6. As a result of using chemical de-icers, the number of injuries resulting from skids in Massachusetts was reduced by about
   A. 35%   B. 45%   C. 55%   D. 65%

6.____

7. According to the above passage, driver visibility can be severely reduced by
   A. sodium chloride deposits on the windshield
   B. glare from salt and snow crystals
   C. salt spray covering the front lights
   D. faulty windshield wipers

7.____

Questions 8-10.

An employee should call the Fire Department for any fire except a small one in a wastebasket. This kind of fire can be put out with a fire extinguisher. If the employee is not sure about the size of the fire, he should not wait to find out how big it is. He should call the Fire Department at once.

Every employee should know what to do when a fire starts. He should know how to use the firefighting tools in the building and how to call the Fire Department. He should also know where the nearest fire alarm box is. But the most important thing for an employee to do in case of fire is to avoid panic.

8. If there is a small fire in a wastebasket, an employee should
   A. call the Fire Department   B. let it burn itself out
   C. open a window   D. put it out with a fire extinguisher

8.____

9. In case of fire, the MOST important thing for an employee to do is to
   A. find out how big it is   B. keep calm
   C. leave the building right away D. report to his boss

9.____

10. If a large fire starts while he is at work, an employee should always FIRST   10.____
    A. call the Fire Department
    B. notify the Housing Superintendent
    C. remove inflammables from the building
    D. use a fire extinguisher

Questions 11-12.

Those correction theorists who are in agreement with severe and rigid controls as a normal part of the correctional process are confronted with a contradiction; this is so because a responsibility which is consistent with freedom cannot be developed in a repressive atmosphere. They do not recognize this contradiction when they carry out their programs with dictatorial force and expect convicted criminals exposed to such programs to be reformed into free and responsible citizens.

11. According to the above passage, those correction theorists are faced with a contradiction who   11.____
    A. are in favor of the enforcement of strict controls in a prison
    B. believe that to develop a sense of responsibility, freedom must not be restricted
    C. take the position that the development of responsibility consistent with freedom is not possible in a repressive atmosphere
    D. think that freedom and responsibility can be developed only in a democratic atmosphere

12. According to the above passage, a repressive atmosphere in a prison   12.____
    A. does not conform to present-day ideas of freedom of the individual
    B. is admitted by correction theorists to be in conflict with the basic principles of the normal correctional process
    C. is advocated as the best method of maintaining discipline when rehabilitation is of secondary importance
    D. is not suitable for the development of a sense of responsibility consistent with freedom

Questions 13-16.

Abandoned cars—with tires gone, chrome stripped away, and windows smashed—have become a common sight on the City's streets. In 2020, more than 72,000 were deposited at curbs by owners who never came back, an increase of 15,000 from the year before and more than 30 times the number abandoned a decade ago. In January, 2021, the City's Environmental Protection Administrator asked the State Legislature to pass a law requiring a buyer of a new automobile to deposit $100 and an owner of an automobile at the time the law takes effect to deposit $50 with the State Department of Motor Vehicles. In return, they would be given a certificate of deposit which would be passed on to each succeeding owner. The final owner would get the deposit money back if he could present proof that he has disposed of his car "in an environmentally acceptable manner." The Legislature has given no indication that it plans to rush ahead on the matter.

13. The number of cars abandoned in City streets in 2010 was MOST NEARLY   13.____
    A. 2,500   B. 12,000   C. 27,500   D. 57,000

14. The proposed law would require a person who owned a car bought before the   14.____
    law was passed to deposit
    A. $100 with the State Department of Motor Vehicles
    B. $50 with the Environmental Protection Administration
    C. $100 with the State Legislature
    D. $50 with the State Department of Motor Vehicles

15. The proposed law would require the State to return the deposit money only   15.____
    when the
    A. original owner of the car shows roof that he sold it
    B. last owner of the car shows proof that he got rid of the car in a
       satisfactory way
    C. owner of the car shows proof that he has transferred the certificate of
       deposit to the next owner
    D. last owner of a car returns the certificate of deposit

16. The MAIN idea or theme of the above article is that   16.____
    A. a proposed new law would make it necessary for car owners in the State
       to pay additional taxes
    B. the State Legislature is against a proposed law to require deposits from
       automobile owners to prevent them from abandoning their cars
    C. the City is trying to find a solution for the increasing number of cars
       abandoned on its streets
    D. to pay for the removal of abandoned cars, the City's Environmental
       Protection Administrator has asked the State to fine automobile owners
       who abandon their vehicles

Questions 17-19.

The German roach is the most common roach in houses in the United State. Adults are pale brown and about ½-inch long; both sexes have wings as long as the body, and can be distinguished from other roaches by the two dark stripes on the pronotum. The female carries its egg capsule protruding from her abdomen until the eggs are ready to hatch. This is the only common house-infesting species which carries the egg capsule for such an extended period of time. A female will usually produce 4 to 8 capsules in her lifetime. Each capsule contains 30 to 48 eggs which hatch out in about 28 days at ordinary room temperature. The completion of the nymph stage under room conditions requires 40 to 125 days. German roaches may live as adults for as long as 303 days.

It is stated about that the German cockroach is the most commonly encountered of the house-infesting species in the United States. The reasons for this are somewhat complex, but the understanding of some of the factors involved are basic to the practice of pest control. In the first place, the German cockroach has a larger number of eggs per capsule and a shorter hatching time than do the other species. It also requires a shorter period from hatching until sexual maturity, so that within a given period of time a population of German roaches will produce a larger number of eggs. Onn the basis of this fact, we can state that this species has a high reproductive potential. Since the female carries the egg capsule during nearly the entire time that the embryos are developing within the egg, many hazards of the environment which may affect the eggs are avoided. This means that more nymphs are likely to hatch and that a larger portion of the reproductive potential is realized. The nymphs which hatch from each egg capsule tend to stay close to each other, and since they are often close to the female at time of hatching, there is a tendency for the population density to be high locally. Being smaller than most of the other roaches, they are able to conceal themselves in many places which are inaccessible to individuals of the larger species. All of these factors combined help to give the German cockroach an advantage with regard to group survival.

17. According to the above passage, the MOST important feature of the German roach which gives it an advantage over other roaches is
    A. distinctive markings
    B. immunity to disease
    C. long life span
    D. power to reproduce

18. An IMPORTANT difference between an adult female German roach and an adult female of other species is the
    A. black bars or stripes which appear on the abdomen of the German roach
    B. German roach's preference for warm, moist places in which to breed
    C. long period of time during which the German roach carries the egg capsule
    D. presence of longer wings on the female German roach

19. A storeroom in a certain housing project has an infestation of German roaches, which includes 125 adult female.
    If the infestation is not treated and ordinary room temperature is maintained in the storeroom, how many eggs will hatch out during the lifetime of these females if they each lay 8 capsules containing 48 eggs each?
    A. 1,500   B. 48,000   C. 96,000   D. 303,000

Questions 20-22.

City governments have long had building codes which set minimum standards for building and for human occupancy. The code (or series of codes) makes provisions for standards of lighting and ventilation, sanitation, fire prevention, and protection. As a result of demands from manufacturers, builders, real estate people, tenement owners, and building-trades unions, these codes often have established minimum standards well below those that the contemporary society would accept as a rock-bottom minimum. Codes often become outdated, so that meager standards in one era become seriously inadequate a few decades later as society's concept of a minimum standard of living changes. Out-of-date codes, when still in use, have sometimes prevented the introduction of new devices and modern building techniques. Thus, it is extremely important that building codes keep pace with changes in the accepted concept of a minimum standard of living.

20. According to the above passage, all of the following considerations in building planning would probably be covered in a building code EXCEPT
    A. closet space as a percentage of total floor area
    B. size and number of windows required for rooms of differing sizes

C. placement of fire escapes in each line of apartments
D. type of garbage disposal units to be installed

21. According to the above passage, if an ideal building code were to be created, how would the established minimum standards in it compare to the ones that are presently set by city governments?
They would
    A. be lower than they are at present
    B. be higher than they are at present
    C. be comparable to the present minimum standards
    D. vary according to the economic group that sets them

21.____

22. On the basis of the above passage, what is the reason for difficulties in introducing new building techniques?
    A. Builders prefer techniques which represent the rock-bottom minimum desired by society.
    B. Certain manufacturers have obtained patents on various building methods to the exclusion of new techniques.
    C. The government does not want to invest money in techniques that will soon be outdated.
    D. New techniques are not provided for in building codes which are not up-to-date.

22.____

Questions 23-25.

A flameproof fabric is defined as one which, when exposed to small sources of ignition such as sparks or smoldering cigarettes, does not burn beyond the vicinity of the source of the ignition. Cotton fabrics are the materials commonly used that are considered most hazardous. Other materials, such as acetate rayons and linens, are somewhat less hazardous, and woolens and some natural silk fabrics, even when untreated, are about the equal of the average treated cotton fabric insofar as flame spread and ease of ignition are concerned. The method of application is to immerse the fabric in a flameproofing solution. The container used must be large enough so that all the fabric is thoroughly wet and there are no folds which the solution does not penetrate.

23. According to the above passage, a flameproof fabric is one which
    A. is unaffected by heat and smoke
    B. resists the spread of flames when ignited
    C. burns with a cold flame
    D. cannot be ignited by sparks or cigarettes
    E. may smolder but cannot burn

23.____

24. According to the above passage, woolen fabrics which have not been flameproofed are as likely to catch fire as _____ fabrics.
    A. treated silk   B. treated acetate rayon
    C. untreated linen   D. untreated synthetic
    E. treated cotton

24.____

25. In the method described above, the flameproofing solution is BEST applied to the fabric by _____ the fabric. 25._____
    A. sponging
    B. spraying
    C. dipping
    D. brushing
    E. sprinkling

KEY (CORRECT ANSWERS)

1.	B	11.	A
2.	B	12.	D
3.	D	13.	A
4.	C	14.	D
5.	A	15.	B
6.	C	16.	C
7.	A	17.	D
8.	D	18.	C
9.	B	19.	B
10.	A	20.	A

21. B
22. D
23. B
24. E
25. C

TEST 2

DIRECTIONS: All questions are to be answered SOLELY on the basis of the information contained in the passage. Each question or incomplete statement is followed by several suggested answers or completions. Select the one that BEST answers the question or completes the statement. *PRINT THE LETTER OF THE CORRECT ANSWER IN THE SPACE AT THE RIGHT.*

Questions 1-4.

Safety belts provide protection for the passengers of a vehicle by preventing them from crashing around inside if the vehicle is involved in a collision. They operate on the principle similar to that used in the packaging of fragile items. You become a part of the vehicle package and you are kept from being tossed about inside if the vehicle is suddenly decelerated. Many injury-causing collisions at low speeds—for example, at city intersections—could have been injury-free if the occupants had fastened their safety belts. There is a double advantage to the driver in that it not only protects him from harm, but prevents him from being yanked away from the wheel, thereby permitting him to maintain control of the car. Since, without seat belts, the risk of injury is about 50% greater, and the risk of death is about 30% greater, the State Vehicle and Traffic Law provided that a motor vehicle manufactured or assembled after June 30, 1964 and designated as a 1965 or later model should have two safety belts for the front seat. It also provides that a motor vehicle manufactured after June 30, 1966 and designated as a 1967 or later model should have at least one safety belt for the rear seat for each passenger for which the rear seat of such vehicle was designed.

1. The principle on which seat belts work is that
   A. a car and its driver and passengers are fragile
   B. a person fastened to the car will not be thrown around when the car slows down suddenly
   C. the driver and passengers of a car that is suddenly decelerated will be thrown forward
   D. the driver and passengers of an automobile should be packaged the way fragile items are packaged

2. We can assume from the above passage that safety belts should be worn at all times because you can never tell when
   A. a car will be forced to turn off onto another road
   B. it will be necessary to shift into low gear to go up a hill
   C. you will have to speed up to pass another car
   D. a car may have to come to a sudden stop

3. Besides preventing injury, an ADDITIONAL benefit from the use of safety belts is that
   A. collisions are fewer
   B. damage to the car is kept down
   C. the car can be kept under control
   D. the number of accidents at city intersections is reduced

4. The risk of death in car accidents for people who don't use safety belts is
   A. 30% greater than the risk of injury
   B. 30% greater than for those who do use them
   C. 50% less than the risk of injury
   D. 50% greater than for those who use them

Questions 5-9.

Any person who is living in New York City and is otherwise eligible may be granted public assistance whether or not he has New York State residence. However, since New York City does not contribute to the cost of assistance granted to persons who are without State residence, the cases of all recipients must be formally identified as to whether or not each member of the household has State residence.

To acquire State residence a person must have resided in New York State continuously for one year. Such residence is not lost unless the person is out of the State continuously for a period of one year or longer. Continuous residence does not include any period during which the individual is a patient in a hospital, an inmate of a public institution or of an incorporated private institution, a resident on a military reservation, or a minor residing in a boarding home while under the care of an authorized agency. Receipt of public assistance does not prevent a person from acquiring State residence. State residence, once acquired, is not lost because of absence from the State while a person is serving in the U.S. Armed Forces or the Merchant Marine; nor does a member of the family of such a person lose State residence while living with or near that person in these circumstances.

Each person, regardless of age, acquires or loses State residence as an individual. There is no derivative State residence except for an infant at the time of birth. He is deemed to have State residence if he is in the custody of both parents and either one of them has State residence, or if the parent having custody of him has State residence.

5. According to the above passage, an infant is deemed to have New York State residence at the time of his birth if
   A. he is born in New York State but neither of his parents is a resident
   B. he is in custody of only one parent, who is not a resident, but his other parent is a resident
   C. his brother and sister are residents
   D. he is in the custody of both his parents but only one of them is a resident

6. The Jones family consists of five members. Jack and Mary Jones have lived in New York State continuously for the past eighteen months after having lived in Ohio since they were born. Of their three children, one was born ten months ago and has been in custody of his parents since birth. Their second child lived in Ohio until six months ago and then moved in with his parents. Their third child had never lived in New York until he moved with his parents to New York eighteen months ago. However, he entered the armed forces one month later and has not lived in New York since that time.
   Based on the above passage, how many members of the Jones Family are New York State residents?
   A. 2   B. 3   C. 4   D. 5

3 (#2)

7. Assuming that each of the following individuals has lived continuously in New York State for the past year and has never previously lived in the State, which one of them is a New York State resident? 7.____
   A. Jack Salinas, who has been an inmate in a State correctional facility for six months of the year
   B. Fran Johnson, who has lived on an Army base for the entire year
   C. Arlene Snyder, who married a non-resident during the past year
   D. Gary Phillips, who was a patient in a Veterans Administration hospital for the entire year

8. The above passage implies that the reason for determining whether or not a recipient of public assistance is a State resident is that 8.____
   A. the cost of assistance for non-residents is not a New York City responsibility
   B. non-residents living in New York City are not eligible for public assistance
   C. recipients of public assistance are barred from acquiring State residence
   D. New York City is responsible for the full cost of assistance to recipients who are residents

9. Assume that the Rollins household in New York City consists of six members at the present time—Anne Rollins, her three children, her aunt, and her uncle. Anne Rollins and one of her children moved to New York City seven months ago. Neither of them had previously lived in New York State. Her other two children have lived in New York City continuously for the past two years, as has her aunt. Anne Rollins' uncle had lived in New York City continuously for many years until two years ago. He then entered the armed forces and has returned to New York City within the past month. 9.____
   Based on the above passage, how many members of the Rollins' household are New York State residents?
   A. 2   B. 3   C. 4   D. 6

Questions 10-12.

The agreement under which a tenant rents property from a landlord is known as a lease. Generally speaking, leases are classified as either short-term or long-term in duration. They are further subdivided according to the method used to determine the amount of periodic rent payments. Of the many types of lease in use, the more commonly used ones are the following:
1. The straight or fixed lease is one in which rent may be paid in equal amounts throughout the duration of the lease. These are usually restricted to short-term leasing, or somewhat longer-term if clauses in the lease provide for periodic escalation of payments as the economy shifts.
2. Percentage leasing, used for short-term commercial leasing, provides the landlord with a stipulated percentage of a tenant's gross sales from goods and services sold on the premises, in addition to a fixed amount of rent.
3. The net lease, generally long-term (ten years or more), requires the tenant to pay all operating costs, including real estate taxes and insurance. In a net-net lease, the tenant further agrees to meet mortgage interest and principal payments.

4. An escalated lease, which is a long-term lease, requires rent to be of a stipulated base amount which periodically is subject to escalation in accordance with cost-of-living index scales, or in direct proportion to taxes, insurance, and operating costs.

10. Based on the information given in the above passage, which type of lease is MOST likely to be advantageous to a landlord if there is a high rate of inflation?
    A. Fixed lease
    B. Percentage lease
    C. Net lease
    D. Escalated lease

11. On the basis of the above passage, which type of lease would generally be MOST suitable for a well-established textile company which requires permanent facilities for its large operations?
    A. Percentage lease and escalated lease
    B. Escalated lease and net lease
    C. Straight lease and net lease
    D. Straight lease and percentage lease

12. According to the above passage, the only type of lease which assures the same amount of rent throughout a specified interval is the _____ lease.
    A. straight
    B. percentage
    C. net-net
    D. escalated

Questions 13-18.

Basic to every office is the need for proper lighting. Inadequate lighting is a familiar cause of fatigue and serves to create a somewhat dismal atmosphere in the office. One requirement of proper lighting is that it be an appropriate intensity. Intensity is measured in foot-candles. According to the Illuminating Engineering Society of New York, for casual seeing tasks such as in reception rooms, inactive file rooms, and other service areas, it is recommended that the amount of light be 30 foot-candles. For ordinary seeing tasks such as reading and work in active file rooms and in mail rooms, the recommended lighting is 100 foot-candles. For very difficult seeing tasks such as accounting, transcribing, and business-machine use, the recommended lighting is 150 foot-candles.

Lighting intensity is only one requirement. Shadows and glare are to be avoided. For example, the larger the proportion of a ceiling filled with lighting units, the more glare-free and comfortable the lighting will be. Natural lighting from windows is not too dependable because on dark wintry days windows yield little usable light, and on sunny, summer afternoons the glare from windows may be very distracting. Desks should not face the windows. Finally, the main lighting source ought to be overhead and to the left of the user.

13. According to the above passage, insufficient light in the office may cause
    A. glare
    B. shadows
    C. tiredness
    D. distraction

14. Based on the above passage, which of the following must be considered when planning lighting arrangements? The
    A. amount of natural light present
    B. amount of work to be done
    C. level of difficulty of work to be done
    D. type of activity to be carried out

15. It can be inferred from the above passage that a well-coordinated lighting scheme is likely to result in
    A. greater employee productivity
    B. elimination of light reflection
    C. lower lighting cost
    D. more use of natural light

15._____

16. Of the following, the BEST title for the above passage is:
    A. Characteristics of Light
    B. Light Measurement Devices
    C. Factors to Consider When Planning Lighting Systems
    D. Comfort vs. Cost When Devising Lighting Arrangements

16._____

17. According to the above passage, a foot-candle is a measurement of the
    A. number of bulbs used
    B. strength of the light
    C. contrast between glare and shadow
    D. proportion of the ceiling filled with lighting units

17._____

18. According to the above passage, the number of foot-candles of light that would be needed to copy figures onto a payroll is _____ foot-candles.
    A. less than 30   B. 350   C. 100   D. 140

18._____

Questions 19-22.

A summons is an official statement ordering a person to appear in court. In traffic violation situations, summonses are used when arrests need not be made. The main reason for traffic summonses is to deter motorists from repeating the same traffic violation. Occasionally, motorists may make unintentional driving errors and sometimes they are unaware of correct driving regulations. In cases such as these, the policy should be to have the Officer verbally inform the motorist of the violation and warn him against repeating it. The purpose of this practice is not to limit the number of summonses, but rather to prevent the issuing of summonses when the violation is not due to deliberate intent or to inexcusable negligence.

19. According to the above passage, the PRINCIPAL reason for issuing traffic summonses is to
    A. discourage motorists from violating these laws again
    B. increase the money collected by the city
    C. put traffic violators in prison
    D. have them serve as substitutes for police officers

19._____

20. The reason a verbal warning may sometimes be substituted for a summons is to
    A. limit the number of summonses
    B. distinguish between excusable and inexcusable violations
    C. provide harsher penalties for deliberate intent than for inexcusable negligence
    D. decrease the caseload in the courts

20._____

21. The author of the above passage feels that someone who violated a traffic regulation because he did not know about the regulation should be
    A. put under arrest
    B. fined less money
    C. given a summons
    D. told not to do it again

22. Using the distinctions made by the author of the above passage, the one of the following motorists to whom it would be MOST desirable to issue a summons is the one who exceeded the speed limit because he
    A. did not know the speed limit
    B. was late for an important business appointment
    C. speeded to avoid being hit by another car
    D. had a speedometer which was not working properly

Questions 24-25.

Physical design plays a very significant role in crime rate. Crime rate has been found to increase almost proportionately with building height. The average number of crimes is much greater in higher buildings than in lower ones (equal to or less than six stories). What is most interesting is that in buildings of six stories or less, the project size or total number of units does not make a difference. It seems that, although larger projects encourage crime by fostering feelings of anonymity, isolation, irresponsibility, and lack of identity with surroundings, evidence indicate that larger projects encompassed in low buildings seem to offset what we may assume to be factors conducive to high crime rates. High-rise projects not only experience a higher rate of crime within the buildings, but a greater proportion of the crime occurs in the interior public spaces of these buildings as compared with those of the lower buildings. Lower buildings have more limited public space than higher ones. A criminal probably perceives that the interior public areas of buildings are where his victims are most vulnerable and where the possibility of his being seen or apprehended is minimal. Placement of elevators, entrance lobbies, and secondary exits all are factors related to the likelihood of crimes taking place in buildings. The study of all of these elements should bear some weight in the planning of new projects.

23. According to the above passage, which of the following BEST describes the relationship between building size and crime?
    A. Larger projects lead to a greater crime rate.
    B. Higher buildings tend to increase the crime rate.
    C. The smaller the number of project apartments in low buildings the higher the crime rate
    D. Anonymity and isolation serve to lower the crime rate in small buildings.

24. According to the above passage, the likelihood of a criminal attempting a mugging in the interior public portions of a high-rise building is good because
    A. tenants will be constantly flowing in and out of the area
    B. there is easy access to fire stairs and secondary exits
    C. there is a good chance that no one will see him
    D. tenants may not recognize the victims of crime as their neighbors

25. Which of the following is *implied* by the above passage as an explanation for the fact that the crime rate is lower in large low-rise housing projects than in large high-rise projects?
    A. Tenants know each other better and take a greater interest in what happens in the project.
    B. There is more public space where tenants are likely to gather together.
    C. The total number of units in a low-rise project is fewer than the total number of units in a high-rise project.
    D. Elevators in low-rise buildings travel quickly, thus limiting the amount of time in which a criminal can act.

25.____

KEY (CORRECT ANSWERS)

1. B
2. D
3. C
4. B
5. D

6. B
7. C
8. A
9. C
10. D

11. B
12. A
13. C
14. D
15. A

16. C
17. B
18. D
19. A
20. B

21. D
22. B
23. B
24. C
25. A

READING COMPREHENSION
UNDERSTANDING AND INTERPRETING WRITTEN MATERIAL
EXAMINATION SECTION
TEST 1

DIRECTIONS: Each question or incomplete statement is followed by several suggested answers or completions. Select the one that BEST answers the question or completes the statement. *PRINT THE LETTER OF THE CORRECT ANSWER IN THE SPACE AT THE RIGHT.*

Questions 1-3.

DIRECTIONS: Questions 1 through 3 are to be answered SOLELY on the basis of the following passage.

Foot patrol has some advantages over all other methods of patrol. Maximum opportunity is provided for observation within range of the senses and for close contact with people and things that enable the patrolman to provide a maximum service as an information source and counselor to the public and as the eyes and ears of the police department. A foot patrolman loses no time in alighting from a vehicle, and the performance of police tasks is not hampered by responsibility for his vehicle while afoot. Foot patrol, however, does not have many of the advantages of a patrol car. Lack of both mobility and immediate communication with headquarters lessens the officer's value in an emergency. The area that he can cover effectively is limited and, therefore, this method of patrol is costly.

1. According to the above passage, the foot patrolman is the eyes and ears of the police department because he is
   A. in direct contact with the station house
   B. not responsible for a patrol vehicle
   C. able to observe closely conditions on his patrol post
   D. a readily available information source to the public

2. The MOST accurate of the following statements concerning the various methods of patrol, according to the above passage, is that
   A. foot patrol should sometimes be combined with a motor patrol
   B. foot patrol is better than motor patrol
   C. helicopter patrol has the same advantages as motor patrol
   D. motor patrol is more readily able to communicate with superior officers in an emergency

3. According to the above passage, it is CORRECT to state that foot patrol is
   A. economical since increased mobility makes more rapid action possible
   B. expensive since the area that can be patrolled is relatively small
   C. economical since vehicle costs need not be considered
   D. expensive since giving information to the public is time consuming

Questions 4-6.

DIRECTIONS: Questions 4 through 6 are to be answered SOLELY on the basis of the following passage.

All applicants for an original license to operate a catering establishment shall be fingerprinted. This shall include the officers, employees, and stockholders of the company and the members of a partnership. In case of a change, by addition or subtraction, occurring during the existence of a license, the person added or substituted shall be fingerprinted. However, in the case of a hotel containing more than 200 rooms, only the officer or manager filing the application is required to be fingerprinted. The police commissioner may also at his discretion exempt the employees and stockholders of any company. The fingerprints shall be taken on one copy of form C.E. 20 and on two copies of C.E. 21. One copy of form C.E. 21 shall accompany the application. Fingerprints are not required with a renewal application.

4. According to the above passage, an employee added to the payroll of a licensed catering establishment which is not in a hotel must
   A. always be fingerprinted
   B. be fingerprinted unless he has been previously fingerprinted for another license
   C. be fingerprinted unless exempted by the police commissioner
   D. be fingerprinted only if he is the manager or an officer of the company

4.____

5. According to the above passage, it would be MOST accurate to state that
   A. form C.E. 20 must accompany a renewal application
   B. form C.E. 21 must accompany all applications
   C. form C.E. 21 must accompany an original application
   D. both forms C.E. 20 and C.E. 21 must accompany all applications

5.____

6. A hotel of 270 rooms has applied for a license to operate a catering establishment on the premises.
   According to the instructions for fingerprinting given in the above passage, the _____ shall be fingerprinted.
   A. officers, employees, and stockholders
   B. officers and the manager
   C. employees
   D. officer filing the application

6.____

Questions 7-9.

DIRECTIONS: Questions 7 through 9 are to be answered SOLELY on the basis of the following passage.

It is difficult to instill in young people inner controls on aggressive behavior in a world marked by aggression. The slum child's environment, full of hostility, stimulates him to delinquency; he does that which he sees about him. The time to act against delinquency is before it is committed. It is clear that juvenile delinquency, especially when it is committed in groups or gangs, leads almost inevitably to an adult criminal life unless it is checked at once.

The first signs of vandalism and disregard for the comfort, health, and property of the community should be considered as storm warnings which cannot be ignored. The delinquent's first crime has the underlying element of testing the law and its ability to hit back.

7. A SUITABLE title for this entire paragraph based on the material it contains is
   A. The Need for Early Prevention of Juvenile Delinquency
   B. Juvenile Delinquency as a Cause of Slums
   C. How Aggressive Behavior Prevents Juvenile Delinquency
   D. The Role of Gangs in Crime

8. According to the above passage, an initial act of juvenile crime USUALLY involves a(n)
   A. group or gang activity
   B. theft of valuable property
   C. test of the strength of legal authority
   D. act of physical violence

9. According to the above passage, acts of juvenile delinquency are MOST likely to lead to a criminal career when they are
   A. acts of vandalism
   B. carried out by groups or gangs
   C. committed in a slum environment
   D. such as to impair the health of the neighborhood

Questions 10-12.

DIRECTIONS: Questions 10 through 12 are to be answered SOLELY on the basis of the following passage.

The police laboratory performs a valuable service in crime investigation by assisting in the reconstruction of criminal action and by aiding in the identification of persons and things. When studied by a technician, physical things found at crime scenes often reveal facts useful in identifying the criminal and in determining what has occurred. The nature of substances to be examined and the character of the examinations to be made vary so widely that the services of a large variety of skilled scientific persons are needed in crime investigations. To employ such a complete staff and to provide them with equipment and standards needed for all possible analyses and comparisons is beyond the means and the needs of any but the largest police departments. The search of crime scenes for physical evidence also calls for the services of specialists supplied with essential equipment and assigned to each tour of duty so as to provide service at any hour.

10. If a police department employs a large staff of technicians of various types in its laboratory, it will affect crime investigation to the extent that
    A. most crimes will be speedily solved
    B. identification of criminals will be aided
    C. search of crime scenes for physical evidence will become of less importance
    D. investigation by police officers will not usually be required

11. According to the above passage, the MOST complete study of objects found at the scenes of crimes is
    A. always done in all large police departments
    B. based on assigning one technician to each tour of duty
    C. probably done only in large police departments
    D. probably done in police departments of communities with low crime rates

11.____

12. According to the above passage, a large variety of skilled technicians is useful in criminal investigations because
    A. crimes cannot be solved without their assistance as a part of the police team
    B. large police departments need large staffs
    C. many different kinds of tests on various substances can be made
    D. the police cannot predict what methods may be tried by wily criminals

12.____

Questions 13-14.

DIRECTIONS: Questions 13 and 14 are to be answered SOLELY on the basis of the following passage.

The emotionally unstable person is always potentially a dangerous criminal, who causes untold misery to other persons and is a source of considerable trouble and annoyance to law enforcement officials. Like his fellow criminals, he will be a menace to society as long as he is permitted to be at large. Police activities against him serve to sharpen his wits and imprisonment gives him the opportunity to learn from others how to commit more serious crimes when he is released. This criminal's mental structure makes it impossible for him to profit by his experience with the police officials, by punishment of any kind or by sympathetic understanding and treatment by well-intentioned persons, professional and otherwise.

13. According to the above passage, the MOST accurate of the following statements concerning the relationship between emotional instability and crime is that
    A. emotional instability is proof of criminal activities
    B. the emotionally unstable person can become a criminal
    C. all dangerous criminals are emotionally unstable
    D. sympathetic understanding will prevent the emotionally unstable person from becoming a criminal

13.____

14. According to the above passage, the effect of police activities on the emotionally unstable criminal is that
    A. police activities aid this type of criminal to reform
    B. imprisonment tends to deter this type of criminal from committing future crimes
    C. contact with the police serves to assist sympathetic understanding and medical treatment
    D. police methods against this type of criminal develop him for further unlawful acts

14.____

Questions 15-17.

DIRECTIONS: Questions 14 through 17 are to be answered SOLELY on the basis of the following passage.

Proposals to license gambling operations are based on the belief that the human desire to gamble cannot be suppressed and, therefore, it should be licensed and legalized with the people sharing in the profits, instead of allowing the underworld to benefit. If these proposals are sincere, then it is clear that only one is worthwhile at all. Legalized gambling should be completely controlled and operated by the state with all the profits used for its citizens. A state agency should be set up to operate and control the gambling business. It should be as completely removed from politics as possible. In view of the inherent nature of the gambling business, with its close relationship to lawlessness and crime, only a man of the highest integrity should be eligible to become head of this agency. However, state gambling would encourage mass gambling with its attending social and economic evils in the same manner as other forms of legal gambling; but there is no justification whatever for the business of gambling to be legalized and then permitted to operate for private profit or for the benefit of any political organization.

15. The central thought of this passage may be CORRECTLY expressed as the   15.____
    A. need to legalize gambling in the state
    B. state operation of gambling for the benefit of the people
    C. need to license private gambling establishments
    D. evils of gambling

16. According to the above passage, a problem of legalized gambling which will   16.____
    still occur if the state operates the gambling business is
    A. the diversion of profits from gambling to private use
    B. that the amount of gambling will tend to diminish
    C. the evil effects of any form of mass gambling
    D. the use of gambling revenues for illegal purposes

17. According to the above passage, to legalize the business of gambling would be   17.____
    A. *justified*, because gambling would be operated only by a man of the highest integrity
    B. *justified*, because this would eliminate politics
    C. *unjustified* under any conditions because the human desire to gamble cannot be suppressed
    D. *unjustified* if operated for private or political profit

Questions 18-19.

DIRECTIONS: Questions 18 and 19 are to be answered SOLELY on the basis of the following passage.

For many years, slums had been recognized as breeding disease, juvenile delinquency, and crime which not only threatened the health and welfare of the people who lived there, but also weakened the structure of society as a whole. As far bac as 1834, a sanitary inspection report in New York City pointed out the connection between unsanitary, overcrowded housing and the spread of epidemics. Down through the years, evidence of slum-produced evils accumulated as the slums themselves continued to spread. This spread of slums was nationwide. Its symptoms and its ill effects were peculiar to no locality, but were characteristic of the country as a whole and imperiled the national welfare.

18. According to the above passage, people who live in slum dwellings 18.____
    A. cause slums to become worse
    B. are threatened by disease and crime
    C. create bad housing
    D. are the chief source of crime in the country

19. According to the above passage, the effects of juvenile delinquency and crime 19.____
    in slum areas were
    A. to destroy the structure of society
    B. noticeable in all parts of the country
    C. a chief cause of the spread of slums
    D. to spread unsanitary conditions in New York City

Questions 20-22.

DIRECTIONS: Questions 20 through 22 are to be answered SOLELY on the basis of the following passage.

Whenever, in the course of the performance of their duties in an emergency, members of the force operate the emergency power switch at any location on the transit system and thereby remove power from portions of the track, or they are on the scene where this has been done, they will bear in mind that, although power is removed, further dangers exist; namely, that a train may coast into the area even though the power is off, or that the rails may be energized by a train which may be in a position to transfer electricity from a live portion of the third rail through its shoe beams. Employees must look in each direction before stepping upon, crossing, or standing close to tracks, being particularly careful not to come into contact with the third rail.

20. According to the above passage, whenever an emergency occurs which has 20.____
    resulted in operating the emergency power switch, it is MOST accurate to state that
    A. power is shut off and employees may perform their duties in comploto safety
    B. there may still be power in a portion of the third rail
    C. the switch will not operate if a portion of the track has been broken
    D. trains are not permitted to stop in the area of the emergency

21. An IMPORTANT precaution which this passage urges employees to follow after 21.____
    operating the emergency power switch is to
    A. look carefully in both directions before stepping near the rails
    B. inspect the nearest train which has stopped to see if the power is on
    C. examine the third rail to see if the power is on
    D. check the emergency power switch to make sure it has operated properly

22. A trackman reports to you, the patrolman, that a dead body is lying on the road bed. You operate the emergency power switch. A train which has been approaching comes to a stop near the scene.
In order to act in accordance with the instructions in the above passage, you should
   A. climb down to the road bed and remove the body
   B. direct the train motorman to back up to the point where his train will not be in position to transfer electricity through its shoe beams
   C. carefully cross over the road bed to the body, avoiding the third rail and watching for train movements
   D. have the train motorman check to see if power is on before crossing to the tracks

22.____

Questions 23-25.

DIRECTIONS: Questions 23 through 25 are to be answered SOLELY on the basis of the following passage.

Pickpockets operate most effectively when there are prospective victims in either heavily congested areas or in lonely places. In heavily populated areas, the large number of people about them covers the activities of these thieves. In lonely spots, they have the advantage of working unobserved. The main factor in the pickpocket's success is the selection of the *right* victim. A pickpocket's victim must, at the time of the crime, be inattentive, distracted, or unconscious. If any of these conditions exist, and if the pickpocket is skilled in his operations, the stage is set for a successful larceny. With the control of winter, the crowds move southward—and so do most of the pickpockets. However, some pickpockets will remain in certain areas all year around. They will concentrate on theater districts, bus and railroad terminals, hotels or large shopping centers. A complete knowledge of the methods of this type of criminal and the ability to recognize them come only from long years of experience in performing patient surveillance and trailing of them. This knowledge is essential for the effective control and apprehension of this type of thief.

23. According to the above passage, the pickpocket is LEAST likely to operate in a
   A. baseball park with a full capacity attendance
   B. subway station in an outlying area late at night
   C. moderately crowded dance hall
   D. overcrowded department store

23.____

24. According to the above passage, the one of the following factors which is NOT necessary for the successful operation of the pickpocket is that
   A. he be proficient in the operations required to pick pockets
   B. the *right* potential victims be those who have been the subject of such a theft previously
   C. his operations be hidden from the view of others
   D. the potential victim be unaware of the actions of the pickpocket

24.____

25. According to the above passage, it would be MOST correct to conclude that police officers who are successful in apprehending pickpockets
    A. are generally those who have had lengthy experience in recognizing all types of criminals
    B. must, by intuition, be able to recognize potential *right* victims
    C. must follow the pickpockets in their southward movement
    D. must have acquired specific knowledge and skills in this field

25._____

KEY (CORRECT ANSWERS)

1.	C	11.	C
2.	D	12.	C
3.	B	13.	B
4.	C	14.	D
5.	C	15.	B
6.	B	16.	C
7.	A	17.	D
8.	C	18.	D
9.	B	19.	B
10.	B	20.	B

21. A
22. C
23. C
24. B
25. D

TEST 2

DIRECTIONS: Each question or incomplete statement is followed by several suggested answers or completions. Select the one that BEST answers the question or completes the statement. *PRINT THE LETTER OF THE CORRECT ANSWER IN THE SPACE AT THE RIGHT.*

Questions 1-2.

DIRECTIONS: Questions 1 and 2 are to be answered SOLELY on the basis of the following passage.

    The medical examiner may contribute valuable data to the investigator of fires which cause fatalities. By careful examination of the bodies of any victims, he not only establishes cause of death, but may also furnish, in many instances, answers to questions relating to the identity of the victim and the source and origin of the fire. The medical examiner is of greatest value to law enforcement agencies because he is able to determine the exact cause of death through an examination of tissue of apparent arson victims. Thorough study of a burned body or even of parts of a burned body will frequently yield information which illuminates the problems confronting the arson investigator and the police.

1. According to the above passage, the MOST important task of the medical examiner in the investigation of arson is to obtain information concerning the
    A. identity of arsonists   B. cause of death
    C. identity of victims   D. source and origin of fires

1._____

2. The central thought of the above passage is that the medical examiner aids in the solution of crimes of arson when
    A. a person is burnt to death
    B. identity of the arsonist is unknown
    C. the cause of the fire is known
    D. trained investigators are not available

2._____

Questions 3-6.

DIRECTIONS: Questions 3 through 6 are to be answered SOLELY on the basis of the following passage.

    A foundling is an abandoned child whose identity is unknown. Desk officers shall direct the delivery, by a policewoman if available, of foundlings actually or apparently under two years of age to the American Foundling Hospital, or if actually or apparently two year of age or over to the Children's Center. In all other cases of dependent or neglected children, other than foundlings, requiring shelter, desk officers shall provide for obtaining such shelter as follows: between 9 A.M. and 5 P.M., Monday through Friday, by telephone direct to the Bureau of Child Welfare, in order to ascertain the shelter to which the child shall be sent; at all other time, direct the delivery of a child actually or apparently under two years of age to the American Foundling Hospital, or if the child is actually or apparently two years of age or over to the Children's Center.

3. According to the above passage, it would be MOST correct to state that
   A. a foundling as well as a neglected child may be delivered to the American Foundling Hospital
   B. a foundling but not a neglected child may be delivered to the Children's Center
   C. a neglected child requiring shelter, regardless of age, may be delivered to the Bureau of Child Welfare
   D. the Bureau of Child Welfare may determine the shelter to which a foundling may be delivered

3.____

4. According to the above passage, the desk officer shall provide for obtaining shelter for a neglected child apparently under two years of age by
   A. directing its delivery to Children's Center if occurrence is on a Monday between 9 A.M. and 5 P.M.
   B. telephoning the Bureau of Child Welfare if occurrence is on a Sunday
   C. directing its delivery to the American Foundling Hospital if occurrence is on a Wednesday at 4 P.M.
   D. telephoning the Bureau of Child Welfare if occurrence is at 10 A.M. on a Friday

4.____

5. According to the above passage, the desk officer should direct delivery to the American Foundling Hospital of any child who is
   A. actually under 2 years of age and requires shelter
   B. apparently under 2 years of age and is neglected or dependent
   C. actually 2 years of age and is a foundling
   D. apparently under 2 years of age and has been abandoned

5.____

6. A 12-year-old neglected child requiring shelter is brought to a police station on Thursday at 2 P.M.
   Such a child should be sent to
   A. a shelter selected by the Bureau of Child Welfare
   B. a shelter selected by the desk officer
   C. the Children's Center
   D. the American Foundling Hospital when a brother or sister under 2 years of age also requires shelter

6.____

Questions 7-10.

DIRECTIONS: Questions 7 through 10 are to be answered SOLELY on the basis of the following passage.

In addition to making the preliminary investigation of crimes, patrolmen should serve as eyes, ears, and legs for the detective division. The patrol division may be used for surveillance, to serve warrants and bring in suspects and witnesses, and to perform a number of routine tasks for the detectives which will increase the time available for tasks that require their special skills and facilities. It is to the advantage of individual detectives, as well as of the detective division, to have patrolmen working in this manner; more cases are cleared by arrest and a greater proportion of stolen property is recovered when, in addition to the detective regularly assigned, a number of patrolmen also work on the case. Detectives may stimulate the interest and participation of patrolmen by keeping them currently informed of the presence, identity or description, hangouts, associates, vehicles, and method of operation of each criminal known to be in the community.

7. According to the above passage, a patrolman should
   A. assist the detective in certain of his routine functions
   B. be considered for assignment as a detective on the basis of his patrol performance
   C. leave the scene once a detective arrives
   D. perform as much of the detective's duties as time permits

8. According to the above passage, patrolmen should aid detectives by
   A. accepting assignments from detectives which give promise of recovering stolen property
   B. making arrests of witnesses for the detective's interrogation
   C. performing all special investigative work for detectives
   D. producing for questioning individuals who may aid the detective in his investigation

9. According to the above passage, detectives can keep patrolmen interested by
   A. ascertaining that patrolmen are doing investigative work properly
   B. having patrolmen directly under his supervision during an investigation
   C. informing patrolmen of the value of their efforts in crime prevention
   D. supplying the patrolmen with information regarding known criminals in the community

10. Which of the following is NOT a result of cooperation between detectives and patrolmen?
    A. A greater proportion of stolen property is recovered.
    B. Detectives have more time to make preliminary investigations.
    C. Detectives have more time to finish tasks requiring their special skills.
    D. Patrolmen may become more interested and participate more in solving the case.

Questions 11-12.

DIRECTIONS: Questions 11 and 12 are to be answered SOLELY on the basis of the following passage.

State motor vehicle registration departments should and do play a vital role in the prevention and detection of automobile thefts. The combatting of theft is, in fact, one of the primary purposes of the registration of motor vehicles. In 2020 there were approximately 61,309,000 motor vehicles registered in the United States. That same year some 200,000 of them were stolen. All but 6 percent have been or will be recovered. This is a very high recovery ratio compared to the percentage of recovery of other stolen personal property. The reason for this is that automobiles are carefully identified by the manufacturers and carefully registered by many of the states.

11. The central thought of this passage is that there is a close relationship between the
    A. number of automobiles registered in the United States and the number stolen
    B. prevention of automobile thefts and the effectiveness of police departments in the United States
    C. recovery of stolen automobiles and automobile registration
    D. recovery of stolen automobiles and of other stolen property

11._____

12. According to the above passage, the high recovery ratio for stolen automobiles is due to
    A. state registration and manufacturer identification of motor vehicles
    B. successful prevention of automobile thefts by state motor vehicle departments
    C. the fact that only 6% of stolen vehicles are not properly registered
    D. the high number of motor vehicles registered in the United States

12._____

Questions 13-16.

DIRECTIONS: Questions 13 through 16 are to be answered SOLELY on the basis of the following passage.

It is not always understood that the term *physical evidence* embraces any and all objects, living or inanimate. A knife, gun, signature, or burglar tool is immediately recognized as physical evidence. Less often is it considered that dust, microscopic fragments of all types, even an odor, may equally be physical evidence and often the most important of all. It is well established that the most useful types of physical evidence are generally microscopic in dimensions, that is, not noticeable by the eye and, therefore, most likely to be overlooked by the criminal and by the investigator. For this reason, microscopic evidence persists for months or years after all other evidence has been removed and found inconclusive. Naturally, there are limitations to the time of collecting microscopic evidence as it may be lost or decayed. The exercise of judgment as to the possibility or profit of delayed action in collecting the evidence is a field in which the expert investigator should judge.

13. The one of the following which the above passage does NOT consider to be physical evidence is a
    A. criminal thought   B. minute speck of dust
    C. raw onion smell   D. typewritten note

13._____

14. According to the above passage, the rechecking of the scene of a crime
    A. is useless when performed years after the occurrence of the crime
    B. is advisable chiefly in crimes involving physical evidence
    C. may turn up microscopic evidence of value
    D. should be delayed if the microscopic evidence is not subject to decay or loss

14._____

15. According to the above passage, the criminal investigator should
    A. give most of his attention to weapons used in the commission of the crime
    B. ignore microscopic evidence until a request is received from the laboratory
    C. immediately search for microscopic evidence and ignore the more visible objects
    D. realize that microscopic evidence can be easily overlooked

16. According to the above passage,
    A. a delay in collecting evidence must definitely diminish its value to the investigator
    B. microscopic evidence exists for longer periods of time than other physical evidence
    C. microscopic evidence is generally the most useful type of physical evidence
    D. physical evidence is likely to be overlooked by the criminal and by the investigator

Questions 17-20.

DIRECTIONS: Questions 17 through 20 are to be answered SOLELY on the basis of the following passage.

Sometimes, but not always, firing a gun leaves a residue of nitrate particles on the hands. This fact is utilized in the paraffin test which consists of applying melted paraffin and gauze to the fingers, hands, and wrists of a suspect until a cast of approximately 1/8 of an inch is built up. The heat of the paraffin causes the pores of the skin to open and release any particles embedded in them. The paraffin cast is then removed and tested chemically for nitrate particles. In addition to gunpowder, fertilizers, tobacco ashes, matches, and soot are also common sources of nitrates on the hands.

17. Assume that the paraffin test has been given to a person suspected of firing a gun and that nitrate particles have been found.
    It would be CORRECT to conclude that the suspect
    A. is guilty   B. is innocent
    C. may be guilty or innocent   D. is probably guilty

18. In testing for the presence of gunpowder particles on human hands, the characteristic of paraffin which makes it MOST serviceable is that it
    A. causes the nitrate residue left by a fired gun to adhere to the gauze
    B. is waterproof
    C. melts at a high temperature
    D. helps to distinguish between gunpowder nitrates and other types

19. According to the above passage, in the paraffin test the nitrate particles are removed from the pores because the paraffin
    A. enlarges the pores   B. contracts the pores
    C. reacts chemically with nitrates   D. dissolves the particles

20. The presence of a residue of nitrate particles on the hands is a COMMON   20.____
    result of
    A. the paraffin test
    B. handling fertilizer
    C. a bullet wound
    D. enlarged pores

KEY (CORRECT ANSWERS)

1.	B	11.	C
2.	A	12.	A
3.	A	13.	A
4.	D	14.	C
5.	D	15.	D
6.	A	16.	C
7.	A	17.	C
8.		18.	A
9.	D	19.	A
10.	B	20.	B

REPORT WRITING
EXAMINATION SECTION
TEST 1

DIRECTIONS: Each question or incomplete statement is followed by several suggested answers or completions. Select the one that BEST answers the question or completes the statement. *PRINT THE LETTER OF THE CORRECT ANSWER IN THE SPACE AT THE RIGHT.*

1. Following are six steps that should be taken in the course of report preparation: 1.____
   I. Outlining the material for presentation in the report
   II. Analyzing and interpreting the facts
   III. Analyzing the problem
   IV. Reaching conclusions
   V. Writing, revising, and rewriting the final copy
   VI. Collecting data

   According to the principles of good report writing, the CORRECT order in which these steps should be taken is:
   A. VI, III, II, I, IV, V
   B. III, VI, II, IV, I, V
   C. III, VI, II, I, IV, V
   D. VI, II, III, IV, I, V

2. Following are three statements concerning written reports: 2.____
   I. Clarity is generally more essential in oral reports than in written reports.
   II. Short sentences composed of simple words are generally preferred to complex sentences and difficult words.
   III. Abbreviations may be used whenever they are customary and will not distract the attention of the reader.

   Which of the following choices correctly classifies the above statements in to those which are valid and those which are not valid?
   A. I and II are valid, but III is not valid
   B. I is valid, but II and III are not valid.
   C. II and III are valid, but I is not valid.
   D. III is valid, but I and II are not valid.

3. In order to produce a report written in a style that is both understandable and effective, an investigator should apply the principles of unit, coherence, and emphasis. 3.____
   The one of the following which is the BEST example of the principle of coherence is
   A. interlinking sentences so that thoughts flow smoothly
   B. having each sentence express a single idea to facilitate comprehension
   C. arranging important points in prominent positions so they are not overlooked
   D. developing the main idea fully to insure complete consideration

123

4. Assume that a supervisor is preparing a report recommending that a standard work procedure be changed.
Of the following, the MOST important information that he should include in this report is
   A. a complete description of the present procedure
   B. the details and advantages of the recommended procedure
   C. the type and amount of retraining needed
   D. the percentage of men who favor the change

5. When you include in your report on an inspection some information which you have obtained from other individuals, it is MOST important that
   A. this information have no bearing on the work these other people are performing
   B. you do not report as fact the opinions of other individuals
   C. you keep the source of the information confidential
   D. you do not tell the other individuals that their statements will be included in your report

6. Before turning in a report of an investigator of an accident, you discover some additional information you did not know about when you wrote the report.
Whether or not you re-write your report to include this additional information should depend MAINLY on the
   A. source of this additional information
   B. established policy covering the subject matter of the report
   C. length of the report and the time it would take you to re-write it
   D. bearing this additional information will have on the conclusions in the report

7. The MOST desirable *first* step in the planning of a written report is to
   A. ascertain what necessary information is readily available in the files
   B. outline the methods you will employ to get the necessary information
   C. determine the objectives and uses of the report
   D. estimate the time and cost required to complete the report

8. In writing a report, the practice of taking up the least important points and the most important points last is a
   A. *good* technique since the final points made in a report will make the greatest impression on the reader
   B. *good* technique since the material is presented in a more logical manner and will lead directly to the conclusions
   C. *poor* technique since the reader's time is wasted by having to review irrelevant information before finishing the report
   D. *poor* technique since it may cause the reader to lose interest in the report and arrive at incorrect conclusions about the report

9. Which one of the following serves as the BEST guideline for you to follow for effective written reports?
   Keep sentences
   A. short and limit sentences to one thought
   B. short and use as many thoughts as possible
   C. long and limit sentences to one thought
   D. long and use as many thoughts as possible

9.____

10. One method by which a supervisor might prepare written reports to management is to begin with the conclusions, results, or summary, and to follow this with the supporting data.
    The BEST reason why management may *prefer* this form of report is that
    A. management lacks the specific training to understand the data
    B. the data completely supports the conclusions
    C. time is saved by getting to the conclusions of the report first
    D. the data contains all the information that is required for making the conclusions

10.____

11. When making written reports, it is MOST important that they be
    A. well-worded
    B. accurate as to the facts
    C. brief
    D. submitted immediately

11.____

12. Of the following, the MOST important reason for a supervisor to prepare good written reports is that
    A. a supervisor is rated on the quality of his reports
    B. decisions are often made on the basis of the reports
    C. such reports take less time for superiors to review
    D. such reports demonstrate efficiency of department operations

12.____

13. Of the following, the BEST test of a good report is whether it
    A. provides the information needed
    B. shows the good sense of the writer
    C. is prepared according to a proper format
    D. is grammatical and neat

13.____

14. When a supervisor writes a report, he can BEST show that he has a understanding of the subject of the report by
    A. including necessary facts and omitting nonessential details
    B. using statistical data
    C. giving his conclusions but not the data on which they are based
    D. using a technical vocabulary

14.____

15. Suppose you and another supervisor on the same level are assigned to work together on a report. You disagree strongly with one of the recommendations the other supervisor wants to include in the report but you cannot change his views.

15.____

Of the following, it would be BEST that
- A. you refuse to accept responsibility for the report
- B. you ask that someone else be assigned to this project to replace you
- C. each of you state his own ideas about this recommendation in the report
- D. you give in to the other supervisor's opinion for the sake of harmony

16. Standardized forms are often provided for submitting reports. Of the following, the MOST important advantage of using standardized forms for reports is that
    - A. they take less time to prepare than individually written reports
    - B. the person making the report can omit information he considers unimportant
    - C. the responsibility for preparing these reports can be turned over to subordinates
    - D. necessary information is less likely to be omitted

17. A report which may BEST be classed as a *periodic* report is one which
    - A. requires the same type of information at regular intervals
    - B. contains detailed information which is to be retained in permanent records
    - C. is prepared whenever a special situation occurs
    - D. lists information in graphic form

18. In the writing of reports or letters, the ideas presented in a paragraph are usually of unequal importance and require varying degrees of emphasis. All of the following are methods of placing extra stress on an idea EXCEPT
    - A. repeating it in a number of forms
    - B. placing it in the middle of the paragraph
    - C. placing it either at the beginning or at the end of a paragraph
    - D. underlining it

Questions 19-25.

DIRECTIONS: Questions 19 through 25 concern the subject of report writing and are based on the information and incidents described in the following paragraph. (In answering these questions, assume that the facts and incidents in the paragraph are true.)

On December 15, at 8 A.M., seven Laborers reported to Foreman Joseph Meehan in the Greenbranch Yard in Queens. Meehan instructed the men to load some 50-pound boxes of books on a truck for delivery to an agency building in Brooklyn. Meehan told the men that, because the boxes were rather heavy, two men should work together, helping each other lift and load each box. Since Michael Harper, one of the Laborers, was without a partner, Meehan helped him with the boxes for a while. When Meehan was called to the telephone in a nearby building, however, Harper decided to lift a box himself. He appeared able to lift the box, but, as he got the box halfway up, he cried out that he had a sharp pain in his back. Another Laborer, Jorge Ortiz, who was passing by, ran over to help Harper put the box down. Harper suddenly dropped the box, which fell on Ortiz' right foot. By this time, Meehan had come out of the building. He immediately helped get the box off Ortiz' foot and had both men lie down. Meehan covered the men with blankets and called an ambulance, which arrived a half hour later. At the hospital, the doctor said that the X-ray results showed that Ortiz' right foot was broken in three places.

19. What would be the BEST term to use in a report describing the injury of Jorge Ortiz? 19.____
    A. Strain   B. Fracture   C. Hernia   D. Hemorrhage

20. Which of the following would be the MOST accurate summary for the Foreman to put in his report of the incident? 20.____
    A. Ortiz attempted to help Harper carry a box which was too heavy for one person, but Harper dropped it before Ortiz got there.
    B. Ortiz tried to help Harper carry a box but Harper got a pain in his back and accidentally dropped the box on Ortiz' foot.
    C. Harper refused to follow Meehan's orders and lifted a box too heavy for him; he deliberately dropped it when Ortiz tried to help him carry it.
    D. Harper lifted a box and felt a pain in his back; Ortiz tried to help Harper put the box down but Harper accidentally dropped it on Ortiz' foot.

21. One of the Laborers at the scene of the accident was asked his version of the incident. 21.____
    Which information obtained from this witness would be LEAST important for including in the accident report?
    A. His opinion as to the cause of the accident
    B. How much of the accident he saw
    C. His personal opinion of the victims
    D. His name and address

22. What should be the MAIN objective of writing a report about the incident described in the above paragraph? To 22.____
    A. describe the important elements in the accident situation
    B. recommend that such Laborers as Ortiz be advised not to interfere in another's work unless given specific instructions
    C. analyze the problems occurring when there are not enough workers to perform a certain task
    D. illustrate the hazards involved in performing routine everyday tasks

23. Which of the following is information *missing* from the above passage but which *should* be included in a report of the incident? The 23.____
    A. name of the Laborer's immediate supervisor
    B. contents of the boxes
    C. time at which the accident occurred
    D. object or action that caused the injury to Ortiz' foot

24. According to the description of the incident, the accident occurred because 24.____
    A. Ortiz attempted to help Harper who resisted his help
    B. Harper failed to follow instructions given him by Meehan
    C. Meehan was not supervising his men as closely as he should have
    D. Harper was not strong enough to carry the box once he lifted it

25. Which of the following is MOST important for a foreman to avoid when writing up an official accident report?
    A. Using technical language to describe equipment involved in the accident
    B. Putting in details which might later be judged unnecessary
    C. Giving an opinion as to conditions that contributed to the accident
    D. Recommending discipline for employees who, in his opinion, caused the accident

KEY (CORRECT ANSWERS)

1.	B		11.	B
2.	C		12.	B
3.	A		13.	A
4.	B		14.	A
5.	B		15.	C
6.	D		16.	D
7.	C		17.	A
8.	D		18.	B
9.	A		19.	D
10.	C		20.	D

21.	C
22.	A
23.	C
24.	B
25.	D

TEST 2

DIRECTIONS: Each question or incomplete statement is followed by several suggested answers or completions. Select the one that BEST answers the question or completes the statement. *PRINT THE LETTER OF THE CORRECT ANSWER IN THE SPACE AT THE RIGHT.*

1. Lieutenant X is preparing a report to submit to his commanding officer in order to get approval of a plan of operation he has developed.
   The report starts off with the statement of the problem and continues with the details of the problem. It contains factual information gathered with the help of field and operational personnel. It contains a final conclusion and recommendation for action. The recommendation is supplemented by comments from other precinct staff members on how the recommendations will affect their areas of responsibility. The report also includes directives and general orders ready for the commanding officer's signature. In addition, it has two statements of objections presented by two precinct staff members.
   Which one of the following, if any, is either an item that Lieutenant X should have included in his report and which is not mentioned above, or is an item which Lieutenant X improperly did include in his report?
   A. Considerations of alternative courses of action and their consequences should have been covered in the report.
   B. The additions containing undocumented objections to the recommended course of action should not have been included as part of the report.
   C. A statement on the qualifications of Lieutenant X, which would support his expertness in the field under consideration, should have been included in the report.
   D. The directives and general orders should not have been prepared and included in the report until the commanding officer had approved the recommendations.
   E. None of the above, since Lieutenant X's report was both proper and complete.

   1.____

2. During a visit to a section, the district supervisor criticizes the method being used by the assistant foreman to prepare a certain report and orders him to modify the method. This change ordered by the district supervisor is in direct conflict with the specific orders of the foreman.
   In this situation, it would be BEST for the assistant foreman to
   A. change the method and tell the foreman about the change at the first opportunity
   B. change the method and rely on the district supervisor to notify the foreman
   C. report the matter to the foreman and delay the preparation of the report
   D. ask the district supervisor to discuss the matter with the foreman but use the old method for the time being

   2.____

3. A department officer should realize that the MOST usual reason for writing a report is to
   A. give orders and follow up their execution
   B. establish a permanent record
   C. raise questions
   D. supply information

4. A very important report which is being prepared by a department officer will soon be due on the desk of the district supervisor. No typing help is available at this time for the officer.
   For the officer to write out this report in longhand in such a situation would be
   A. *bad*; such a report would not make the impression a typed report would
   B. *good*; it is important to get the report in on time
   C. *bad*; the district supervisor should not be required to read longhand reports
   D. *good*; it would call attention to the difficult conditions under which this section must work

5. In a well-written report, the length of each paragraph in the report should be
   A. varied according to the content
   B. not over 300 words
   C. pretty nearly the same
   D. gradually longer as the report is developed and written

6. A clerk in the headquarters office complains to you about the way in which you are filing out a certain report.
   It would be BEST for you to
   A. tell the clerk that you are following official procedures in filling out the report
   B. ask to be referred to the clerk's superior
   C. ask the clerk exactly what is wrong with the way in which you are filling out the report
   D. tell the clerk that you are following the directions of the district supervisor

7. The use of an outline to help in writing a report is
   A. *desirable*, in order to insure good organization and coverage
   B. *necessary*, so it can be used as an introduction to the report itself
   C. *undesirable*, since it acts as a straightjacket and may result in an unbalanced report
   D. *desirable*, if you know your immediate supervisor reads reports with extreme care and attention

8. It is advisable that a department officer do his paper work and report writing as soon as he has completed an inspection MAINLY because
   A. there are usually deadlines to be met
   B. it insures a steady work-flow
   C. he may not have time for this later
   D. the facts are then freshest in his mind

9. Before you turn in a report you have written of an investigation that you have made, you discover some additional information you didn't know about before. Whether or not you re-write the report to include this additional information should depend MAINLY on the
   A. amount of time remaining before the report is due
   B. established policy of the department covering the subject matter of the report
   C. bearing this information will have on the conclusions of the report
   D. number of people who will eventually review the report

10. When a supervisory officer submits a periodic report to the district supervisor, he should realize that the CHIEF importance of such a report is that it
    A. is the principal method of checking on the efficiency of the supervisor and his subordinates
    B. is something to which frequent reference will be made
    C. eliminates the need for any personal follow-up or inspection by higher echelons
    D. permits the district supervisor to exercise his functions of direction, supervision, and control better

11. Conclusions and recommendations are usually placed at the end rather than at the beginning of a report because
    A. the person preparing the report may decide to change some of the conclusions and recommendations before he reaches the end of the report
    B. they are the most important part of the report
    C. they can be judged better by the person to whom the report is sent after he reads the facts and investigators which come earlier in the report
    D. they can be referred to quickly when needed without reading the rest of the report

12. The use of the same method of record-keeping and reporting by all agency sections is
    A. *desirable*, MAINLY because it saves time in section operations
    B. *undesirable*, MAINLY because it kills the initiative of the individual section foreman
    C. *desirable*, MAINLY because it will be easier for the administrator to evaluate and compare section operations
    D. *undesirable*, MAINLY because operations vary from section to section and uniform record-keeping and reporting is not appropriate

13. The GREATEST benefit the section officer will have from keeping complete and accurate records and reports of section operations is that
    A. he will find it easier to run his section efficiently
    B. he will need less equipment
    C. he will need less manpower
    D. the section will run smoothly when he is out

14. You have prepared a report to your superior and are ready to send it forward. But on re-reading it, you think some parts are not clearly expressed and your superior ay have difficulty getting your point.
    Of the following, it would be BEST for you to
    A. give the report to one of your men to read, and if he has no trouble understanding it send it through
    B. forward the report and call your superior the next day to ask whether it was all right
    C. forward the report as is; higher echelons should be able to understand any report prepared by a section officer
    D. do the report over, re-writing the sections you are in doubt about

14._____

15. The BEST of the following statements concerning reports is that
    A. a carelessly written report may give the reader an impression of inaccuracy
    B. correct grammar and English are unimportant if the main facts are given
    C. every man should be required to submit a daily work report
    D. the longer and more wordy a report is, the better it will read

15._____

16. In writing a report, the question of whether or not to include certain material could be determined BEST by considering the
    A. amount of space the material will occupy in the report
    B. amount of time to be spent in gathering the material
    C. date of the material
    D. value of the material to the superior who will read the report

16._____

17. Suppose you are submitting a fairly long report to your superior.
    The one of the following sections that should come FIRST in this report is a
    A. description of how you gathered material
    B. discussion of possible objections to your recommendations
    C. plan of how your recommendations can be put into practice
    D. statement of the problem dealt with

17._____

Questions 18-20.

DIRECTIONS: A foreman is asked to write a report on the incident described in the following passage. Answer Questions 18 through 20 based on the following information.

On March 10, Henry Moore, a laborer, was in the process of transferring some equipment from the machine shop to the third floor. He was using a dolly to perform this task and, as he was wheeling the material through the machine shop, laborer Bob Greene called to him. As Henry turned to respond to Bob, he jammed the dolly into Larry Mantell's leg, knocking Larry down in the process and causing the heavy drill that Larry was holding to fall on Larry's foot. Larry started rubbing his foot and then, infuriated, jumped up and punched Henry in the jaw. The force of the blow drove Henry's head back against the wall. Henry did not fight back; he appeared to be dazed. An ambulance was called to take Henry to the hospital, and the ambulance attendant told the foreman that it appeared likely that Henry had suffered a concussion. Larry's injuries consisted of some bruises, but he refused medical attention.

18. An adequate report of the above incident should give as minimum information the names of the persons involved, the names of the witnesses, the date and the time that each event took place, and the
    A. names of the ambulance attendants
    B. names of all the employees working in the machine shop
    C. location where the accident occurred
    D. nature of the previous safety training each employee had been given

18._____

19. The only one of the following which is NOT a fact is
    A. Bob called to Henry
    B. Larry suffered a concussion
    C. Larry rubbed his foot
    D. the incident took place in the machine shop

19._____

20. Which of the following would be the MOST accurate summary of the incident for the foreman to put in his report of the accident?
    A. Larry Mantell punched Henry Moore because a drill fell on his foot and he was angry. Then Henry fell and suffered a concussion.
    B. Henry Moore accidentally jammed a dolly into Larry Mantell's foot, knocking Larry down. Larry punched Henry, pushing him into the wall and causing him to bang his head against the wall.
    C. Bob Greene called Henry Moore. A dolly than jammed into Larry Mantell and knocked him down. Larry punched Henry who tripped and suffered some bruises. An ambulance was called.
    D. A drill fell on Larry Mantell's foot. Larry jumped up suddenly and punched Henry Moore and pushed him into the wall. Henry may have suffered a concussion as a result of falling.

20._____

Questions 21-25.

DIRECTIONS: Questions 21 through 25 are to be answered ONLY on the basis of the information provided in the following passage.

A written report is a communication of information from one person to another. It is an account of some matter especially investigated, however routine that matter may be. The ultimate basis of any good written report is facts, which become known through observation and verification. Good written reports may seem to be no more than general ideas and opinions. However, in such cases, the facts leading to these opinions were gathered, verified, and reported earlier, and the opinions are dependent upon these facts. Good style, proper form, and emphasis cannot make a good written report out of unreliable information and bad judgment; but, on the other hand, solid investigation and brilliant thinking are not likely to become very useful until they are effectively communicated to others. If a person's work calls for written reports, then his work is often no better than his written reports.

21. Based on the information in the above passage, it can be concluded that opinions expressed in a report should be
    A. based on facts which are gathered and reported
    B. emphasized repeatedly when they result from a special investigation
    C. kept to a minimum
    D. separated from the body of the report

    21.____

22. In the above passage, the one of the following which is mentioned as a way of establishing facts is
    A. authority
    B. communication
    C. reporting
    D. verification

    22.____

23. According to the above passage, the characteristic shared by ALL written reports is that they are
    A. accounts of routine matters
    B. transmissions of information
    C. reliable and logical
    D. written in proper form

    23.____

24. Which of the following conclusions can logically be drawn from the information given in the above passage?
    A. Brilliant thinking can make up for unreliable information in a report.
    B. One method of judging an individual's work is the quality of the written reports he is required to submit.
    C. Proper form and emphasis can make a good report out of unreliable information.
    D. Good written reports that seem to be no more than general ideas should be rewritten.

    24.____

25. Which of the following suggested titles would be MOST appropriate for this passage?
    A. Gathering and Organizing Facts
    B. Techniques of Observation
    C. Nature and Purpose of Reports
    D. Reports and Opinions: Differences and Similarities

    25.____

KEY (CORRECT ANSWERS)

1.	A	11.	C
2.	A	12.	C
3.	D	13.	A
4.	B	14.	D
5.	A	15.	A
6.	C	16.	D
7.	A	17.	D
8.	D	18.	C
9.	C	19.	B
10.	D	20.	B

21. A
22. D
23. B
24. B
25. C

TEST 3

DIRECTIONS: Each question or incomplete statement is followed by several suggested answers or completions. Select the one that BEST answers the question or completes the statement. *PRINT THE LETTER OF THE CORRECT ANSWER IN THE SPACE AT THE RIGHT.*

Questions 1-5.

DIRECTIONS: The following is an accident report similar to those used in departments for reporting accidents. Questions 1 through 5 are be answered using ONLY the information given in this report.

ACCIDENT REPORT

FROM: John Doe	DATE OF REPORT: June 23	
TITLE: Sanitation Worker		
DATE OF ACCIDENT: June 22 time 3 AM PM	CITY: Metropolitan	
PLACE: 1489 Third Avenue		
VEHICLE NO. 1	VEHICLE NO. 2	
OPERATOR: John Doe, Sanitation Worker Title	OPERATOR: Richard Roe	
VEHICLE CODE NO: 14-238	ADDRESS: 498 High Street	
LICENSE NO.: 0123456	OWNER: Henry Roe ADDRESS: 786 E.83 St.	LIC. NO.: 5N1492
DESCRIPTION OF ACCIDENT: Light green Chevrolet sedan while trying to pass drove in to rear side of sanitation truck which had stopped to collect garbage. No one was injured but there was property damage.		
NATURE OF DAMAGE TO PRIVATE VEHICLE: Right front fender crushed, bumper bent		
DAMAGE TO CITY VEHICLE: Front of left rear fender pushed in. Paint scraped.		
NAME OF WITNESS: Frank Brown	ADDRESS: 48 Kingsway	
SIGNATURE OF PERSON MAKING THIS REPORT John Doe	BADGE NO.: 428	

1. Of the following, the one which has been omitted from this accident report is the
   A. location of the accident
   B. drivers of the vehicles involved
   C. traffic situation at the time of the accident
   D. owners of the vehicles involved

   1.____

2. The address of the driver of Vehicle No. 1 is not required because he
   A. is employed by the department   B. is not the owner of the vehicle
   C. reported the accident   D. was injured in the accident

   2.____

3. The report indicates that the driver of Vehicle No. 2 was PROBABLY
   A. passing on the wrong side of the truck
   B. not wearing his glasses
   C. not injured in the accident
   D driving while intoxicated

   3.____

4. The number of people *specifically* referred to in this report is 4.____
   A. 3 B. 4 C. 5 D. 6

5. The license number of Vehicle No. 1 is 5.____
   A. 428 B. 5N1492 C. 14-238 D. 0123456

6. In a report of unlawful entry into department premises, it is LEAST important to include the 6.____
   A. estimated value of the property missing
   B. general description of the premises
   C. means used to get into the premises
   D. time and date of entry

7. In a report of an accident, it is LEAST important to include the 7.____
   A. name of the insurance company of the person injured in the accident
   B. probable cause of the accident
   C. time and place of the accident
   D. names and addresses of all witnesses of the accident

8. Of the following, the one which is NOT required in the preparation of a weekly functional expense report is the 8.____
   A. hourly distribution of the time by proper heading in accordance with the actual work performed
   B. signatures of officers not involved in the preparation of the report
   C. time records of the men who appear on the payroll of the respective locations
   D. time records of men working in other districts assigned to this location

KEY (CORRECT ANSWERS)

1. C   5. D
2. A   6. B
3. C   7. A
4. B   8. B

REPORT WRITING

EXAMINATION SECTION

TEST 1

DIRECTIONS: Each question or incomplete statement is followed by several suggested answers or completions. Select the one that BEST answers the question or completes the statement. *PRINT THE LETTER OF THE CORRECT ANSWER IN THE SPACE AT THE RIGHT.*

Questions 1-10.

DIRECTIONS: Questions 1 through 10 are to be answered SOLELY on the basis of the following passage and Stolen Vehicle Report Form, which appears on the following page. The form contains 43 numbered boxes. Read the passage and look at the form before answering the questions.

Police Officers Walton and Wright, patrolling in their radio patrol car in the industrial area of the 29th Precinct, were dispatched to 523 Johnson Boulevard at 10:30 A.M. on October 30, 2020 by the Police Radio Dispatcher. The Dispatcher had received a telephone call from a Ms. Ann Graham at 10:28 A.M. that her friend's car was being stolen from in front of her house.

Officers Walton and Wright arrived at 523 Johnson Boulevard at 10:32 A.M. Ms. Graham was waiting outside and informed them that the car had already been stolen. She stated that her friend, Samantha Merlin, had gone on vacation to California three days before and had left her car in Ms. Graham's care. Ms. Graham had parked the car in front of her own house the night before.

Ms. Graham stated that she looked out of her window at 10:25 A.M. that day and saw a strange man breaking into the car using a wire coat hanger. The car's hood was raised. She ran to her telephone to call the police. When she returned to her window, she saw the man doing something under the hood and, within a minute, he drove the car away. She had been too frightened to try to stop him, and there was no one else on the street.

Ms. Graham described the car as a black 2002 Buick 2-door sedan, New York license plate number 113-ABT, Vehicle Identification Number 7641239877. She stated that her friend, Ms. Merlin, lives at 1905 Junis Road, her telephone number is 978-4123, she is unmarried, 30 years old, and will return from vacation on November 13. Until then, she can be reached by telephone at 213-804-9112. She is employed at the law firm of Adams and Adams, 360 Park Avenue, as an office manager.

Ms. Graham described the man who stole the car as white, in his early twenties, about 5'7", 155 lbs., and wearing blue pants, a black jacket, and an earring in his left ear. He had dark brown, short curly hair.

Ms. Graham gave her telephone number as 275-8722 and stated that she is divorced, employed as a securities analyst at F.G. Sutton and Company, 125 Wall Street, and is 32 years old. Her birth date is June 13, 1976. Her telephone number at work is 217-7273.

2 (#1)

STOLEN VEHICLE REPORT FORM

COMPLAINT INFORMATION	Complaint Number (1)	Precinct (2)	Date Complaint Reported (3)	Time Reported (4)	Place Complaint Taken (5)
VEHICLE DESCRIPTION	Year (6)	Make (7)	Color (8)		License Number (9)
	I.D. Number (10)		Type (11)		Location of Theft (122)
OWNER INFORMATION	Name (13)		Address (14)		Home Telephone (15)
	Age (16)		Marital Status (17)		Occupation (18)
	Business Address (19)			Business Telephone (20)	
WITNESS INFORMATION	Name (21)		Address (22)		Home Telephone (23)
	Age (24)		Marital Status (25)		Occupation (26)
	Business Address (27)			Business Telephone (28)	
	Witness' Description of Incident (29)				
DESCRIPTION OF SUSPECT	Name (If Known) (30)	Age (31)	Race (32)	Sex (33)	Height (34)	Weight (35)	Hair (36)
	Eyes (37)		Clothing (38)		Distinctive Marks (39)		
	Other (40)						
OFFICER INFORMATION	Name (41)			Date (42)			
	Shield Number (43)						

1. Which one of the following should be entered in Box 3?
   A. June 13
   B. October 13
   C. October 30
   D. November 13

1.____

2. Which one of the following should be entered in Box 31? 2.____
   A. Late teens   B. Early twenties   C. 30   D. 32

3. Which one of the following should be entered in Box 12? 3.____
   In front of
   A. 1905 Junis Road   B. 523 Johnson Boulevard
   C. 125 Wall Street   D. 360 Park Avenue

4. Which one of the following should be entered in Box 8? 4.____
   A. Blue   B. Brown   C. Black   D. Red

5. Which one of the following should be entered in Box 11? 5.____
   A. 2-door sedan   B. 4-door sedan
   C. 4-door station wagon   D. 2-door sportscar

6. Which one of the following should be entered in Box 15? 6.____
   A. 804-9112   B. 217-7273   C. 275-8722   D. 978-4123

7. Which one of the following should be entered in Box 17? 7.____
   A. Married   B. Legally separated
   C. Single   D. Divorced

8. Which one of the following should be entered in Box 21? 8.____
   A. Samantha Merlin   B. Samantha Graham
   C. Ann Merlin   D. Ann Graham

9. Which one of the following should be entered in Box 26? 9.____
   A. Securities analyst   B. Housewife
   C. Office Manager   D. Secretary

10. Which one of the following should be entered in Box 40? 10.____
    A. Scar on left cheek   B. Earring in left ear
    C. Short curly brown hair   D. Blue pants, black jacket

Questions 11-20.

DIRECTIONS: Questions 11 through 20 are to be answered SOLELY on the basis of the following story and Complaint Report Form.

Officers Fred Johnson and Carl Adams, patrolling in their radio car in the Riverfront section of Precinct #8, were dispatched to 124 Selwyn Lane at 3:23 P.M. on April 26 by the dispatcher. The dispatcher had received a telephone call at 3:20 P.M. from a Mrs. Green who said that her house had been burglarized and all of the contents of her house had been stolen.

Officers Johnson and Adams arrived at 124 Selwyn Lane at 3:28 P.M. Mrs. Green and two neighbors were waiting for them on the front steps. The Officers parked their patrol car in front of the house and locked the doors. Mrs. Green explained that she is a schoolteacher and her husband is a lawyer. They usually leave the house around 8:00 A.M. each morning. She is the first to arrive home since school lets out at 3:00 P.M. She tells the Officers that today, when she arrived home, she found the door to her house slightly open. She was frightened and went to her neighbor's house. Both women then returned to 124 Selwyn and, upon entering the house, found that the contents of the house had been removed. At that point, Mrs. Green called the Police Department.

While Officer Johnson took statements from Mrs. Green and Mrs. Walters, her neighbor, Officer Adams questioned other residents of the street. Most of the other residents were standing outside of the Green's house.

Mrs. Schneider, age 56, who lives 5 doors down at 138 Selwyn, told Officer Adams that she arrived home at 2:45 P.M. She then told Adams that she saw a large truck parked near 124 Selwyn and remembers wondering if anyone new was moving into the neighborhood. She remembers the truck was dented, painted bright blue with a white top, and it had New Jersey plates. Also she was able to describe one of the suspects. She saw him get into the truck before it pulled away. The man was white, about 6'2" tall, about 220 lbs., and thinning brown hair. He was wearing a pair of dirty white overalls and brown work boots. He appeared to walk with a limp. There was another man already in the truck, and Mrs. Schneider described him as a very short Black man wearing a white hat. Mrs. Schneider said the truck turned left on Second Street as it pulled away.

Mrs. Jones, Mrs. Dartnell, and Mrs. Leopold, when questioned by Officer Adams, said that they saw nothing. They were all at Mrs. Leopold's house playing cards and didn't come outside until they heard Mrs. Green screaming.

Officer Adams found that Mrs. Schneider's home phone number was 683-2291 and that she lives alone. Officer Johnson found that both Mrs. Green and her neighbor were 48 years of age and that the school's telephone number was 925-6394. Mrs. Walters' home telephone number is 683-7642, and she lives with her husband at 126 Selwyn Lane. Mr. Green's office number is 238-4296. It is located at 555 Fifth Avenue, Suite 816.

Officers Johnson and Adams then completed the complaint form. The complaint number assigned by the dispatcher was 479638G.

5 (#1)

COMPLAINT REPORT				
COMPLAINT INFORMATION	Complaint Number (1)	Precinct (2)	Date of Complaint (3)	Time of Complaint (4)	Place Complaint Taken (5)
INFORMATION ABOUT PERSON MAKING COMPLAINT	Name of Person Making Complaint (6) Last Name First Name Middle		Address of Person Making Complaint (7) Street City State	
	Age (8)	Marriage (9) Married ☐ Not-Married ☐	Occupation (If Any) (10)	
	Spouse's Occupation (If Any) (11)		Spouse's Business Address (12) Street City State	
WITNESS INFORMATION	Name of Witness (If Any) (13) Last Name First Name Middle		Address of Witness (If Any) (14) Street City State	
	Age (15)	Occupation (If Any) (16)		
	Spouse's Occupation (If Any) (17)		Spouse's Business Address (18) Street City State	
DESCRIPTION OF INCIDENT	Description (19)			
DESCRIPTION OF SUSPECTS (if Any)	Suspect #1	Name (20)	Age (21)	Race (22) *white*	Sex (23) *male*	Height (24)	Weight (25)	Hair (26)	Eyes (27)
	Suspect #2	Name (28)	Age (29)	Race (30) *black*	Sex (31) *male*	Height (32)	Weight (33)	Hair (34)	Eyes (35)
	Suspect #3	Name (36)	Age (37)	Race (38)	Sex (39)	Height (40)	Weight (41)	Hair (42)	Eyes (43)
	Special Suspect Description (44) Suspect Number _____		Description (45) *Walked with limp*	
SUSPECT VEHICLE DESCRIPTION (If Any)	Year (46)	Make (47)	Color (48)	License Number 49)
OFFICER INFORMATION	Name (50)			Date (51)
	Shield No. (52)			

11. Which one of the following should be entered in Box 4?   11._____
    A. 8:00 AM   B. 2:45 PM   C. 3:20 PM   D. Not known

12. Which one of the following should be entered in Box 6?   12._____
    A. Mrs. Schneider   B. Mrs. Green
    C. Officer Johnson   D. Not known

13. Which one of the following should be entered in Box 7?   13._____
    A. 138 Selwyn Lane   B. 125 Selwyn Lane
    C. 124 Selwyn Lane   D. Not known

14. Which one of the following should be entered in Box 8? 14._____
    A. 48   B. 52   C. 46   D. Not known

15. Which one of the following should be entered in Box 10? 15._____
    A. Lawyer   B. Widow   C. Teacher   D. Not known

16. Which one of the following should be entered in Box 11? 16._____
    A. Lawyer   B. Widow   C. Teacher   D. Not known

17. Which one of the following should be entered in Box 13? 17._____
    A. Mrs. Green   B. Mrs. Schneider
    C. Mrs. Leopold   D. Not known

18. Which one of the following should be entered in Box 16? 18._____
    A. Lawyer   B. Teacher   C. Widow   D. Not known

19. Which one of the following should be entered in Box 26? 19._____
    A. Black   B. Brown   C. Blonde   D. Not known

20. Which one of the following should be entered in Box 44? 20._____
    A. 1   B. 2   C. 3   D. Not known

KEY (CORRECT ANSWERS)

1. C   11. C
2. B   12. B
3. B   13. C
4. C   14. A
5. A   15. C

6. D   16. A
7. C   17. B
8. D   18. D
9. A   19. B
10. B   20. A

TEST 2

DIRECTIONS: Each question or incomplete statement is followed by several suggested answers or completions. Select the one that BEST answers the question or completes the statement. *PRINT THE LETTER OF THE CORRECT ANSWER IN THE SPACE AT THE RIGHT.*

Questions 1-10.

DIRECTIONS: Questions 1 through 10 are to be answered SOLELY on the basis of the following story and Complaint Report Form.

Officers Hunt and Torry respond to a suspected burglary-in-process call at 285 E. Reed Street. They arrive there at 2:32 P.M. A man wearing gray slacks, white dress shirt, and red tie is standing in front of the store yelling, *Stop, robbers!* He is pointing east. Officer Hunt sees three men running about one hundred and fifty feet away. He immediately starts to chase after them. One suspect is 5'9" and weighs about 140 lbs. He has black hair in an Afro cut and is wearing tan pants with a blue work shirt. He is wearing white tennis shoes with blue stripes. He turns the corner and runs south on Elm Street. Another one is 6'2" and weighs about 200 lbs. He has long dark brown hair and is wearing a green headband, white jacket, and blue jeans. He is carrying a brown paper bag in his left hand. He also turns south on Elm. The third man is 5'9" and weighs about 180 lbs. He has long dark brown hair and is wearing a white cap. He is wearing blue jeans and a light blue jacket with a white stripe around it. He continues running east on Reed.

Officer Torry questions the man in the red tie and finds he is the manager of the Elite Jewelry Store and that he has just been robbed by the men running away. Torry radios in the information and continues his questioning. The manager, Mr. Oscar Freehold, says that he was showing a ruby and diamond necklace to Mrs. Mandt, a customer, when these men entered the store. One of them, the tallest one, pointed a gun at Freehold and grabbed the necklace. He put the necklace in the pocket of his white jacket. The other two men were shorter and the same height. The heaver one of the two opened the cash register and emptied the money into a brown paper bag.

The thinner short man opened a display case and put several sapphire and emerald rings in his pants pocket. He then took a knife from his pocket and held it on Mrs. Mandt. The tall one forced Mr. Freehold to open the safe. The tall one took jewels and money from the safe and put them in another brown paper bag. The three men ran out.

Officer Hunt chased the two suspects who turned south on Elm Street. At the next corner, they turned east on Maple. They ran one block to the corner of Beech, where the one with the Afro cut turned south. The other suspect got into a car and drove east on Maple. It was a dark blue 2018 Ford sedan with New York license number 677-HKL. As he drove east on Maple, he sideswiped a 2016 red Dodge and a 2019 tan Volvo.

Officer Hunt returns to the jewelry store and radios in the additional information. Officer Torry completes the Complaint Report.

2 (#2)

COMPLAINT REPORT					
COMPLAINT INFORMATION	Complaint Number (1)	Precinct (2)	Date of Complaint (3)	Time of Complaint (4)	Place Complaint Taken (5)
INFORMATION ABOUT PERSON MAKING COMPLAINT	Name of Person Making Complaint (6) Last Name First Name Middle			Address of Person Making Complaint (7) Street City State	
	Age (8)	Marriage (9) Married ☐ Not-Married ☐		Occupation (If Any) (10)	
	Spouse's Occupation (If Any) (11)			Spouse's Business Address (12) Street City State	
WITNESS INFORMATION	Name of Witness (If Any) (13) Last Name First Name Middle			Address of Witness (If Any) (14) Street City State	
	Age (15)	Occupation (If Any) (16)			
	Spouse's Occupation (If Any) (17)			Spouse's Business Address (18) Street City State	
DESCRIPTION OF INCIDENT	Description (19)				

DESCRIPTION OF SUSPECTS (if Any)	Suspect #1	Name (20)	Age (21)	Race (22)	Sex (23) *male*	Height (24) 5'9"	Weight (25) 140	Hair (26)	Eyes (27)
	Suspect #2	Name (28)	Age (29)	Race (30) *black*	Sex (31) *male*	Height (32) 6'2"	Weight (33) 200	Hair (34)	Eyes (35)
	Suspect #3	Name (36)	Age (37)	Race (38)	Sex (39) *male*	Height (40) 5'9"	Weight (41) 180	Hair (42)	Eyes (43)
	Special Suspect Description (44) Suspect Number _____				Description (45) *Walked with limp*				

SUSPECT VEHICLE DESCRIPTION (If Any)	Year (46)	Make (47)	Color (48)	License Number 49)
OFFICER INFORMATION	Name (50) Shield No. (52)		Date (51)	

1. Which of the following should be entered in Box 6? 1.____
   A. Officer Hunt   B. Mr. Oscar Freehold
   C. Mrs. Mandt   D. Not known

2. Which of the following should be entered in Box 10? 2.____
   A. Jewelry store manager   B. Police officer
   C. Clerk   D. Not known

3. Which of the following should be entered in Box 13? 3.____
   A. Mr. Oscar Freehold   B. Mrs. Mandt
   C. Officer Hunt   D. Not known

4. Which of the following should be entered in Box 14? 4._____
   A. East Reed Street B. East Elm Street
   C. South Beech Street D. Not known

5. Which of the following should be entered in Box 26? 5._____
   A. Blonde B. Brown C. Black D. Not known

6. Which of the following should be entered in Box 34? 6._____
   A. Blonde B. Brown C. Black D. Not known

7. Which of the following should be entered in Box 42? 7._____
   A. Blonde B. Brown C. Black D. Not known

8. Which of the following should be entered in Box 46? 8._____
   A. 2016 B. 2018 C. 2019 D. Not known

9. Which of the following should be entered in Box 48? 9._____
   A. Green B. Tan C. Blue D. Not known

10. Which of the following should be entered in Box 50? 10._____
    A. Officer Hunt B. Officer Freehold
    C. Officer Torry D. Not known

Questions 11-20.

DIRECTIONS: Questions 11 through 20 are to be answered SOLELY on the basis of the following story and Arrest Form.

Officer John Smith, on foot patrol near a delicatessen, heard a man's cry for help. When he reached the man, Peter Laxalt Green, Green told him that he had just been robbed by a young white male who could be seen running down the street. The officer ran after the youth and saw him jump into a 2019 two-door white Buick, New York plate number 761-QCV. While the youth was trying to start the car, the officer caught up with him and arrested him in front of 49 Second Avenue, Brooklyn. The arrest took place ten minutes after the robbery occurred. The officer brought his prisoner to the 65th Precinct station house at 57 Second Avenue, Brooklyn. At the station house, thirty minutes after the robbery, it was determined that the prisoner's legal name was John Wright Doman and his nickname was *Beefy*. Mr. Doman lives at 914 East 140th Street, Brooklyn, Apartment 3G, telephone number 737-1392. He was born in Calgary, Canada, on February 3, 2005. He became a U.S. citizen on February 3, 2012. His Social Security number is 056-46-7056. Doman is not married. He is employed at the Bollero Wine Company, 213 Fourth Avenue, Brooklyn. An arrest report was prepared at the Precinct. The number assigned to the report was 17460.

At the station house, Mr. Green described the incident in detail. Mr. Green stated that at 11:55 P.M. on July 18, 2023, a young, heavy-set white male, 5'11" tall, weighing 220 pounds, with brown hair and blue eyes, entered Mr. Green's delicatessen, at 141 Second Avenue, Brooklyn, New York. Green, who lives in the apartment above the delicatessen, asked him if he could help him. The male replied, *Yes, you can*, and then immediately pulled out a knife. Mr.

4 (#2)

Green then noticed that the male had a red tattoo of an ax on his right arm. The male demanded that Mr. Green give him all the money from the cash register or else Mr. Green would get hurt. Mr. Green picked up a bottle that was on the counter and threw it at the male, striking him in the chest. The male fled from the delicatessen and headed south on Second Avenue. Mr. Green then ran out of the delicatessen and yelled for the police.

Mr. Green was born on March 17, 1969. His business phone number is 871-3113; his home phone number is 330-5286.

ARREST REPORT					
ARREST INFORMATION	Arrest Number (1)	Precinct (2)	Date of Arrest (3)	Time of Arrest (4)	Place of Arrest (5)
DESCRIPTION OF INCIDENT	Date & Time (6)			Prisoner's Weapon (Description) (7)	
	Prisoner's Auto (color, year, make, model, license plate number, state) (8)				
	Location of Incident (be specific) (9)			Type of Business (10)	
DESCRIPTION OF PRISONER	Last Name First Name Middle (11)			Date of Birth (12)	
	Age (13)	Sex (14)	Race (15)	Eyes (16)	Hair (17)	Weight (18)	Height (19)
	Address City State			Apt. No. (21)	Home Phone Number (22)
	Place of Birth (23)		Citizenship (24) Citizen ☐ Non-citizen ☐		Marital Status (25)
	Social Security Number (26)		Where Employed (Company and Address) (27)		
	Nickname (28)	Scars, Tattoos (Describe fully and give location) (29)			
DESCRIPTION OF COMPLAINANT	Last Name First Name Middle (30)			Date of Birth (31)	
	Address City State (32)			Telephone Numbers Business: (33) Home: (34)	

11. Which of the following should be entered in Box 3? _____, 2018
    A. February 3   B. March 17   C. July 18   D. July 19

12. Which of the following should be entered in Box 4?
    A. 11:55 P.M.   B. 12:05 A.M.   C. 12:25 A.M.   D. 12:35 A.M.

5 (#2)

13. Which of the following should be entered in Box 6?   13.____
    A. 7/18/23, 11:55 P.M.   B. 7/18/23, 11:55 A.M.
    C. 7/19/23, 11:55 P.M.   D. 7/19/23, 11:55 A.M.

14. Which of the following should be entered in Box 7?   14.____
    A. Ax   B. Gun   C. Bottle   D. Knife

15. Which of the following should be entered in Box 8?   15.____
    White _____ Buick, _____, New York
    A. 2019; two-door; 761-QCV   B. 2020; four-door; 762-QCV
    C. 2019; two-door; 761-VCQ   D. 2020; four-door; 167-QCV

16. Which of the following should be entered in Box 12?   16.____
    A. 3/17/69   B. 2/3/05   C. 7/18/05   D. 2/3/12

17. Which of the following should be entered in Box 27?   17.____
    Bollero _____, Brooklyn, N.Y.
    A. Beer Company, 213 Fourth Avenue
    B. Wine Company, 213 Fourth Avenue
    C. Beer & Wine Company, 213 Second Avenue
    D. Wine Company, 213 Fourth Street

18. Which of the following should be entered in Box 32? _____, Brooklyn.   18.____
    A. 49 Second Avenue   B. 57 Second Avenue
    C. 141 Second Avenue   D. 914 East 140th Street

19. Which of the following should be entered in Box 33?   19.____
    A. 330-1392   B. 330-5286   C. 737-1392   D. 871-3113

20. Which of the following should be entered in Box 28?   20.____
    A. Doman   B. Axe   C. Beefy   D. Maniac

KEY (CORRECT ANSWERS)

1.	B	11.	D
2.	A	12.	B
3.	B	13.	A
4.	D	14.	D
5.	C	15.	A
6.	B	16.	B
7.	B	17.	B
8.	B	18.	C
9.	C	19.	D
10.	C	20.	C

BASIC FUNDAMENTALS OF REPORT WRITING

CONTENTS

INSTRUCTIONAL OBJECTIVES	1
CONTENT	1
Introduction	1

1. Types of Reports
   - The Formal Report — 1
   - The Informal Report
   - The Semi-Formal Report

2. Examples of Reports — 2
   - School Setting
     - The Formal Report
     - The Semi-Formal Report
     - The Informal Report
   - Public Service Agencies
     - Police Reporting
     - Other Reporting Areas

3. The Report Writer — 4

4. Choosing Best Words — 4
   - Use Proper Word for Intended Meaning
   - Eliminate Slang in Reports

5. Choosing Best Phrases — 6
   - Don't Use Weasel Words
   - Cliches to Avoid
   - Don't Use Excess Wordage
   - Don't Be Pompous

6. Writing Sentences — 8
   - Be Simple
   - Keep Active
   - Don't be Wordy

7. Writing a Good Paragraph — 10
   - Developing a Paragraph
   - Paragraph Construction

8. Special Word Forms — 10
   - Using Numbers Correctly
   - Using Abbreviations Correctly
   - Using Contractions Correctly
   - Using Capital Letters Correctly
   - Using Punctuation Correctly
     - The Comma
     - The Semicolon
     - The Colon

9. Using the Dictionary in Report Writing — 13
   - Dictionary Usage
   - Dictionary Content
   - Word Division

10. Summation — 14

STUDENT LEARNING ACTIVITIES	15
TEACHER MANAGEMENT ACTIVITIES	15
EVALUATION QUESTIONS	17

BASIC FUNDAMENTALS OF REPORT WRITING

INSTRUCTIONAL OBJECTIVES

1. Ability to understand how reports are used.
2. Ability to form an appreciation for the importance of effective report writing in public service occupations.
3. Ability to define and differentiate between the types of reports.
4. Ability to select the proper form for a report.
5. Ability to recognize the steps in preparing a good report.
6. Ability to demonstrate a knowledge of correct word usage and its importance in a report.
7. Ability to demonstrate the proper grammatical structure in report writing.
8. Ability to explain the importance of using a dictionary in report writing.

CONTENT

INTRODUCTION

A report is the communication of information in the most convenient form to someone who wants or needs it. It is difficult to overstate the importance of reports in our complex society today. They provide the data on which far-reaching decisions and policy are determined. A report that is not accurate or that is incomplete may cause the writer and the receiver misunderstanding, antagonism, and costly errors. Repeated errors in reports may well cost the writer his position.

Many of the reports that public service workers make are oral ones. However, the more important reports are always required to be in writing.

A report is always addressed to someone - the audience. The audience is usually a superior who needs the information to determine what action to take or what recommendations to pass ori to his superior. The good report writer analyzes the audience to which the report will be directed.

○ Should the report be a formal document or should the report be an informal memo?

○ How will the audience use the report?

○ Will it be passed along to others in the organization, or people in other areas?

The report writer's answers to questions such as these may well determine the format that is selected for the report.

1. TYPES OF REPORTS

<u>The Formal Report</u>. Formal reports usually follow a format prescribed by the agency or department. A central office typically supplies the form on which the report is to be prepared and submitted. A copy of a previous

report is frequently used as a guideline in preparing the new one. This procedure saves considerable time and makes it easier for the central office to analyze and interpret the information contained in the report.

The Informal Report. Another type of report, the informal one, frequently takes the form of a note or memo requesting additional supplies, services, or providing suggestions for the supervisor or a fellow worker. The informal report could possibly contain abbreviations, first names, and technical jargon that would be meaningless to anyone not acquainted with the situation in which it was written.

The Semi-Formal Report. A semi-formal report fits between the casual or informal memo and the highly structured and authoritative formal report. The semi-formal report is to be considered more important than the informal one and consequently is written with more thought and care than the informal report.

2. EXAMPLES OF REPORTS

School Setting. The various types of reports may be illustrated in school settings:

- *The Formal Report*. Progress reports, attendance reports, accident reports, and classroom reports prepared by students; these are all examples of well-structured formal reports. The importance of such reports is great. For example, the attendance reports determine how many teachers will be added or deleted from the faculty, in addition to being the basis for computing the state's financial contribution to the local school district.

- *The Semi-Formal Report* is illustrated by the office referral requesting action because of a student's behavior. It may result in a student-administrator conference, a parent conference, or even student suspension from school.

- *The Informal Report*. The note that a teacher leaves in the school mail for the staff assistant in charge of audiovisual equipment requesting service on the malfunctioning movie projector is an example of an informal report.

Public Service Agencies. The public-service report writer will find that he is writing:

- About specific subjects, and about various technicalities or events associated with the governmental agency or a responsibility assigned to it.

- With certain formal elements, such as the technical vocabulary of the department and the use of forms prepared by the department or agency.

- With an attitude of impartiality and objectivity, taking extreme care to convey information accurately and concisely, and with no attempt to arouse emotions.

Police Reporting - An illustration which would be meaningful to students may be made by examining what a policeman would include in a report when investigating an automobile accident. The policeman's report must contain such specific facts as:

- The names, addresses, phone numbers, ages, drivers' license numbers, and the identification of witnesses to the accident.

- Where the accident occurred - address.

- Description of the accident scene.

- The witnesses' observations - obtaining not only their account of events, but from what point they observed the event, and what they were doing at the time.

- Time and day of the accident.

- Weather conditions at the time of accident.

- The location of traffic signals, stop signs, skid marks, traffic lanes, etc.

- Description of the injuries, If any, or lack of apparent injuries.

- Description of the automobiles involved and apparent damages.

The investigating officer will have a pad of accident report forms which will outline the information needed. This insures that in the emotion and tension of the accident scene the investigating officer will be reminded of the information that he needs to include in the report. Numbers will be used to code certain information. This speeds up the writing, simplifies the recording and filing of the information, and makes the report less emotional.

The accident report will be of major importance when the insurance companies settle the claim. If there is a dispute over the settlement, the police report will be entered into the court record. The officer who wrote the report will also have to testify. The testimony may not be called for years after the accident and the officer will have to use the report to refresh his memory. It would probably be difficult for the officer otherwise to recall all of the events or even to notice them all at the time, as he may have had to direct traffic, administer first aid, call an ambulance, and keep curious bystanders out of the way. Even though human life may have been lost or saved by the policeman's actions on the scene, the primary issues in which the court or insurance adjusters will be interested are the facts in his report.

Other Reporting Areas - There are other workers in the public service area, such as teachers' aides, recreation aides, and forestry aides, who are likely to be required to complete accident reports while on the job. While their reports may not be as sensational as the police report, they are important and may be used in subsequent litigation.

It should also be pointed out that any report may have far-reaching ramifications. However, it is wise to be especially careful if a financial settlement between two adversaries will be affected by the report.

3. THE REPORT WRITER

Regardless of the type of report that is being prepared, the key to a good report is a good writer. The writer is the prime mover of the entire process. He gathers the material, interprets it, organizes it, and chooses the vocabulary. The writer imposes meaning merely by determining whether to make the report a formal, a semi-formal, or an informal one.

The reader is led to an understanding by an orderly presentation of the facts. The facts are determined by the writer's examination and observations of the situation or activity. The report's validity hinges upon the competence and objectivity of the writer and the accuracy of his observations.

Competence in report writing means that an individual has acquired the technique of careful inquiry. This may be illustrated by the police officer at the scene of the accident. He will take statements from witnesses, take measurements of skid marks, inspect and record the automobiles' registrations, and inspect the scene of the accident for real evidence that may have been instrumental in the cause of the accident, such as flat tires, conditions of the tires on the automobiles, mechanical defects, health of the drivers, etc. The report writer must acquire the habit of orderly thinking from problems to solutions, and learn to write an exact statement.

A good report communicates deaf ideas in simple language. The organization is orderly and fast moving. It is easy to read and uses visual aids where they will best carry forward the message. These skills are required of almost every member of governmental agencies. Management quickly recognizes competence in the preparation of reports. The individual who writes them well will assume a position of leadership at every level where accurate data supplies the basis for a difficult decision.

4. CHOOSING BEST WORDS

A major aspect of clear and concise report writing is being careful to select the proper word to express the thought exactly.

Use Proper Word for Intended Meaning. Since any one word may have a number of different meanings in different contexts, the writer must be certain that the word chosen is appropriate to convey the intended meaning within the human situation in which it is used. Paul Douglas, in his book

Communicating Through Reports, illustrates this point with "word." He lists twelve different meanings, ranging from the preacher expounding the *Word* (scripture) to the wife's having the *last word* (decision). This relationship of meaning to the environment and circumstances of its use is known as *context*.

Nearly all words mean more than they seem to mean; they possess associative meanings, almost outlying areas of suggestive values. The bare dictionary meaning of a word is its *denotation*. The *connotation* of a word relates to the suggestions and associations which have surrounded it.

For example, a dictionary definition of the word "gold" is "a precious yellow metal which is highly malleable and ductile. This is its denotation. But along with its denotative meaning, gold has also been associated with wealth, value, color, and power. These characteristics are the connotations of gold.

Beyond the core of the dictionary definition are suggestions, associations, and implications. Connotations must be watched as they have practical consequences for the report writer. Words and phrases with unpleasant connotations may become fighting words which blind the reader to anything else in the report. The following words are a few that have negative suggestions: mistakes, inefficient, death, refuse, error, rejecting, prohibited, unfair, poor judgment, and failed.

The writer may avoid irritation by choosing words with positive or neutral connotations. Note the difference in meaning of the following words:

- car, automobile, limousine
- inebriated, intoxicated, drunk
- portly, stout, obese
- smell, smell bad, stink
- slow, lazy, sluggish
- firm, obstinate, pigheaded
- Negro, colored man, black man
- dog, hound, mongrel

To use words both accurately and effectively, one must understand their connotations as well as their denotations. Social welfare aides, employment service workers, and probation services aides need to be especially alert to those words which are unique to the groups of people they serve. When wishing to express something with literal accuracy, the report writer will rely wholly upon the standards set by the department or dictionary definitions.

<u>Eliminate Slang in Reports</u>. *Slang should not be used in reports except when reporting dialogue.* There are several reasons for not using slang:

- First, many slang words and expressions are so short-lived that they will be outmoded before the report will have lived its useful life.

- Second, the use of slang expressions may be an excuse for not searching for the exact words to express the meaning.

Many slang expressions are only rubber stamps; to refer to a person as a "dude" hardly expresses exactly any critical judgment or intelligent description. To argue that such a word conveys precisely the intended meaning is to reveal a poverty of vocabulary, or careless thinking and laxness. The most serious charge against slang is that it becomes a substitute for thinking. Public service workers are likely to encounter the following slang:

- grubby
- get burned
- the boss
- real cool dude
- far out
- right on
- groovy
- bummer
- a drag
- rip off
- split
- low rider
- doing your own thing
- busted

The list could go on indefinitely. It would be very difficult to get a widely acceptable definition for any one of the above slang words. *Slang does express feeling, but when writing reports, the main concern is facts, not feelings.*

5. **CHOOSING BEST PHRASES**

   Don't Use Weasel Words. Other words to avoid in writing reports are what some authors call "weasel words." *A weasel word is a phrase that rids the writer of any responsibility for a statement.* By the use of the weasel word, the writer attempts to wriggle out of a position of accountability for an observation, inference, or statement, as may be seen by these examples:

   - It would be difficult to estimate ...

   - It is too early to say whether ...

   - It is generally believed that ...

   - It would appear that ...

   - There may be a tendency toward ...

   Weasel words are usually used with the passive voice, which is discussed later in this unit under "Writing Sentences."

   Clichés to Avoid. Public-service workers, like many other report writers, too often use words and phrases which are trite, outworn, commonplace, and flat stereotypes. Here are some examples of cliches which should be avoided:

   - It certainly merits study ...

- We will see what may be done ...

- This suggestion certainly has merit ...
- The matter is receiving our closest attention ...
- We will explore every avenue ...
- The handwriting on the wall ...
- Let's get down to brass tacks ...
- Naturally, the child's interest is our concern ...
- Fools rush in ...
- In the last analysis ...
- No thinking man ...
- The skeleton in the closet ...
- Let sleeping dogs ...

Cliches are similar to slang in that they are but rubber stamps, "stereotyped plates" of thought and expression. They save the writer the trouble of thinking exactly what he means. Consequently, they get in the way of clear and concise report writing.

<u>Don't Use Excess Wordage</u>. Diction, to be effective, must be as economical as possible. Necessary words should not be omitted nor should the report be sketchy. However, wordiness should be avoided as it lessens the force of expression. *In forceful writing, the ratio of ideas to words is high.* Conciseness alone will not achieve effective writing, but it is extremely difficult to write forcefully if you use two or three words to convey the idea which one word would express. Note these examples of excess or "superfluous" words:

- absolutely parallel
- first beginnings
- free gratis
- someone I met up with
- perfect circle
- the sunset in the west
- resume again
- join together

<u>Don't be Pompous</u>. When it is possible to reduce a group of words to a single word, it should be done. Here are some examples of economy in diction that are achieved by reducing pompous phrases to more natural words:

Pompous	Natural
in the nature of	like
for the purpose of	for
prior to	before
subsequent to	after
despite the fact that	though
give consideration to	consider
give instruction to	instruct
is due in large measure to	is due largely to
confidential nature	confidential information

6. WRITING SENTENCES

<u>Be Simple</u>. *One of the most important rules to follow in writing a report is to keep your sentences short, usually twenty words or less.* Language, like a machine, will be the most efficient when it operates on the principle that the more simple and better arranged the parts, the greater the effect which is produced. The subject-verb-object sentence is the best arrangement of parts in the simple report.

<u>Keep Active</u>. Verbs should be kept active. Avoid the passive voice; this puts excess words in a sentence, and its dullness derives as much from its extra wordage as from its impersonality. <u>John was hit by Don</u> says no more than <u>Don hit John</u> but takes 66 percent more words.

The passive voice's inevitable "was" and "by" do nothing but connect; worse, all the "was's" and "by's" and "has been's" actually get in the way of words carrying the meaning. It's like underbrush, it slows you down and hides what the report reader should see.

The passive voice, in its wordiness, is likely to be unclear even on the surface. When it eliminates the subject of the verb, as it usually does, it is intrinsically unclear. For example, a sentence written in the passive voice will often begin: "This evidence has been selected because...." The reader cannot tell who did the selecting. Does the writer mean that he picked it or does he describe some process of popular selection? It is usually surmised that the writer did the selecting, but why doesn't he say so and save a word and avoid confusion? "I selected this evidence because...." *The report writer should be careful not to leave the reader with any assumptions or implications.*

<u>Don't be Wordy</u>. Government writing is often noted for its wordiness. The following example is taken from a World War II price control regulation:

"Ultimate consumer means a person or group of persons, generally constituting a domestic household, who purchase eggs generally at the individual stores or retailers or purchase and receive deliveries of eggs at the place of abode of the individual or domestic household from producers or retail route sellers and who use such eggs for their consumption or food." This statement may be changed, without changing its meaning, by reducing it to:

"Ultimate consumers are people who buy eggs to eat them."

A good writer sees sharply what he wants to say, says directly what he sees, edits what he says, and takes pain to ease his reader's task. The example just given illustrates how much more readable a short sentence is than a long one.

7. WRITING A GOOD PARAGRAPH

The next major step after writing sentences is the construction of paragraphs. A good paragraph will clearly state the central ideas, it will fill in supporting details, and show how the central idea relates to the ideas which precede and follow it. The proper length of a paragraph is much like Abraham Lincoln's idea of a speech; it should be long enough to reach the end. There are exceptions, however. A report writer should be critical of his writing when a page of typewritten copy contains more than three or less than one complete paragraph.

Developing a Paragraph. There are many different ways of developing a paragraph in a report. The entry-level public-service worker may well utilize a variation of the following patterns of development:

- *Definition and description*. The writer gives his reader all the concepts he needs to follow the presentation.

- *Historical summary*. The writer briefs the reader on where the problem came from and why it is a problem. It provides a perspective for the problem.

- *Case history*. The report writer details an actual record for the reader.

- *Description of a process*. The report describes in detail how factors work together to produce a certain result.

- *Occasional summary*. The writer restates the essential data and ties facts together to clarify them for the reader.

- *Cause and effect*. The writer explains the forces that pro-duce certain consequences.

- *Examination of alternatives*. The writer may present the material so that the reader can make an examination of alternatives and their possible consequences.

- *Directive*. The reader will be told what to do. The writer may describe steps to be taken.

Paragraph Construction. Regardless of the paragraph's development, a well-constructed paragraph will be correct, clear, and effective. Eight desirable paragraph characteristics are listed below:

- A good paragraph contains an implied or expressed topic sentence.

- A good paragraph is never sketchy or incomplete. It contains a complete body of thought.

- A good paragraph is mechanically correct. It is properly indented or otherwise set off. It correctly represents every change of speaker in dialogue.

- A good paragraph is unified. Extraneous details are eliminated.

- A good paragraph contains material arranged in proper order. Good arrangement of ideas demonstrates logical thinking on the part of the writer.

- A good paragraph should make orderly clear progress and there should be clear passage from one paragraph to another.

- A good paragraph will be of suitable length.

- A good paragraph is well proportioned to the importance of the content. The longest paragraph of the report should not deal with the least significant idea.

8. SPECIAL WORD FORMS

The report writer will need to know how to handle such other items as abbreviations and numbers, in addition to writing clear sentences in well constructed paragraphs.

Using Numbers Correctly. Nearly all reports contain numbers. Should the number be written out or should it be shown in figures? Many reports consist primarily of numbers. Such reports call for the use of figures. However, other reports which are not primarily numerical reports may leave the writer in doubt as to how the numbers should be shown. The following suggestions may be helpful:

- Numbers requiring the use of more than one word or a hyphenated word are usually written as figures.

- A number which begins a sentence is written as a word; if this is awkward or inconsistent with the rest of the text, replace the sentence.

- Numbers under ten are usually written as words unless they appear in writing which is full of numbers.

- Numbers that express dimensions are usually written as figures.

- Numbers which contain decimal fractions are always written as figures.

- Any number naming a common fraction is usually written as a hyphenated word.
- Numbers in any sentence in which other numbers are to occur in figure form are usually written in figures.

- Numbers that tell either time, date, or percentage are usually written in figures.

- Numbers above ten naming streets are usually written as figures with the indicators of pronounciation, -st, -nd, -th, attached.

- Round numbers, such as "thousands," are usually written as words except where numbers are occurring very frequently.

- Any number appearing occasionally and simple enough to express in one word is usually written as a word.

- Numbers appearing as two separate categories, one after the other, are usually written as words for the first category and as figures for the second. (five 2x4 boards)

The report writer should remember that the above guidelines are suggestions and that some of them may actually contradict each other. Common sense should determine whether or not a number be written as a figure or a word.

<u>Using Abbreviations Correctly</u>. Abbreviations are found more often in reports than in any other form of writing. Although the use of abbreviations is a healthy part of the style of field reports, it is definitely limited and kept in check by both tradition and common sense. *Only those abbreviations which will be easily understood by the reader are to be used.* Many agencies or departments will have a number of abbreviations that they use regularly, particularly in informal reports. Handbooks or manuals issued by the department will list these and the new worker should memorize them. The use of abbreviations has met with limited success because of the time saved in writing certain reports; the use should be very restricted in formal reports.

There are several rules regarding the general idea of permissible abbreviations in report writing:

- Whenever abbreviations have been used so long that they have assumed vocabulary status, they should be used. Some such abbreviations are Mr., Mrs., B.C., A.D., FBI, CIA, a.m., p.m. (Each job family will have a number of abbreviations of its own.)
- Whenever the names of units are preceded by numerals, it is usually best to abbreviate the names of the units. For instance:

    a. The auto was going 75-mph in the 25-mph zone.
    b. It was 65° F today.
    c. The unit has a 3-hp engine.

- If an abbreviation makes an English word (as for example, in. for inches), use a period. Otherwise, most good writers do <u>not</u> use periods in <u>most</u> cases.

If a term must be repeated many times in a report, that term calls for explanation and thereafter possible abbreviation, regardless of what it is.

Using Contractions Correctly. A contraction is a form of abbreviation. It is a word written with an apostrophe to indicate the omission of a letter. Contractions should be used very seldom in formal reports, but are common in semiformal and informal ones. Field reports are full of abbreviations and contractions as their use can greatly speed up the process of gathering data in the field.

Using Capital Letters Correctly. Report writing calls for no departure from the conventional rules for the use of capital letters. Proper names, names of cities and states, official titles, and organizations are always captalized. There are two practices common to reports:

- Capitalize all important words in titles, division headings, side headings, and captions. By "important" is meant all words except articles, prepositions, and conjunctions.

- Capitalize Figure, Table, Volume, Number as part of titles. Thus, reference would be made to Figure 4, Table 2, etc.

When in doubt, do not capitalize.

Using Punctuation Correctly. Clear communication is dependent upon yet another aspect of written language, punctuation. Every sentence begins with a capital letter, and ends with either a period, question mark, or exclamation point. Punctuation which does not contribute to the clarity of thought should be avoided. Most of the difficulties with punctuation arise out of the use of the comma, semicolon, and colon. For information on other punctuation, see any good handbook of grammar.

The Comma. The principal uses of the comma are:

- Between independent clauses connected by a coordinating conjunction (and, but, for, or, nor, yet). But if commas are used in any of the independent clauses constituting a sentence, a semicolon must be used between the clauses.

- After introductory clauses or phrases preceding the main clause of the sentence.

- Between items in a series.

- Around parenthetical phrases, appositives, and nonrestric-tive modifiers.

The Semicolon. The semicolon is almost as strong a mark of separation as the period. It is chiefly used between the independent clauses not connected with one of the coordinating conjunctions, and between clauses connected with a coordinating conjunction which are long, or unrelated, or contain commas.

The Colon. The colon signals that something is to follow. It is a mark introducing lists, series, and quotations. It is used as a salutation in a business letter, in separating the hours and minutes in a statement of time, or in separating volume and pages in a bibliographical entry.

9. <u>USING THE DICTIONARY IN REPORT WRITING</u>

<u>Dictionary Usage</u>. The report writer should be aware of the fact that most dictionaries have a section listing the principal rules of capitalization, punctuation, and spelling. A dictionary should be considered one of the necessary tools for good report writing, together with the pencil and paper. The report writer should be using the dictionary for the following purposes:

- To determine the exact meaning of a word.

- To determine the correct spelling.

- To determine whether or not a word should be capitalized.

- To determine how a word should be divided at the end of a line.

- To determine correct pronunciation.

- To determine whether or not a hyphen should be used in a compound word.

<u>Dictionary Content</u>. In addition, the dictionary also has a list of common foreign words and phrases. It is obvious that much of the material that a report writer must master is to be found in a dictionary. The excellent report writer has the ability to select the exact word. No one can buy, sell, write letters, use the telephone, give orders, make a speech, or prepare a report, except by using words. Everything else being equal, the individual who knows the most about words will be the most successful in his occupation. *To develop the mastery of language necessary to use the exact word, the writer must know how to use the dictionary skillfully and he must use it frequently.*

The dictionary is a tool that will always be needed by the educated person. As a matter of fact, the better educated a person is, the more likely he is to refer frequently to a dictionary.

<u>Word Division</u>. One use of the dictionary mentioned above is for determining the correct place to divide a word at the end of a line. Since more errors are made in dividing words at the end of a line than in spelling them, capitalizing them, or in using them, it is important that the report writer learn to divide words correctly. Below are eight rules for dividing words at the end of a line:

- Never divide a word of one syllable.

- Do not divide a word of four letters.

- A one-letter syllable at the beginning of a word, or a one or two-letter syllable at the end of a word must not be separated from the rest of the word. (Examples: "about" not "a-bout"; "ready" not "read-y.")

- When a word containing three or more syllables is to be divided at a one-letter syllable, the one-letter syllable should be written on the first line rather than on the second. (Example: "maga-zine" not "mag-azine.")

- When a word is to be divided at a point where two vowels that are pronounced separately come together, these vowels should be divided into separate syllables. (Example: "continu-ation" not "continua-tion.") Note that this rule is an exception to the one stated above.

- A syllable that does not contain a vowel must not be separated from the remainder of the word. (Example: "wouldn't" not "would-n't.")

- Avoid dividing hyphenated words, such as "self-conscious," except at the hyphen.

- When a final consonant is doubled before a suffix, the additional consonant should be placed with the suffix. (Example: "run-ning" not "runn-ing.")

When in doubt about the proper syllable makeup of a word, consult the dictionary. Do not guess at the division of a word.

10. **SUMMATION**

English grammar essentials, such as correct punctuation, capitalization, syllabication, and correct use of numbers and abbreviations, are all part of the skills that the successful report writer has at his disposal. The beginning public-service worker is well advised to obtain a list of the words that appear frequently in his job family, or are a part of the technical or professional vocabulary, and memorize them. Common report forms should be reviewed and used as a guide for making observations and examinations of data when preparing to write a report. The writer may find that maps are needed to show geographical location, charts to visualize statistical data, or tables to determine relationships. Clarity will be the guide dictating how any idea may best be communicated to the reader.

In conclusion, the report writer must know what details to look for, must select the proper format for the report, must select the best possible words that do not have any emotional connotations and build them into short, effective sentences. Paragraphs must be developed by the writer around the central thoughts, leaving nothing to be imagined by the reader. The importance of word relationship and idea sequence is crucial.

Remember, a report is written to express an idea, not to impress a superior.

STUDENT LEARNING ACTIVITIES	○ Write a report explaining a career choice.
	○ View the six films trips, *Constructing Reports,* and evaluate the information they contain.
	○ Complete the matching vocabulary exercise prepared by the teacher for the occupation group selected by the student.
	○ Demonstrate a knowledge of the active and passive verbs in report writing by changing a report prepared by the teacher from the passive voice to the active.
	○ List three words having unfavorable connotations and explain how they could be particularly embarrassing to the writer.
	○ Identify the type of paragraph development used in each of the paragraphs which the teacher has prepared.
	○ Keep a notebook for discussion notes and class handouts.
	○ Take a diagnostic test, and complete remedial lessons, if needed, on punctuation and capitalization.
	○ Complete a dictionary assignment.
	○ Prepare reports describing the events in a simulated classroom interruption.
	○ Prepare a group report on the students' attendance in class, citing the percentage of absentees each day. Compare Monday to Tuesday, etc., and list the frequency of reasons for the absences.
	○ Evaluate the reports prepared by the class members in the above two activities.
TEACHER MANAGEMENT ACTIVITIES	○ Prepare a bulletin board display illustrating the components of a good report.
	○ Review the materials in the local audiovisual library to locate teaching aids that are readily available.
	○ Make arrangements for showing the movie, *Writing a Good Paragraph.*
	○ Make arrangements to show the filmstrips in the series: *Constructing Reports.* (6 filmstrips)
	○ Prepare discussion notes on the types of reports, and the importance and purpose of each type.
	○ Collect examples of reports from the eight job families in the Public Service Occupation area.

- Prepare a vocabulary list of technical and professional words from each of the public-service entry-level job families.

- Prepare matching exercises for the vocabulary words and their definitions for each of the major job groups.

- Prepare overlays for use with an overhead projector illustrating good and bad reports.

- Prepare a list of sentences containing passive-voice verbs which the students are to change to active verbs.

- Prepare a discussion of word meanings and emphasize the importance of connotation.

- Obtain or write, and present, paragraphs illustrating the seven ways of developing a paragraph.

- Plan simulated situations from which the students will have to prepare reports.

- Prepare a handout for students containing suggestions for the use of numbers in reports.

- Prepare discussion notes for the use of abbreviations in reports.

- Prepare a diagnostic quiz on punctuation marks and capitalization.

- Discuss and test the use of the dictionary in the classroom.

- Prepare a student handout on the eight rules for dividing words at the end of a line.

EVALUATION QUESTIONS
Basic Report Writing

1. Public service workers are likely to write:

    A. Formal reports
    B. Informal reports
    C. Semi-formal reports
    D. All of the above

2. Which statement is untrue?

    A. A good report writer does not have to be exact about facts
    B. A good report writer writes objectively and accurately about his observations
    C. A good report writer uses visual aids where they will help put over the message
    D. A good report writer gathers his material in an orderly way

3. Police reports are important because:

    A. They help settle arguments
    B. They help refresh the officer's memory
    C. Financial settlements may be involved
    D. All of the above

4. Which statement is not true?

    A. A good paragraph contains materials arranged in random order
    B. The length of the paragraph is suited to its importance
    C. A good paragraph is mechanically correct - indented or set off
    D. A good paragraph should make orderly, clear passage from one paragraph to another

5. A good paragraph should:

    A. Include all minor details
    B. Contain a topic sentence
    C. Leave out the main ideas
    D. Leave out the important details

6. Inaccurate and incomplete reports can cause:

    A. Misunderstanding
    B. Anger
    C. Costly errors
    D. All of the above

7. Writers do not refer to dictionaries when they need to know: 7.____

   A. Correct spelling
   B. How a word should be divided
   C. Detailed information about a subject
   D. Whether a hyphen should be used

8. Good report writers use: 8.____

   A. Slang as much as possible
   B. Words with unpleasant meanings
   C. Phrases that rid the writer of responsibility
   D. None of the above

9. When writing a report, it is best to use: 9.____

   A. Phrases that are used over and over
   B. Short, simple sentences
   C. As many words as possible
   D. An inactive tone

10. Which statement is incorrect?   10.____

    A. A number which begins a sentence is written as a figure
    B. Numbers under ten are usually written as words
    C. Numbers requiring the use of more than one word are usually written as figures
    D. Numbers which contain decimal fractions are always written as figures

11. Contractions are seldom used in: 11.____

    A. Field reports   B. Semi-formal reports
    C. Formal reports   D. Informal reports

12. Titles and the names of organizations are: 12.____

    A. Never capitalized
    B. Not capitalized in informal reports
    C. Sometimes capitalized in formal reports
    D. Always capitalized

13. After introductory clauses or phrases, one should use: 13.____

    A. A period   B. A comma
    C. A question mark   D. An exclamation mark

14. Between long, unrelated clauses that are connected with a conjunction, one should use: 14.____

    A. A period   B. A question mark
    C. A semi-colon   D. A colon

KEY (CORRECT ANSWERS)

1. D
2. A
3. D
4. A
5. B

6. D
7. C
8. D
9. B
10. A

11. C
12. D
13. B
14. C

BASIC FUNDAMENTALS OF WRITTEN COMMUNICATION

CONTENTS	Page
INSTRUCTIONAL OBJECTIVES	1
CONTENT	1
Introduction	1
1. Business Writing	1
Letters	
Selet the letter type	
Select the Right Format	
Know the Letter Elements	
Be Breef	
Use Concrete Nouns	
Use Active Verbs	
Use a Natural Tone	
Forms	4
Memoranda	5
Minutes of meetings	5
Short Reports	6
News Releases	8
2. Reporting on a Topic	9
Preparation for the Report	9
What is the Purpose of the Report?	
What Questions Should it Answer?	
Where Can the Relevant information be obtained?	
The Text of the Report	10
What Are the Answers to the Questions?	
Organizing the Report	
The Writer's Responsibilities	11
Conclusions and Recommendations	11
3. Persuasive Writing	11
General Guidelines for Writing	11
Persuasively	
Know the Source Credibility	
Avoid Overemotional Appeal	
Consider the Other Man's Point of wiew	
Interpersonal Communications	12
Conditions of Persuading	
The Persuassion campain	
4. Instructional Writing	13
Advances Organizers	
Practice	
Errorless Learning	
Feedback	
STUDENT LEARNING ACTIVITIES	16
TEACHERS MANAGEMENT ACTIVTIES	17
EVALUATION QUESTIONS	19

BASIC FUNDAMENTALS OF WRITTEN COMMUNICATION

INSTRUCTIONAL OBJECTIVES

1. Ability to write legibly.
2. Ability to fill out forms and applications correctly.
3. Ability to take messages and notes accurately.
4. Ability to write letters effectively.
5. Ability to write directions and instructions clearly.
6. Ability to outline written and spoken information.
7. Ability to persuade or teach others through written communication.
8. Ability to write effective overviews and summaries.
9. Ability to make smooth transitions within written communications.
10. Ability to use language forms appropriate for the reader.
11. Ability to prepare effective informational reports.

CONTENT

INTRODUCTION

Public-service employees are required to prepare written communications for a variety of purposes. Written communication is a fundamental tool, not only for the public-service occupations, but throughout the world of work. Many public-service occupations require written communication with ordinary citizens of diverse backgrounds, so the trainee should develop the ability to write in simple, nontechnical language that the ordinary citizen will understand.

This unit is designed to develop the student's ability to communicate effectively in writing for a number of different purposes and in a number of different formats. Whatever the particular purpose or format, however, effective writing will require the writer:

- to have a clear idea of his purpose and his audience;
- to organize his thoughts and information in an orderly way;
- to express himself concisely, accurately, and concretely;
- to report relevant facts;
- to explain and summarize ideas clearly; and
- to evaluate the effectiveness of his communication.

1. BUSINESS WRITING

   Several forms of written communication tend to recur frequently in most public-service agencies, including:
   - letters
   - forms
   - memoranda
   - minutes of meetings
   - short reports
   - telegrams and cables
   - news releases
   - and many others

   The public-service employee should be familiar with the principles of writing in these forms, and should be able to apply them in preparing effective communications.

   Letters

   Every letter sent from a public-service agency should be considered an ambassador of goodwill. The impression it creates may mean the difference between favorable public attitudes or unfavorable ones. It may mean the difference between creating a friend or an enemy for the agency. Every public-service employee has a responsibility to serve the public effectively and to provide services in an efficient and courteous manner. The letters an agency sends out reflect its attitudes toward the public.

The impression a letter creates depends upon both its appearance and its tone. A letter which shows erasures and pen written corrections gives an impression that the sending agency is slovenly. Similarly, a rude or impersonal letter creates the impression that the agency is insensitive or unfeeling. In preparing letters, the employee should apply principles of style and tone which will serve to create the most favorable impression.

Select the Letter Type. The two most common types of business letters are letters of inquiry and letters of response - that is, "asking" letters and "answering" letters. Whichever type of letter the employee is asked to write, the following guidelines will simplify the task and help to achieve a style and tone which will create a favorable impression on the reader.

Select the Right Format. Several styles of letter format are in common use today, including:

- the indented format,
- the block format, and
- the semi-block format.

Modified forms of these are also in use in some offices. The student should become familiar with the formats preferred for usage in his office, and be able to use whichever form the employer requests.

Know the Letter Elements. Every letter includes certain basic elements, such as:

- the letterhead, which identifies the name and address of the sender.
- the date on which the letter was transmitted.
- the inside address, with the name, street, city, and state of the addressee.
- the salutation, greeting the addressee.
- the body, containing the message.
- the complimentary close, the "good-bye" of the business letter.
- the signature, handwritten by the sender.
- the typed signature, the typewritten name and title of the sender.

In addition, several other elements are occasionally found in business letters:

- the *attention line,* directing the letter to the attention of a particular individual or his representative.
- the *subject line,* informing the reader at a glance of the subject of the letter.

- the *enclosure notation,* noting items enclosed with the letter.
- the *copy notation,* listing other persons who receive copies of the letter.
- the *postscript,* an afterthought sometimes (but not normally) added following the last typed line of the letter.

Be *Brief.* Use only the words which help to say what is needed in a clear and straightforward manner. Do not repeat information already known to the reader, or contained elsewhere in the letter. Likewise, do not repeat information contained in the letter being answered. Rather than repeat the content of a previous letter, one can say something like, "Please refer to our letter dated March 5:"

An employee can shorten his letters by using single words that serve the same function as longer phrases. Many commonly used phrases can be replaced by single words. For example,

Phrase	Single word
in order to	to
in reference to in	about
the amount of	for, of
in a number of cases	some
in view of	because
with regard to	about, in

Similarly, avoid the use of adjectives and nouns that are formed from verbs. If the root verbs are used instead, the writing will be more concise and more vivid. For example,

Noun form	Verb form
We made an adjustment on our books	We adjusted our books
We are sorry we cannot make a replacement of	We are sorry we cannot replace
Please make a correction in our order	Please correct our order

Be on the lookout for unnecessary adjectives and adverbs which tend to clutter letters without adding information or improving style. Such unnecessary words tend to distract the reader and make it more difficult for him to grasp the main points. Observe how the superfluous words, italicized in the following example, obscure the meaning: "You may be *very much* disappointed to learn that the *excessively large* demand for our *highly popular recent* publication, 'Your Income Taxes,' has led to an *unexpected* shortage of this *attractive* publication and we *sadly* expect they will not be replenished until *quite* late this year."

Summarizing, then, a *good letter is simple and clear, with short, simple words, sentences, and paragraphs. Related parts of sentences and paragraphs are kept together and placed in an order which makes it easy for the reader to follow the main thoughts.*

Be Natural. Whenever possible, use a human touch. Use names and personal pronouns to let the reader know the letter was written by a person, not an institution. Instead of saying, "It is the policy of this agency to contact its clients once each year to confirm their status," try this: "Our policy, Mr. Jones, is to confirm your status once each year."

Use Concrete Nouns. Avoid using abstract words and generalizations. Use names of objects, places, and persons rather than abstractions.

Use Active verbs. The passive voice gives a motionless, weak tone to most writing. Instead of "The minutes were taken by Mrs. Smith," say, "Mrs. Smith took the minutes." Instead of "The plans were prepared by the banquet committee," say, "The banquet committee prepared the plans."

Use a Natural Tone. Many people tend to become hard, cold, and unnatural the moment they write a letter. *Communicating by letter should have the same natural tone of conversation used in everyday speech.* One way to achieve a natural and personal tone in the majority of letters is through the use of personal pronouns. Instead of saying, "Referring to your letter of March 5, reporting the non-receipt of goods ordered last February 15, please be advised that the goods were shipped as requested," say, "I am sorry to hear that you failed to receive the items you ordered last February 15. We shipped them the same day we received your letter."

Forms

In most businesses and public service agencies, repetitive work is simplified by the use of *forms*. Forms exist for nearly every purpose imaginable: for ordering supplies, preparing invoices, applying for jobs, applying for insurance, paying taxes, recording inventories, and so on. While the forms encountered in different agencies may differ widely, several principles should be applied in completing any form.

- *Legibility.* Entries on forms should be clear and legible. Print or type wherever possible. When space provided is insufficient, attach a supplementary sheet to the form.

- *Completeness.* Make an entry in every space provided on the form. If a particular space does not apply to the applicant, enter there the term "N/A" (for "not applicable"). The reader of the completed form will then know that the applicant did not simply overlook that space.

- *Conciseness.* Forms are intended to elicit a maximum amount of information in the least possible space. When completing a form, it is usually not necessary to write complete sentences. Provide the necessary information in the least possible words.

- *Accuracy*. Be sure the information provided on the form is accurate. If the entry is a number, such as a social security number or an address, double-check the correctness of the number. Be sure of the spelling of names, No one appreciates receiving a communication in which his name is misspelled.

Memoranda

The written communications passing between offices or departments are usually transmitted in a form known as *"interoffice memorandum."* The headings most often used on such "memos" are:

- TO: identifying the addressee,
- FROM: identifying the sender or the originating office,
- SUBJECT: identifying briefly the subject of the memo,
- DATE: identifying the date the memo was prepared.

Larger agencies may also use headings such as FILE or REFERENCE NO. to aid in filing and retrieving memoranda.

In writing a memo, many of the same rules for letter-writing may be applied. Both the appearance and tone of the memo should create a pleasing impression. The format should be neat and follow the standards set by the originating office. The tone should be friendly, courteous, and considerate. The language should be clear, concise, and complete.

Memos usually dispense with salutations, complimentary closings, and signatures of the writers. In most other respects, however, the memorandum will follow the rules of good letter-writing.

Minutes of Meetings

Most formal public-service organization conduct meetings from time to time at which group decisions are made about agency policies, procedures, and work assignments. The records of such meetings are called *minutes*.

Minutes should be written as clearly and simply as possible, summarizing only the essential facts and decisions made at the meeting. While some issue may have been discussed at great length, only the final decision or resolution made of it should be recorded in the minutes. Information of this sort is usually included:

- Time and place of the call to order,
- Presiding officer and secretary,
- Voting members present (with names, if a small organization),

- Approval and corrections of previous minutes,
- Urgent business,
- Old business,
- New business,
- Time of adjournment,
- Signature of recorder.

Minutes should be written in a factual and objective style. The opinions of the recorder should not be in evidence. Every item of business coming up before a meeting should be included in the minutes, together with its disposition. For example:

- "M/S/P (Moved, seconded, passed) that Mr. Thomas Jones take responsibility for rewriting the personnel procedures manual."
- "Discussion of the summer vacation schedule was tabled until the next meeting."
- "M/S/P, a resolution that no client of the agency should be kept waiting more than 20 minutes for an interview."

Note that considerable discussion may have surrounded each of the above items in the minutes, but that only the topic and its resolution are recorded.

Short Reports

The public-service employee often is called upon to prepare a short report gathering and interpreting information on a single topic. Reports of this kind are sometimes prepared so that all the relevant information may be assembled in one place to aid the organization in making certain decisions. Such reports may be read primarily by the staff of the organization or by others closely related to the decision-making process.

Reports may be prepared at other times for distribution to the public or to other agencies and institutions. These reports may serve the purpose of informing public opinion or persuading others on matters of public policy.

Whatever the purpose of the short report, its physical appearance and style of presentation should be designed to create a favorable impression on the reader. Even if the report is distributed only within the writer's own unit, an attractive, clear, thorough report will reflect the writer's dedication to his assignment and the pride he takes in his work.

Some guidelines which will assist the trainee in preparation of effective short reports include use of the following:

- A good quality paper;
- Wide and even margins, allowing binding room;

- An accepted standard style of typing;
- A title page;
- A table of contents (for more lengthy reports only);
- A graphic numbering or outlining system, if needed for clarity;
- Graphics and photos to clarify meaning when useful;
- Footnotes, used sparingly, and only when they contribute to the report;
- A bibliography of sources, using a standard citation style.

A discussion of the organization of content for informational reports follows later in this document.

News Releases

From time to time, the public-service employees may be called upon to prepare a news release for his agency. Whenever the activities of the agency are newsworthy or of interest to the public, the agency has an obligation to report such activities to the press. The most common means for such reporting is by using the press release. Most newspapers and broadcasting stations are initially informed of agencies' activities by news releases distributed by the agencies themselves. Thus, the news release is a basic tool for communicating with the public served by the agency.

The news release is written in news style, with these basic characteristics:

- Sentences are short and simple.

- Paragraphs are short (one or two sentences) and relate to a single item of information.

- Paragraphs are arranged in *inverted order* — the most important in information appears first.

- The first or *lead* paragraph summarizes the entire story. If the reader went no further, he would have the essential information.

- Subsequent paragraphs provide further details, the most important occurring first.

- Reported information is attributed to sources; that is, the source of the news is reported in the story.

- The expression of the writer's opinions is scrupulously avoided.

- The 5 W's (who, what, why, where, when) are included.

News releases should be typed double spaced on standard 8 1/2 x 11 paper, with generous margins and at least 2" of open space above the lead paragraph. Do not write headlines - that is the editor's job. At the top of the first page of the release include the name of the agency releasing the story and the name and phone number of the person to contact if more information is needed. If the release runs more than one page, end each page with the word "-more-" to indicate that more copy follows. End the release with the symbols "###" to indicate that the copy ends at that point.

Accuracy and physical appearance are essential characteristics of the news release. Typographical errors, or errors of fact, such as misspelled names, lead editors to doubt the reliability of the story. Great care should be taken to assure the accuracy and reliability of a news release.

2. REPORTING ON A TOPIC

At one time or another, most public-service employees will be asked to prepare a report on some topic. Usually the need for the report grows out of some policy decision contemplated by the agency for which full information must be considered. For example:

- Should the agency undertake some new project or service?
- Should working conditions be changed?
- Are new specialists needed on the staff?
- Or should a branch office be opened up?

Or any of a hundred other such decisions which the agency must make from time to time.

When called upon to prepare such a report, the employee should have a model to follow which will guide his collection of information and will help him to prepare an effective and useful report.

As with other forms of written communication, both the physical appearance and content of the report are important to create a favorable impression and to engender confidence. The physical appearance of such reports has been discussed earlier; additional suggestions for reports are given in Unit 3. Basic guidelines follow below for organizing and preparing the content.

Preparation for the Report

What is the Purpose of the Report? The preparer of the report should have clearly in mind why the report is needed:

- What is the decision being contemplated by the agency?
- To what use will the report be put?

Before beginning to prepare the report, the writer should discuss its purpose fully with the decision-making staff to articulate the purpose the report is intended to serve. If the employee is himself initiating the report, it would be well to discuss its purpose with colleagues to assure that its purpose is clear in his own mind.

What Questions Should the Report Answer? Once the purpose of the report is clear, the questions the report must answer may begin to become clear. For example, if the decision faced by the agency is whether or not to offer a new service, questions may be asked such as these:

- What persons would be served by the new service?

- What would the new service cost?
- What new staff would be needed?
- What new equipment and facilities would be needed?
- What alternative ways exist for offering the service?
- How might the new service be administered?

And so on. Unless the purpose of the report is clear, it is difficult to decide what specific questions need to be answered. Once the purpose is clear, these questions can be specified.

Where Can the Relevant Information be Obtained? Once the questions are clear in the writer's mind, he can identify the information he will need to answer them. Information may usually be obtained from two general sources:

- *Relevant documents.* Records, publications, and other reports are often useful in locating the information needed to answer particular questions. These may be in the files of the writer's own agency, in other agencies, or in libraries.

- *Personal contacts.* Persons in a position to know the needed information may be contacted in person, by phone, or by letter. Such contacts are especially important in obtaining firsthand accounts of previous experience.

The Text of the Report

What are the Answers to the Questions? Once the relevant in-formation is in hand, the answers to the questions may be assembled.

- What does the information reveal? This activity amounts to summarizing the information obtained. It often helps to organize this summary around the specific questions asked by the report. For example, if the report asks in one part, "What are the costs of the new service likely to be?" one section of the report should summarize the information gathered to answer this question.

Organizing the Report. The organization of a report into main and subsections depends upon the nature of the report. Reports will differ widely in their organization and treatment. In general, however, the report should generally follow the pattern previously discussed. That is, reports which generally include the following subjects in order will be found to be clear in their intent and to communicate effectively:

- *Description of problem or purpose.* Example: "One problem facing our agency is whether or not we should extend our hours of operation to better serve the public. This report is intended to examine the problem and make recommendations."

- *Questions to be answered.* Example: "In examining this problem, answers were sought to the following questions: What persons would be served? What would it cost? What staff would be needed?"

- *Information sources.* Example: "To answer these questions, letters of complaint for the past three years were examined. Interviews with clients were conducted by phone and in person, phone interviews were conducted with the agency directors in Memphis, Philadelphia, and Chicago."

- *Summary of findings.* Example: "At least 25 percent of the agency's clients would be served better by evening or Saturday service. The costs of operating eight hours of extended service would be negligible, since the service could be provided by rescheduling work assignments. The present staff report they would be inconvenienced by evening and Saturday work assignments."

<u>The Writer's Responsibilities.</u> It is the writer's responsibility to address finally the original purpose of the report. Once the questions have been answered, an informed judgment can be made as to the decision facing the agency. It is at this stage that the writer attempts to draw conclusions from the information he has gathered and summarized. For example, if the original purpose of the report was to help make a decision about whether or not the agency should offer a new service, the writer should draw conclusions from the information and recommend either for or against the new service.

<u>Conclusions and Recommendations.</u> Example: "It appears that operating during extended hours would better serve a significant number of clients. The writer recommends that the agency offer this new service. The present staff should be given temporary assignments to cover the extended hours. As new staff are hired to replace separating persons, they should be hired specifically to cover the extended hours."

3. <u>PERSUASIVE WRITING</u>

Often in life, people are called upon to persuade individuals and groups to adopt ideas believed to be good, or attitudes favorable to ideas thought to be worthwhile or behavior believed to be beneficial. The public service employee may find he must persuade the staff of his own agency, his superiors, the clients of the agency, or the general public in his community.

Persuading others by means of written and other forms of communication is a difficult task and requires much practice. Some principles have emerged from the study of persuasion which may provide some guidelines for developing a model for persuasive writing.

General Guidelines for Writing Persuasively

Know the Credibility of the Source. People are more likely to be persuaded by a message they perceive originates from a trustworthy source. Their trust is enhanced if the source is seen as authoritative, or knowledgeable on the issue discussed in the message. Their trust is increased also if the source appears to have nothing to gain either way, has no vested interest in the final decision. Then, the assertions made in persuasive writing should be backed up by referencing trustworthy and disinterested information sources.

Avoid Overemotional Appeals. Appealing to the common emotions of man—love, hate, tear, sex, etc.—can have a favorable effect on the outcome of a persuasive message. But care should be taken because, if the appeal is too strong, it can lead to a reverse effect. For example, if an agency wanted to persuade the public to get chest X-rays, it would have much greater chance of success if it adopted a positive and helpful attitude rather than trying to frighten them into this action. For instance, appealing mildly to the sense of well-being which accompanies knowledge of one's own good health, instead of shocking the public by showing horror pictures of patients who died from lack of timely X-rays.

Consider the Other Man's Point of View. To persuade another to one's own point of view, should the writer include information and arguments contrary to his own position? Or should he argue only for his own side?

Generally, it depends on where most of the audience stand in the first place. If most of the audience already favor the position being advocated, then the writer will probably do better including only information favorable to his position. However, if the greater part of the audience are likely to oppose this position, then the writer would probably be better off including their arguments also. In this case, he may be helping his cause by rebutting the opposing arguments as he introduces them into the writing.

An example of this technique might occur in arguing for such an idea as a four-day, forty-hour workweek. Thus: "Many people feel that the ten-hour day is too long and that they would arrive home too late for their regular dinner hour. But think! If you have dinner a littler later each night, you'll have a three-day weekend every week. More days free to go fishing, or camping. More days with your wife and children." That is good persuasive writing!

Interpersonal Communications

The important role of interpersonal communication in persuading others—face-to-face and person-to-person communications—has been well documented. Mass mailings or printed messages will likely have less effect than personal letters and conversations between persons already known to each other. In any persuasion campaign the personal touch is very important.

An individual in persuading a large number of persons will likely be more effective if he can organize a letter-writing campaign of persuasive messages written by persons favorable to his position to their friends and acquaintances, than if his campaign is based upon sending out a mass mailing of a printed message.

Conditions for Persuading. In order for an audience of one or many to be persuaded in the manner desired, these conditions must be met:

- the audience must be *exposed* to the message,
- members of the audience must *perceive* the intent of the message,
- they must *remember* the message afterwards,
- each member must *decide* whether or not to adopt the ideas.

Each member of the audience will respond to a message differently. While every person may receive the message, not everyone will read it. Even among those who read it, not everyone will perceive it in the same way. Some will remember it longer than others. Not everyone will decide to adopt the ideas. These effects are called *selective exposure, selective perception, selective retention,* and *selective decision*.

The Persuasion Campaign. How can one counteract these selective effects in persuading others? One thing that is known is that *people tend to be influenced by persuasive messages which they are already predisposed to accept*. This means a person is more likely to persuade people a little than to persuade them a lot.

In planning a persuasion campaign, therefore, the messages should be tailored to the audiences. Success will be more likely if one starts with people who believe *almost* as the writer wants to persuade them to believe—people who are most likely to agree with the position advocated.

The writer also wants to use arguments based on values the particular audience already accepts. For example, in advocating a new teen-age job program, he might argue with business men that the program will help business; with parents, that it will build character; with teachers, that it is educational; with taxpayers, that it will reduce future taxes; and so on.

The idea is to find some way to make sure that each member of the particular audiences reached can see an advantage for himself, and for the writer to then tailor the messages for those audiences.

4. **INSTRUCTIONAL WRITING**

Another task that the public-service employee may expect to face from time to time is the instruction of some other person in the performance of a task. This may sometimes involve preparing written instructions to other employees in the unit, or preparing a training manual for new employees.

It may sometimes involve preparing instructional manuals for clients of the unit, such as "How to Apply for a Real Estate License," "How to Bathe your Baby," or "How to Recognize the Symptoms of Heart Disease."

Whatever the purpose or the audience, certain principles of instruction may be applied which will help make more effective these instructional or training communications. These are: *advance organizers, practice, errorless learning,* and *feedback.*

Advance Organizers

At or near the beginning of an instructional communication, it helps the learner if he is provided with what can be called an "advance organizer." This element of the communication performs two functions:

- it provides a framework or "map" for the leader to organize the information he will encounter,
- it helps the learner perceive his purpose in learning the tasks which will follow.

The first paragraphs in this section, for example, serve together as an advance organizer. The trainee is informed that he may be called upon to perform these tasks in his job *(perceived purpose),* and that he will be instructed in advance organizers, practice, errorless learning, and feedback *(framework, or "map").*

Practice

The notion of *practice makes perfect* is a sound instructional principle. When trying to teach someone to perform a task by means of written communication, the writer should build in many opportunities for practicing the task, or parts of it. This built-in practice should be both appropriate and active:

- *Appropriate practice* is practice which is directly related to learning the tasks at hand.

- *Active practice* is practice in actually performing the task at hand or parts of it, rather than simply reading about the task, or thinking about it.

By inserting questions into the text of the communication, by giving practice quizzes, exercises, or field work, one can build into his instructional communication the kind of practice necessary for the reader to readily learn the task.

Errorless Learning

The practice given learners should be easy to do. That is, they should not be asked to practice a task if they are likely to make a lot of mistakes. When a mistake is practiced it is likely to recur again and again, like spelling "demons," which have been spelled wrong so often it's difficult to recall the way they should be spelled. Because it is better to practice a task right from the first, it is important that learners do not make errors in practice.

- One method for encouraging correct practice is to give the reader hints, or *prompts*, to help him practice correctly.

- Another method is to instruct him in a logical sequence a little bit at a time. Don't try to teach everything at once. Break the task down into small parts and teach each part of the task in order. Then give the learner practice in each part of the task before giving him practice in the whole thing.

- A third way of encouraging errorless learning is to build in practice and review throughout the communication. The learner may forget part of the task if the teacher doesn't review it with him from time to time.

Remember, people primarily learn from what they do, so build in to the instructional communication many opportunities for the learner to practice correctly all of the parts of the task required for learning, first separately and then all together.

Feedback

The reader, or learner, can't judge how well he is learning the task unless he is informed of it. In a classroom situation, the teacher usually confirms that the learner has been successful, or points out the errors he made, and provides additional instruction. An instructional communication can also help learners in the same way, by providing *feedback* to the learner.

Following practice, the writer should include in his instructional communication information which will let the reader know whether he performed the task correctly. In case he didn't, the writer should also include some further information which will help the reader perform it correctly next time. This feedback, then, performs two functions:

- it helps the learner confirm that his practice was done correctly, and

- it helps him correct his performance of the task in case he made any errors.

Feedback will be most helpful to the learner if it occurs immediately following practice. The learner should be brought to know of his success or his errors just as soon as possible after practice.

STUDENT LEARNING ACTIVITIES

- Write "asking" and "answering" letters, and answer a letter of complaint, using the format assigned by the teacher.

- Write memoranda to other "offices" in a fictitious organization. Plan a field trip using only memos to communicate with other students in the class.

- Take minutes of a small group meeting. Or attend a meeting of the school board and take minutes.

- Write a short report on a public service occupation of special interest to you.

- Write a 15-word telegram reserving a single room at a hotel and asking to be picked up at the airport.

- Write a news release announcing a new service offered to the public by your agency.

- Based upon hearing a reading or pretaping of a report, summarize the report in news style.

- View films on effective communication, for example, *Getting the Facts, Words that Don't Inform,* and *A Message to No One.*

- For a given problem or purpose, compile a list of specific questions you would need to answer to write a report on the topic.

- For a given list of questions, discuss and compile a list of information sources relevant to the questions.

- As a member of a group, consider the problem of "What field trip should the class take to help students learn how to write an effective news release?" What questions will you need to answer? Where will you obtain your information?

- As a member of a group, gather the information and prepare a short report based on it for presentation to the class.

- Write a report on a problem assigned by your teacher.

- Write a brief persuasive letter to a friend on a given topic. Assume he does not already agree with you. Apply principles of source credibility, emotional appeals, and one or both sides of the issue to persuade him.

- Plan a persuasive campaign to persuade a given segment of your community to take some given action.

- Write a short instructional communication on a verbal learning task assigned by your teacher.

- Write a short instructional communication on a learning task which involves the operation of equipment.

- Try your instructional communications with a fellow student to check for errors during practice.

TEACHER MANAGEMENT ACTIVITIES

- Have students practice letter writing. Assign letters of "asking" and "answering." Read them a letter of complaint and ask them to write an answering letter. Establish common rules of format and style for each assignment. Change the rules from time to time to give practice in several styles.

- Have small groups plan an event, such as a field trip, assigning the various tasks to one another using only memoranda. Evaluate the effectiveness of each group's memo writing by the speed and completeness of their planning.

- Have the class attend a public meeting. Assign each the task of taking the minutes. Evaluate the minutes for brevity and completeness.

- Encourage each student to prepare a short report on a public service occupation of special interest to himself.

- Give the students practice in writing 15-word telegrams.

- Have the students prepare a news release announcing some new service offered to the public, such as "Taxpayers can now obtain help from the Internal Revenue Service in completing their income tax forms as a result of a new service now being offered by the agency."

- Give the students practice in summarizing and writing leads by giving them the facts of a news event and asking them to write a one or two-sentence lead summarizing the significant facts of the event.

- Read a speech or a story. Have students write a summary and a report of the speech or story in news style.

- Show films on effective communication, for example, *Getting the Facts, Words that Don't Inform,* and *A Message to No One.*

- State a general problem and have each student prepare a list of the specific questions implied by the problem.

- State a list of specific questions and discuss with the class the sources of information which might bear upon each of the questions.

- Have small groups consider and write short reports jointly on the general problem, "What field trip should the class take to help students learn how to write an effective news release?" Have each group identify the specific questions to be answered, with sources for needed information.

- Have each student identify and prepare a short report on a general problem of interest.

- Assign students to work in groups of three or four to draft a letter to a friend to persuade him to make a contribution to establish a new city art museum.

- Assign the students to groups of five or six, each group to map out a persuasive campaign on a given topic. Some topics are "Give Blood," "Get Chest X-Ray," "Quit Smoking," "Don't Litter," "Inspect Your House Wiring," etc.

- Have each student identify a simple verbal learning task and prepare an instructional communication to teach that task to another student not familiar with the task.

- Have each student prepare an instructional manual designed to train someone to operate some simple piece of equipment, such as an adding machine, a slide projector, a tape recorder, or something of similar complexity.

- Have each student try his instructional communication out on another student, unfamiliar with the task. He should observe the activities and responses of the trial student to identify errors made in practice. He should revise the communication, adding practice, review, and prompts wherever needed to reduce errors in practice.

EVALUATION QUESTIONS

Written Communications

1. Which type of letter would be correct for a public service worker to send?

   A. A letter containing erasures
   B. A letter reflecting goodwill
   C. A rude letter
   D. An impersonal letter

2. Memos usually leave out:

   A. Complimentary closings
   B. The name of the sender
   C. The name of the addressee
   D. The date the memo was sent

3. A good business letter would not contain:

   A. Short, simple words, sentences, and paragraphs
   B. Information contained in the letter being answered
   C. Concrete nouns and active verbs
   D. Orderly placed paragraphs

4. In writing business letters it is important to:

   A. Use a conversational tone
   B. Use a hard, cold tone
   C. Use abstract words
   D. Use a passive tone

5. Messages between departments in an agency are usually sent by:

   A. Letter
   B. Memo
   C. Telegram
   D. Long reports

6. Repetitive work can be simplified by the use of:

   A. Memos
   B. Telegrams
   C. Forms
   D. Reports

7. In filling out forms and applications, it is important to be:

   A. Legible
   B. Complete
   C. Accurate
   D. All of the above

8. Memos should be: 8.____

   A. Clear
   B. Brief
   C. Complete
   D. All of the above

9. Minutes of meetings should not include: 9.____

   A. The opinions of the recorder
   B. The approval of previous minutes
   C. The corrections of previous minutes
   D. The voting members present

10. Reports are written by public service workers to: 10.____

    A. Assemble information in one place
    B. Aid the organization in making decisions
    C. Inform the public and other agencies
    D. All of the above

11. News releases should include: 11.____

    A. A lead paragraph summarizing the story
    B. Long paragraphs about many topics
    C. The writer's opinion
    D. All of the above

12. Readers of news releases and reports are influenced by the: 12.____

    A. Content of the material
    B. Accuracy of the material
    C. Physical appearance of the material
    D. All of the above

13. The contents of a report should include: 13.____

    A. A description of the problem
    B. The questions to be answered
    C. Unimportant information
    D. A summary of findings

14. People tend to be influenced easier if: 14.____

    A. They can see something in the position that would be advantageous to them
    B. They are almost ready to agree anyhow
    C. The appeal to the emotions is not overly strong
    D. All of the above

KEY (CORRECT ANSWERS)

1. B
2. A
3. B
4. A
5. B

6. C
7. D
8. D
9. A
10. D

11. A
12. D
13. C
14. D

www.ingramcontent.com/pod-product-compliance
Lightning Source LLC
Chambersburg PA
CBHW082038300426
44117CB00015B/2530